ALTERNATIVES TO NEOLIBERALISM
Towards equality and democracy

Edited by Bryn Jones and Mike O'Donnell

First published in Great Britain in 2017 by

Policy Press
University of Bristol
1-9 Old Park Hill
Bristol
BS2 8BB
UK
t: +44 (0)117 954 5940
pp-info@bristol.ac.uk
www.policypress.co.uk

North America office:
Policy Press
c/o The University of Chicago Press
1427 East 60th Street
Chicago, IL 60637, USA
t: +1 773 702 7700
f: +1 773-702-9756
sales@press.uchicago.edu
www.press.uchicago.edu

© Policy Press 2017

British Library Cataloguing in Publication Data
A catalogue record for this book is available from the British Library

Library of Congress Cataloging-in-Publication Data
A catalog record for this book has been requested

ISBN 978-1-4473-3114-8 hardcover
ISBN 978-1-4473-3118-6 ePub
ISBN 978-1-4473-3119-3 Mobi
ISBN 978-1-4473-3115-5 ePdf

The right of Bryn Jones and Mike O'Donnell to be identified as editors of this work has been
asserted by them in accordance with the Copyright, Designs and Patents Act 1988.

Cover design by Andrew Corbett
Front cover image: Shutterstock
Printed and bound in Great Britain by by CPI Group (UK) Ltd,
Croydon, CR0 4YY
Policy Press uses environmentally responsible print partners

MIX
Paper from
responsible sources
FSC® C013604

This volume is dedicated to the memory of Frank 'Stretch' Longstreth – colleague, critic and friend.

Contents

List of figures, tables and boxes

Figures

Tables

Box

List of abbreviations

AGM	Annual general meeting
BBC	British Broadcasting Association
BoE	Bank of England
BMA	British Medical Association
BREXIT	British exit from the EU
BRICS	Brazil, Russia, India, China
B-S-M	Black-Scholes-Merton
CBs	Central banks
CDU	Christian Democratic Party (Germany)
CEO	Chief executive officer
CIA	Central Intelligence Agency
CORE	Coalition for Corporate Responsibility
CSO	Civil society organisation
CSR	Corporate Social Responsibility
DiEM25	Democracy in Europe Movement 2025
DSGE	Dynamic Scholastic General Equilibrium
ECB	European Central Bank
EMH	Efficient Market Hypothesis
EMU	European Monetary Union
EU	European Union
FED	Federal Reserve System for United States banking
FTT	Financial transactions tax
GATT	General Agreement on Tariffs and Trade
G-C	Gaussian copula
GDP	Gross domestic product
GHG	Greenhouse gas
GMB	General trade union, UK (ex-General Municipal and Boiler Makers)
G20	Assembly for 20 of the world's largest economies
HBOS	Halifax Bank of Scotland
INGOs	International nongovernmental organisations
OECD	Organisation of Economic Co-operation and Development
IMF	International Monetary Fund
IPPR	Institute for Public Policy Research
MPC	Monetary Policy Committee of Bank of England
NAFTA	North Atlantic Free Trade Agreement
NC	Nomination Committee for appointing company directors

NCVO	National Council for Voluntary Organisations
NEDs	Non-executive directors
NEF	New Economics Foundation
NGO	Nongovernmental organisation
NHS	National Health Service
NSMs	New social movements
ONS	Office of National Statistics
QE	Quantitative easing
SDP	Social Democratic Party (Germany)
SDS	Students for a Democratic Society (United States)
SMOs	Social Movement Organisations
SNP	Scottish National Party
ST/EM	Share traded/executive managed corporation
TTIP	Transatlantic Trade and Investment Partnership
TUC	Trades Union Congress
UK	United Kingdom
UN	United Nations
UNITE	Britain's largest trade union
US/USA	United States (of America)
VAT	Value-added tax
WTO	World Trade Organization

Notes on contributors

Ted Benton is Emeritus Professor of the University of Essex. He has published extensively on social theory, ecological sociology and entomology. He is an active field naturalist and a member of the Red-Green study group and Green Party.

Anna Coote, Principal Fellow at the New Economics Foundation, has written widely on social justice, sustainable development, working time, public health policy, public involvement and democratic dialogue, gender and equality; including, most recently, NEF publications: *Local early action: How to make it happen*; *People, planet power: Towards a new social settlement* and *Time on our side: Why we all need a shorter working week*.

Colin Crouch is a Professor Emeritus of the University of Warwick and external scientific member of the Max Planck Institute for the Study of Societies at Cologne.

Andrew Cumbers is Professor of Regional Political Economy at the University of Glasgow. His book, *Reclaiming Public Ownership: Making Space for Economic Democracy* (Zed), won the 2015 Gunnar Myrdal Prize.

Kevin Farnsworth is Reader in Comparative and Global Social Policy, University of York, and coeditor of the *Journal of International and Comparative Social Policy*.

Jeremy Gilbert is Professor of Cultural and Political Theory at the University of East London and a political activist. He was written widely on politics, music, and contemporary culture; including: *Common Ground: Democracy and Collectivity in an Age of Individualism* (Pluto, 2013).

Zoë Irving, Senior Lecturer in Comparative and Global Social Policy, University of York and coeditor of the *Journal of International and Comparative Social Policy*, currently publishes on the politics of austerity and welfare, and the relationship between population size and social policy development.

Sukhdev Johal is Professor of Accounting and Strategy at Queen Mary University London and a member of the Centre for Research on Socio-Cultural Change.

Bryn Jones (former Senior Lecturer, University of Bath) author of *Corporate Power and Responsible Capitalism*, has taught, researched and published on economic and political change in European, Asian and North American societies.

Michael Moran is Professor of Government at Alliance Business School, University of Manchester, and a member of the Centre for Research on Socio-Cultural Change.

Mike O'Donnell, recently retired as Professor of Sociology at Westminster University, has taught widely in Britain and the United States, publishing in social theory, social movements and identity and difference.

Grahame F. Thompson is Associate Research Fellow at the CAST research programme and NordSTEVA at Copenhagen University and Emeritus Professor of Political Economy at the Open University, England. His chapter is part of a research project: 'Financial (In-) Security in a Period of Central Bank led Capitalism'.

Karel Williams is Professor of Accounting and Political Economy, Alliance Business School, University of Manchester, and director of the Centre for Research on Socio-Cultural Change.

Acknowledgements

The editors would like to thank staff at Policy Press, particularly Laura Vickers, Rebecca Tomlinson and Andy Chadwick, for their patience and help in the commissioning and preparation of this volume. For helpful comments at the Bath University seminar thanks go to: Kimber, Helen and Pandora Longstreth; and for advice on draft chapters thanks to Peter Cressey, Phil DeSouza, Leah DeSouza-Jones and an anonymous reviewer. Theo Papadopoulos gave invaluable advice on several editorial decisions. Of course, surviving errors and flaws remain the responsibility of the editors.

Foreword

This important book is part of the emergent social science paradigm that both analyses the neoliberal transformation of society and offers the conceptual tools needed for an alternative vision.

'Democracy' is offered as an alternative principle of social organisation to replace the current privileging of 'markets' as the best form of societal governance. Markets are shown to need regulation in order to reduce fraud, corruption and abuse of power.

My own work on the concept of 'crisis' is echoed in the way that some of the crisis of neoliberalism is analysed to demonstrate how neoliberal values have become endemic in social and cultural as well as economic relations. The different aspects of that crisis are shown to be interconnected, as it cascades through one social institution to another.

The significance of multiple inequalities is demonstrated in detail. Building on recent scholarship, it examines the underlying, destructive dynamic of neoliberalism, not only for class divisions, but also for gender, ethnicity, generation and citizenship.

Throughout the book, selective use of Karl Polanyi's theory of countermovement and transformation, informs alternative policy proposals. The book also builds on the classic sociological heritage that understands society as a whole, as a social system, rather than as numerous discrete institutions to be analysed separately within a set of narrow specialisms.

The book offers a contribution to policy making and the reinvigoration of the critical and politically relevant uses of sociology and other social sciences, to help develop the knowledge base needed to build a better world.

Sylvia Walby
Distinguished Professor of Sociology, UNESCO Chair in Gender
Research, Lancaster University
Director, Violence and Society UNESCO Centre, Lancaster University

Editors' preface

As we prepare this book for publication the UK, and much of Europe, is riven by the spectre of the UK's withdrawal from the European Union. Donald Trump's impending presidency may have wider implications for the conduct of neoliberal governance. However, these two expressions of popular discontent are unlikely to change substantially neoliberalism's unequal relations of power and resources, which are detailed below. In some respects they may even intensify them. Eminent economists such as Stiglitz and Krugman have produced devastating diagnoses of the economic flaws of neoliberal capitalism which led to the 2008 financial crash.

Yet these critiques, as well as more recent depictions of wider, catastrophic social consequences, like Alain Touraine's *After the Crisis* (2014), have barely influenced political and business leaders. These are apparently accepting of continuing financial and economic instability, uncertainty and repressive austerity. Waves of protest and a rising tide of social movement disillusion with global capitalism continue, captured in a litany of outrage in George Monbiot's 2016 denunciation of the UK's version of the neoliberal regime (*How Did We Get into This Mess?*). Monbiot rightly blames the political and economic stasis and manifold social distress on the regime's unshaken commitment to the ideas and policies of 'neoliberalism'. Moreover, as he shrewdly observes, this is an ideology which is all the more effective by being largely unnamed in public discourse, yet all-pervasive in society.

Amongst academics, campaigners and radical, fringe journalism there is no shortage of critiques and calls for resistance. Our own account of neoliberalism, given in the Introduction, summarises some of these critical aspects. However, the main thrust of this book is to provide potential alternatives, both as synoptic, coherent perspectives and also as specific policy recommendations and suggestions. These would both break with neoliberalism and provide reference points for politicians and activists to promote a more equal, more secure and genuinely freer society. Such developments would depend on collective efforts far beyond what is possible in a single volume such as this. However, we hope this collection will assist the wider movement for change to pursue, adapt and advance these or related ideas.

Neoliberalism penetrates and shapes the lives of the general public, yet few encounter let alone use the term. Its original scope, as a belief in and promotion of free market exchanges of private property, has been stretched to describe a variety of still evolving ideas and practices.

Essentially, however, neoliberalism continues to maintain commitment to the market, not only as the central economic mechanism, but also as the main means of solving political and social issues. As such, neoliberalism is an ideology that has shaped politics, and social and economic policy, throughout the world – but especially in the United Kingdom and its international relationships, most recently with the EU. This book aims both to describe and clarify these developments and also to present a spectrum of alternatives. These range from reforms for 'regime change', to curb market excesses but within a basic capitalist framework, to reforms that could lead on to 'system change' – that is, beyond market capitalism. We emphasise, however, that our editorial theme does not assume a reform/revolution dichotomy. Accumulations of reform could remain simply as reforms; or they could amount, eventually, to system change; such as the removal of private or corporate control of financial capital.

There is now considerable opposition to various *consequences* of neoliberalism. The EU referendum showed much hostility to the 'free movement of labour'. Also a majority of voters in the 2015 UK general election chose parties which rejected basic elements of the neoliberal consensus: welfare austerity, corporate control of public services, as well as the open labour markets which stimulate immigration. However, neither the idea nor the term 'neoliberalism' featured explicitly in the opposition parties' campaigns, with the partial exception of the Green Party's housing policy which aimed to 'to throw off the shackles of market ideology'. In all, 15 million voters overtly or implicitly opposed policies based on neoliberalism.

Yet most were probably unaware of the full nature of what they were rejecting. By contrast, in academic debate and social justice campaigns the extent of neoliberalism and its consequences are common knowledge and staples of debate. One aim of this book is to channel this coverage to issues of broader electoral relevance. The book's Introduction explains in detail why the extent and implications of neoliberalism need to be more widely recognised and understood, along with the nature and relevance of alternatives that have already been proposed – several of which are evaluated by our contributors in subsequent chapters, such as those by Gilbert, Coote, and Johal, Moran and Williams.

Despite its domination of public, popular and policy discourses (Hall et al 2015),what academics, journalists and activists call 'neoliberalism' is actually a mosaic of ideas and practices, threaded through academic theory, business ideology and political thought, as well as policy making. The electorate can assess and respond to the performance of a political party but a barely perceived ideology is an altogether more slippery matter. Moreover, its influence and evolution occurs within everyday public, business and financial, as well as political spheres. However, there have been few attempts to translate the many analyses of neoliberalism into overarching political and policy alternatives for a specific country such as the UK. This is the focus of the present collection and the editors' concluding assessment.

In March 2015 our contributors came together at a symposium in the University of Bath held in memory of Frank Longstreth, lecturer at the university, who died in 2014. Frank's work in the 'new institutionalist' approach to political economy and his interest in Karl Polanyi's theories of the social embeddedness of markets provided a backdrop to the symposium themes, which is reflected in several of the contributions.

In Part One, Jeremy Gilbert assesses the range of contending alternatives and the most likely combinations of forces and ideas to realise the most convincing approaches for change. Ted Benton sets out the 'Red–Green' alternatives which combine environmental and socialist imperatives irreconcilable with the logic of market capitalism. Anna Coote describes similar priorities but also policy ideas framed in the discourse of a 'new social settlement' in which capitalism is reformed by a more democratic and environmentally focused social democracy. Mike O'Donnell's chapter addresses how the implementation of popularly based 'institutional democracy' could undermine neoliberalism and become the foundation for a more participatory and fairer alternative society – a theme explored in more detail in Parts Two and Three.

Part Two moves on to examine the scope for limited reforms to the prevailing regime, particularly relationships between economic and governance constraints and policy alternatives. Farnsworth and Irving examine international evidence on the limitations to and reversals of austerity programmes – sites where neoliberalism is being variously modified or contested. Grahame F. Thompson scrutinises the nature and limits of changes in financial and monetary policy making, chiefly through an analysis of the expanded role of the Bank of England. Bryn Jones and Mike O'Donnell examine one of the most important, and topical, institutional constraints on progressive change in the form of the neoliberal governance of the EU – an institutional complex whose relationship to the UK could, at the time of going to press, undergo fundamental change following the outcome of the 'Brexit' vote; with potentially profound consequences for the neoliberal regime.

Jones' own chapter reassesses the significance of corporate power for neoliberalism, as well as alternative and democratic governance models for these citadels of elite hegemony. Johal, Moran and Williams provide complementary proposals for accountability and local democratic supervision of businesses and employment in what they call the 'foundational' sectors of the national economy. Part Three deals with a broader range of 'alternatives for ownership, control, and democracy'. Crouch sets out the case for a revitalised form of social democracy which prioritises the needs and interests of women and proposes them as the principal agents of change. Jones and Mike O'Donnell widen this focus on change agents by assessing the significance of social movements' strategies and goals, as vehicles for promoting more democratic and socially just alternatives. Andrew Cumbers offers a rethink on the long-standing, but often neglected, role for economic democracy, showing how public ownership can still be a revitalised alternative if modelled on popular ownership forms already practised overseas. The Conclusion chapter brings together the different threads of economic ownership and democracy with the prioritisation of environmental and gender issues in relation to the kinds of discourse and politics likely to progress them. Reworking Polanyi's concept of 'the commons', it reasserts the fundamental point that the economy should be embedded in society and primarily serve the public good ahead of private interest.

The crystallisation of a potentially anti-neoliberal policy portfolio for the Labour Party opposition, signalled by the Corbyn and McDonnell leadership, is evaluated in this chapter. However, it is worth stressing that the options and ideas this book, or similar others, offer to activists, policy makers and politicians will not, on their own, advance a realisable challenge to the current neoliberal dominance. The success of neoliberalism shows that promising ideas have to be complemented by, and embedded in, broader intellectual and ideological paradigms and social movements. Hopefully, critics, commentators, activists, policy makers and politicians, all frustrated by the neoliberal hegemony, will find here elements from which a convincing alternative perspective and compatible policies can be constructed – in other words, templates to help move the opposition to neoliberalism beyond its present, stalled, emphasis on critique and resistance.

INTRODUCTION

The open-market society and its opponents: an overview

Bryn Jones and Mike O'Donnell

The neoliberal paradigm extends far more widely and deeply than sets of party or government policies. As George Monbiot has written, it is the mainly anonymous character of neoliberalism which enables it to be simultaneously all-pervasive, yet unnoticed as an ideology (Monbiot, 2016). Our assumption is that policy makers, political actors and activists will not develop genuine alternatives until the phenomenon, its impacts and implications are fully identified, 'named and shamed'. For elements of neoliberal ideology now dominate in the media, business and social institutions, as well as the political and policy-making sphere.

Trapped in this barely acknowledged paradigm, centre-left politicians and policy makers usually talk as though progress can be achieved by minor modifications; such as public-private partnerships, or 'better regulation'. So we begin by exploring why and how, particularly in the UK, neoliberalism became an all-encompassing and politically dominant ideology and discourse, with multiple, adverse, social and economic impacts. We go on to explain some authoritarian and even incipiently totalitarian tendencies in neoliberalism which undermine democratic governance and the integrity of civil society. What could reverse these trends and their pernicious consequences?

To this end we assess, in the final sections of this Introduction, some of the principal existing alternatives: socialist and social democratic paradigms which combine social justice with feminist aims and related 'lifeworld' values of egalitarian, community relationships (Habermas, 1981), as well as ideas from social-Green movements. Chapters by Benton, Coote, Crouch, and Jones and O'Donnell (Chapters Three, Two, Ten and Twelve, and Conclusion) provide more detail on the significance and relevance of some of these perspectives. While Jeremy Gilbert, in Chapter One, provides a wider description and analysis of the different anti-neoliberal arguments and discourses. Comprehensive blueprints for alternatives to the broader capitalist system are not our concern here. Instead our focus is on the current, neoliberal regime of that system, in both its British and global forms. Further, in our judgement, the several varieties of capitalism – some uncompromisingly market-based, others more social democratic – show that significant regime change is possible. While the proposals offered here could eventually contribute to system change, the pressing need is for more realisable alternatives to both neoliberalism and right-wing, nationalistic populism.

As editors we put forward an overall synthesis of the different contributions, which consists of a radical but realisable set of political and policy ideas. In terms explained below, we propose a tripartite rebalancing of the currently distorted relationship between a market economy, the political system and civil society. In this rebalancing, equality would be pursued by effecting a shift in relative power to members and representatives of civil society. Economic development would be centred not so much on the macroeconomy, but on the foundational and core economy on which the personal and community relationships of the 'lifeworld' are based. The needs and interests of women's roles would be at the heart of this equalisation and rebalancing. It would be constituted through extensions of democratic participation at all levels and institutions of society, including those where neoliberalism is currently strongest.

Beginnings and ambitions

It is not the intrinsic appeal or credibility of neoliberalism's economic theories that explain why it was so widely adopted. Rather it was imposed mainly through the use of political and economic power and influence. Its challenge to the ascendant Keynesian political economy of state-centred economic development began early in post-war Europe. Reinforcement came from the United States, principally the hugely influential Chicago School of economists. Chicagoans and their fellow travellers extended ideas about market behaviour into the fields of government policy, law, history and economics. In the 1970s economists with Chicago links took posts under Pinochet's dictatorship and deregulated Chilean markets.

A breakthrough in using economic power for neoliberal ends came when an early advocate, US Treasury Secretary William E. Simon, succeeded in making the 1976 IMF loan to the UK's Labour government conditional on swingeing public spending cuts. This was a decisive blow against the Keynesian welfare state paradigm. It marked the beginning of the end of guaranteed funding for welfare state provision in the UK. Simon went on to make a fortune from leveraged buyouts on Wall Street and, via free-market think tanks such as the Olin Foundation, to promote the application of 'Chicago economics' concepts into university law faculties (PhilanthropyRoundtable, nd). The UK Labour government began the welfare retrenchment and experimentation with 'monetarist' economics as a response to the 'stagflation' recession of the mid-1970s (Jones, 2013). By 1980, Britain's Hayekian Institute of Economic Affairs was extending similar concepts for public policy analysis even for intangibles such as love and marriage (Papps, 1980).

By 1981, Rose Friedman and Chicago guru Milton Friedman (1981, p xxi) could proclaim an intellectual 'tide ... turning' in the Anglophone world and Western Europe, while, 'in many ... countries around the world, there is a growing recognition of the dangers of big government'. The phrase 'in many countries around the world' conveys the beginnings of the intellectual capture of international politics and governance. However, in many cases this course was pushed not by intellectual persuasion and enthusiastic imitation, but by a powerful armoury of pressure, including: American transnational corporations' investment clout; American control and influence on the key regulating bodies of the world economy – the IMF, the World Bank and the World Trade Organization (replacing the GATT in 1995); American aid and other incentives; and, in some cases, military force.

As exemplified by Margaret Thatcher's 1979 UK election, success with right-wing principles, such as the paramountcy of law and order and property rights, meshed neoliberalism with the outlook of conservatives in the UK and US (Amable, 2011, pp 21-22). Often, however, this conservative bias is camouflaged. Unlike neoliberal philosophers and social scientists, political parties rarely present their ideas as consistent theories. Policies are nuanced and/or simplified to win over mass media and key voters. The 1997-2010 Labour governments' 'Third Way' merely superimposed more socially responsible support for disadvantaged groups onto the core of neoliberal economic policy. The Conservatives continued to campaign on a broadly neoliberal platform of austerity in both the 2010 and 2015 UK elections. However, their welfare spending cuts were selectively targeted on working-age, poor and younger people, rather than to the benefits of older and people more likely to vote Conservative. Neoliberalism's capture of the EU (analysed in Chapter Six) has led to post-Crash austerity in several European states; and, as job-seeking young workers have flocked to the UK, to the anti-immigration hysteria propagated by right-wing (but closet neoliberal) populism and the 'Brexit' campaign: 'hiding behind nationalist flag waving' as Crouch (Chapter Ten), puts it.

Neoliberal ideology and its reality

> As Keynes observed of 'madmen in authority', the present government is 'distilling its frenzy from some academic scribbler of a few years back' – in this case the ideology of the so-called Washington Consensus, with its cult of competition and markets and its absurd belief in rational choice. (neurosurgeon Henry Marsh, *Guardian*, 21 October 2015)

Because neoliberalism is disproportionately supported by the very wealthiest and most privileged in society, it can justifiably be designated as an ideology in the classic Marxist sense: an outlook which distorts in order to protect or promote the interests of the dominant social groups. Yet neoliberalism is not merely an apologetic ideology. Ideological elements are part of a discourse running from the more scientifically formulated models of formal economics to the practical sentiments of everyday life. For systematic analyses of neoliberalism's discursive nuances see Amable (2011), Mirowski (2013) and Ventura (2012).

The principles associated with Chicagoan or Hayekian neoliberal theory outlined below, such as 'rational choice', act as a sort of universal grammar of concepts. This grammar provides the underlying structure for derivative discourses in more practical, applied and policy contexts. The Conservative–Liberal Democrat Coalition government in the UK established a 'behavioural insights team' in the Cabinet Office. This 'Nudge Unit' uses economic modelling to predict the incentives to change individual behaviours deemed to be socially, medically or environmentally negative. Influential derivatives abound in political and public-facing language. Literary reviewer Steven Poole points to the 'supermarketisation' of the language of politicians, PR professionals and public organisations, with their policy, electoral and service 'offers' and 'choices' to the media and general public (Poole, 2015). Neoliberalism's classic grammar and vocabulary, however, can be applied, by its experts and analysts, as a 'gold standard' for monitoring and correcting these vernaculars, where necessary. Analysis of routes out of neoliberalism therefore needs to begin with a dissection of this conceptual grammar.

Contradicting both Marxism and most of classical sociology, Hayek's doctrine extols Adam Smith's notion of the 'invisible hand' of individual economic choices as constitutive of the 'spontaneous order' of markets (Petsoulas, 2001). Milton Friedman described Hayek's: 'profound distinction between an imposed order and an order that develops without conscious intention out of the voluntary interaction of individuals' (Friedman, 1977, pp xxii–xxiii). Guided by incentives and responsibility, the rational choices of autonomous subjects are deemed to be expressed in 'spontaneous orders' which emerge from the myriad of individual market decisions. Except for the few carefully circumscribed exceptions described below, this reductionist view of social affairs sees collective institutions, which are not founded on atomised individual choice, as either illegitimate or unnatural, or both. Hayek's extreme individualism, shared with fellow Austrian (later American) luminary, Ludwig von Mises, had a moral dimension which has proved useful in political advocacy. Hayek's seminal book, *The Road to Serfdom* (1944), associated 'excessive' state power with the risk of totalitarianism, with 'freedom' as primarily economic freedom. In the USA, the Friedmans' *Free to Choose* slipped ethical justifications into their 'positive economics' disdain for state activity. Ironically, neoliberalism's ubiquitous and insidious presence, derived from its capture of state power, allows a reversal of these charges: neoliberalism itself now generates a creeping totalitarianism.

Neoliberals anathematised state or local government provision of health, social welfare and house-building because it pre-empted a role for private firms and associations. As David Harvey, a prominent critic of neoliberalism, summarises: 'The role of the state is to create and preserve an institutional framework appropriate to such practices' (Harvey, 2005, p 2). Neoliberals seldom express similar concern about analogous powers accruing to giant business corporations. Instead, Chicagoans attempted to redefine these firms as, essentially, bundles of individual transactions; but, outside the neoliberal bubble, such sophistries have proven unconvincing, even to managerial pundits (Denning, 2013). Business 'competition', as Fligstein (1993) and others have convincingly demonstrated, rests on corporations' shifting strategies of control over consumers, finance, technology, or over one another.

Neoliberalism's takeoff and global expansion through the 1980s and 1990s inevitably made it something more than its pioneers anticipated or relished; for example, in the extent to which large-scale transnational corporations dominate and even weaken allegedly competitive markets. Nor perhaps did they fully anticipate the seepage of neoliberal values and practices into everyday life, forming, at least in the commercial sphere, a near-global level of shared norms, driven by the market logic of commodity and service production for profit and consumption.

Drawing on Raymond Williams, Patricia Ventura even argues that neoliberalism has created a 'cultural logic' characterised by 'a structure of feeling' that permeates beyond economic affairs to individuals' social, cultural and personal behaviour, thus rooting it more firmly than abstract doctrines could achieve alone. She links Williams' analysis to Foucault's theory of governmentality which, as well as describing the intent and policy of neoliberal government, has the effect of structuring

> the way subjects think about the practices, techniques and rationalities used to govern them and which they use to govern themselves. Neoliberal government represents the population's wellbeing as intimately tied to individual's ability to make market principles the guiding values of their lives, to see themselves as products to create, sell, and optimize. (Ventura, 2012, p 2)

However, as she also suggests, the reality of neoliberalism turns the individual into the opposite of its supposed free market agent. The core neoliberal role of consumer choice is subverted and contradicted by market institutions. Advertisers actively prevent rational autonomy for target customers – notably its development in children. Marketing and advertising ploys bypass conscious calculation by, for example, hooking into humans' addictive tendencies for sugar and saturated fats in food products (BMA, 2015).

Inside the workplace brutal market freedoms are complemented by intensified forms of control to rival the worst nightmares of Max Weber and Franz Kafka. In predominantly computer-based work routines, communications, as orders and directions, cascade down through various management levels to the mass of employees, who have virtually no authority and minimal scope for creativity. As in the ubiquitous call centres, authority in personal contacts with the public is limited to rule implementation and enforcement, without creative interaction. In the state-engineered economic upturn after 2011 a huge proportion of the vaunted new jobs were part-time or in self-employment (ONS, 2013, 2014). Neoliberalism can therefore be defined as an abstract label covering a diffuse but systemic discourse embodied in the dominance of market-like practices over social life and governance. It is not so much the imposition of textbook market systems which links discourse with practice but a pervasive commodification of most aspects of personal, public and cultural life, and well-being.

Inconvenient realities: free markets or new corporate baronies and empires?

Media outrage at the perceived powers of trade union 'barons' in the 1970s and 1980s has not been matched by a recognition of the much greater oligarchic powers of organised business, especially over-fragmented under-unionised and weakly regulated labour markets. Neoliberal ideology vaunts individualism but it is huge transnational corporations which dominate the national and global economies: originally as new businesses floated on the 1990s' tide of market freedoms and entrepreneurship in the uncharted, new world of the internet. However, the 'heroic' individuals behind 'the cloud' and the likes of Amazon, Apple and Google have evolved into gigantic, though largely invisible, bureaucracies, embodying grossly uneven rewards, status and power. This now typical path of business evolution has partly been obscured by corporations' ideology of 'techie' informality and personal internet communication; potentially anytime and anywhere.

Instead of a market nirvana of unrestrained competition, internet enterprises are often oligopolies dominated by a few mega-corporations (Jones, 2015; and Chapter Eight below). More recent decentralised corporations such as Uber, Deliveroo and Airbnb – hyped as part of a new, cool, 'sharing economy' – have mushroomed largely by avoiding regulations and taxes for licensed accommodation or taxi drivers. The standard costs of, and obligations to, regular employees are removed by using casual and often underpaid workers (Slee, 2016). Our economy is based on the ideology of the market rather than its substance. In the neoliberal vision, however, the actual or potential competitors are presumed to abound in the wider international market (see Jones, 2015, pp 79–80).

Indeed, Thatcherism's long-term 'game-changer' was the opening of the British economy to overseas investment and a reduction of government investment into British industry. Predominantly British-owned manufacturing shrank but imports from overseas-owned industry increased. By 2015 over 50% of the top FTSE 100 companies were not majority British-owned (Wilks, 2013). Financial firms in the City of London were opened up to overseas banks and businesses, largely at the expense of smaller established ones. Such reforms intensified Britain's dependency on overseas capital. These and further relaxations under New Labour and the Clinton Democrats, led to the subprime mortgage crash of 2007, the near collapse of the international banking system in 2008 and the austerity programmes designed to reduce the exposure of financiers' lending to nation states. Even after the crash, world trade in merchandise exports, at an annual total of $18,301 billion (WTO, 2014), lagged behind international financial trades of $5345 billion dollars a day (Bank for International Settlements, 2013). The implication of these developments for the distribution of power and decision making, particularly in Britain, is discussed later (Chapters Eight and Nine).

A more insidious consequence – magnified through intergovernmental promotion of a global investment system – was its expansion of rentier capital as the dominant interest in almost all business activity. Enterprises and banks have constantly sought to match their returns for investors to the best levels on offer in this financialised global system. Because financial profit became almost the sole end, rather than a means for business growth, firms maximise 'shareholder value'. Corporate businesses sacrifice long-term investment in environmental sustainability, research and development, skills and stable employment in order to reward investors (Lazonick and O'Sullivan, 2000; Dore, 2008; Erturk et al, 2008; Jones and Nisbet, 2011). Increasing casual and 'zero-hours' employment contracts, and general employment insecurity through redundancies and 'sweated labour', transfers more 'value' to investors – conspicuously in the supply chains of fashionable, 'new economy' corporations such as Amazon and eBay. In many sectors a precariat (Standing, 2011) of insecure and impecunious workers has been created.

The main cause of the 2007–8 financial crash and its chaotic social and political consequences was, ultimately, this tunnel-vision search for the highest returns (Luyendijk, 2015). The neoliberal mission was to shift governance and accountability from the state to markets. In reality, as comprehensively detailed by academic studies (Vogel, 1996; Jones, 2015), this shift has actually been to the pseudo-markets dominated by corporations. Yet state powers have not been superseded. Some 'markets' are actually bureaucratically regulated contracting systems franchised by the state (see, inter alia, Jones, 2015; Wilks, 2013). More generally, as Mirowski (2013) observes, the state has new coercive powers to create and enforce market-like processes.

However, the focus of state powers is slanted by the simultaneously glamorous and menacing trope of 'globalisation', for trade, finance and fiscal policies, through international pacts and agreements: the World Trade Organization, Basel Agreements, and trade bloc regulations, such as those of NAFTA or the European Union. The earliest of these strictures, in the so-called Washington Consensus, was described as a 'golden straitjacket' for state policy makers because 'gold' flooded in as international finance and investment; but restrictions on states' ability to regulate these flows imposed a straitjacket. Neoliberal globalisation may now be stalling. Even weak global growth in a world of depressed incomes is only achieved by ultimately unsustainable personal debt (Telegraph, nd). The so-called Doha Round of negotiations to extend multilateral free trading, begun in 2001, is practically moribund. Some states, including India, Russia and the USA, bend or ignore rules to protect industries such as steel (Elliot, 2015; Evenett and Fritz, 2015). Yet, though fraying, the straitjacket remains. Paradoxically, the promised 'independence' from EU membership, could drive a UK seeking trade elsewhere further into this global web of rules (Donnan, 2016).

Neoliberal governance: a soft totalitarianism?

Similar to Ventura, above, Wendy Brown (2015) critically modifies Foucault's idea of governmentality to describe the above characteristics as the economisation of society, which spans law, bureaucratic regulation, the direction of government expenditure and, ultimately, the general culture. William Davies (2014) vividly depicts one rampant manifestation: as the all-pervasive and stress-inducing measurement and calculation with numerical ranking or 'starring' of every kind of activity. For Brown, neoliberalism's 'totalising' character involves: extending 'economic rationality to all aspects of thought and activity', using the state in 'direct service to the economy', while organising it as an enterprise with a 'market rationality'. Because of the 'hegemony of rational choice theory in the human sciences … as an objective branch of knowledge', individuals are identified as 'entrepreneurial rather than moral subjects in areas such as social policy' (Brown, 2003).

Television programmes such as *The Apprentice*, *Dragons' Den*, *Homes under the Hammer*, *Safe as Houses* encourage aspects of the 'entrepreneurship' role. Meanwhile some voluntary sector organisations are becoming less 'charitable' and 'more market driven, client driven, self-sufficient, commercial or business like' (Dart, 2004, p 414; Evans et al, 2005; McKay et al, 2011). As further evidence consider the dominance of the political system by corporations (Wolin, 2008), disciplining of labour through punitive welfare 'conditionality' and trade union curbs, propagation of neoliberal and pro-market ideology through a network of right-wing media, a compliant BBC (Mills, 2015), and state policies which enforce competition in education, health care and employment services while simultaneously amplifying neoliberal values.

Neoliberals' distrust of electoral democracy also suggests that these encroachments may indeed encourage a more disturbing 'soft totalitarianism'. In the 1970s advocates such as the Financial Times pundit Samuel Brittan edged away from electoral accountability, decrying the capitulation of parliamentary democracy to voters' economically unrealisable expectations (Brittan, 1975). Hayek himself championed some types of dictatorship; commending Chile's Pinochet regime for protecting and promoting 'free' markets in ways that elected governments would not. Margaret Thatcher, the recipient of these views, politely demurred.

> in Britain with our democratic institutions and the need for a high degree of consent, some of the measures adopted in Chile are quite unacceptable. Our reform must be in line with our traditions and our Constitution ... But I am certain we shall achieve our reforms in our own way and in our own time. Then they will endure. (Thatcher, 1982)

And endure they have. But only by sidelining, manipulating or exploiting the inadequacies of the British system of democracy.

The UK is not a monolithically authoritarian state, but its representative democracy is a particularly restrictive one; allowing it to function as the vehicle for elite interests rather than for the general good (see Chapter Thirteen) and thus for the imposition of market models. At no time did a majority of UK voters, let alone the registered electorate, vote for Thatcherite 'reforms'. Social surveys showed that a majority still supported broadly social democratic policies (Talbot, 2013). However, academic research has vindicated Monbiot's early warnings of the corporate 'take-over of the state' (Monbiot, 2000). Legitimating their roles and advice in neoliberal language, business elites not only now influence government policy – and civil society NGOs (Jones, 2007) – they directly formulate it (Wilks, 2013). Neoliberal stalwarts such as Cabinet Secretary and ex-McKinsey and Morgan Stanley employee Jeremy Heywood have been at the heart of government for decades. They have, with some success, sought to convert the officially neutral civil service into a market-inspired corporate simulacrum (Beckett, 2016).

When the full scope of neoliberal hegemony is surveyed, and considering Crouch's similar diagnosis in Chapter Ten, a powerful totalitarian tendency is visible (Monbiot, 2016). 'Totalitarian' in the sense defined by social philosopher John Gray (1993, p 157) as: 'a project of suppressing civil society ... within which divergent values and beliefs may [otherwise] co-exist in peace'. Though more circumspect, Wendy Brown nevertheless concurs on 'principles and institutions of democracy … becoming … ideological shells' (Brown, 2003). Changing the scale of this societal regime and its 'detached democracy' thus constitutes an immense challenge. Soft totalitarianism does not directly suppress critique and condemnation of neoliberals, but these are relatively easy and unthreatening acts. However, as the next section shows, construction of politically plausible alternatives within this hermetic system of politics, media and policy making is an altogether greater challenge.

Challenges to the neoliberal consensus

Spawned in opposition to other leading paradigms, particularly of the left, neoliberalism has continued, successfully, to discredit attempts to rehabilitate them. Moreover, as Monbiot (2016) has commented: 'It is hard to mobilise people around old ideas'. However, efforts to re-establish and often to revise older models are increasing. In Chapter One, Jeremy Gilbert provides a detailed analysis of the various types of oppositional politics and discourse currently ranged against neoliberal ideas and realities. Here we examine those political and social movement-inspired discourses closest to the alternative model outlined in our concluding chapter.

Resurgent socialism or regenerated social democracy?

Interest in socialist politics, albeit diluted, continues to revive (Jeffries, 2012). Syriza, an amalgam of leftists, greens and feminists which led Greek opposition to EU neoliberalism and austerity had a predominantly socialistic outlook. A veteran, self-confessed socialist MP, Jeremy Corbyn, won election to become the new leader of the British Labour Party. The only avowed socialist in the US Congress, Bernie Sanders, rivalled establishment figure Hillary Clinton to be Democratic Party candidate for the US presidency. However, if socialism is defined, as it usually was, as democratic or popular control of capital, then such resurgent currents are incomplete reincarnations. Their goals of state intervention, quasi-Keynesian investment and demand management, plus restorations of state welfare services, are closer to the pre-neoliberal, dominant social democracy of Western capitalism.

The New Labour governments of Blair and Brown and their counterparts elsewhere in Europe effectively abandoned such tenets of social democracy. As a leading New Labour strategist of the 1990s put it:

> In government, ... they would not explicitly prioritise a lessening of inequalities ... [for] intellectually Thatcherite neoliberalism was triumphant, and ... the post-war welfare state consensus had irretrievable broken down. (Liddle, 2007, p 2)

Some influential voices on the academic left see this trend away from social democracy as terminal. *The Kilburn Manifesto* sees the 'ethos of social democracy' as 'evaporated' (Hall et al, 2015). Others, such as Colin Crouch (see Chapter Ten), are more hopeful that renewed social democracy can appeal to a moderate left Labour government and its supporters. National comparisons – see Farnsworth and Irving, Chapter Five – show that it can flourish in a national context within an inimical neoliberal international framework.

Renewed focus on the traditional social democratic concern with inequality gives wider, normative legitimacy to the fiscal redistribution advocated by updated social democratic approaches such as A.B. Atkinson (2014), Peter Hain (2015) and Will Hutton (2015). When the poor are penalised more than the rich, even demagogic politicians will struggle with austerity appeals for solidarity and sacrifice. Blatant inequality also delegitimises market paradigms when the more disadvantaged compete with the privileged. Even leading US neoliberal Alan Greenspan, ex-chairman of the Federal Reserve bank, has ranked inequality as the 'most dangerous' trend afflicting America (Tett, 2014). Wilkinson and Pickett's (2009) best-seller correlated inequality with higher social and health costs for life expectancy, child mortality, obesity, homicide, imprisonment rates, mental illness, teenage births, social mobility and low trust. Formal civil equality is negated when the resources needed merely to live a decent life depend on purchasing power and when political influence depends on lobbying capacity. Both socialism and social democracy therefore insist on defined socioeconomic rights for individuals as prerequisites for equal citizenship. An insistence which directly contradicts tendentious neoliberal tropes of 'opportunity', 'flexibility' and 'deregulation'.

Thomas Piketty's influential dissection of the widening of wealth and income distributions under neoliberalism broadens Atkinson's similar diagnosis for the UK. Piketty supports fairly conventional social democratic reforms (better education, a unified retirement scheme based on equal rights to individual accounts, and higher top rates of income tax), plus a more radical progressive global tax on capital (Picketty, 2014). Atkinson, Hutton, and Hain propose rebalancing bargaining power between employers and workers and consumers and big businesses, rectifying horizontal inequality between 'race … gender, sexual orientation, age, disability or faith' (Hain, 2015, p 154), and between generations. Hutton, and Hain, prescribe universal benefits and pensions, living-wage levels, with Atkinson proposing guarantees for small savers and – more distinctively – an equal 'participation income' (see below). Complemented by a 'change in values to question high pay at the top', such measures seem plausible. The broader question, explored in Chapters Nine, Eleven and Twelve, is how these values can be activated and by whom. The prescription of a symbolic presence by trade union or employee representatives on company boards (Hutton, 2015; Hain, 2015) – even recently floated by new Tory Prime Minister Theresa May – would not seem to be powerful enough for such a major shift.

Even more problematic, however, is that Hutton, Hain and similar social democrats base their strategy for greater equality and renewed social security on redistribution from the proceeds of economic growth. This traditional but usually failed approach of the social democratic left in the UK is problematic for three reasons:

1. It is effectively a bet on a volatile, internationalised economy, over which UK policy makers have no control and little influence.
2. It assumes, fallaciously, that the UK has a homogenous, competitive market economy which is amenable to precise management ('steerage') by technocratic elites and the government. As Johal, Moran and Williams explain in Chapter Nine, the UK is the locus of several economic subsystems with varying degrees of dependency on central macroeconomic factors such as interest rates or tax changes.
3. Proposing to base social policy on economic management submits and subjects governments to a whole array of policy actors, from the IMF and banking sector to think tanks and business lobbies. The risks to a growth-for-equality strategy from these and other interests is increased, because the debates and political dispute will be conducted mainly on the terrain of conventional economic discourse. Dilution, modification and, yes, subversion by rival growth policies of neoliberals is likely. Cue pressure for new forms of privatisation, de-regulation and commoditisation of state services or familial roles the better to secure 'growth'.

Hay and Payne's (2015) manifesto proposes a variation on such a growth-focused transformation. Their proposals for a 'civic capitalism' would substitute a compound index of variables such as health, wellbeing, inequality, longevity and sustainable energy use for traditional criteria such as GDP. An attractive idea but one which would also most likely be disputed and challenged by entrenched 'expert' interests, and be unlikely to get much popular recognition and support. To guide and support the relevant state intervention, Hall and Payne, like Atkinson, argue for a 'minimum set of values'. But the achievement of these values is consigned to some future and undefined process of 'public deliberation, debate and consultation' (Hay and Payne, 2014, p 17). In Michael Moran's (2015) view this whole approach relies on moralised re-regulation steered by technocratic and, by extension, elitist controls. In other words, a continuation of the democratic deficits – re-evaluated in the chapters by Cumbers, Jones, O'Donnell, and our Conclusion chapter – which facilitated neoliberalism. Feminist social democratic renewal inspired partly by social justice movements analysed below promises a more potent social democracy.

Marxist solutions

Since its heyday in the tumultuous mid to late 20th century, Marxist socialism has fragmented and relocated in a number of different discourses and guises. But, as erstwhile adherents have acknowledged, as an integrated theory of socioeconomic crisis and political action, Marxism has become a creed without a movement (Schwartz, 2013). Marxist analyses have informed significant elements of the anti-globalisation movement, but not the alter-globalisation movement. In other words, Marxism remains as an analytical weapon but not as a popular guide to mobilisation or a new institutional order to replace international capitalism. The forensic analysis of *The Class Struggles in France* (Marx, 1969) certainly did not inform the potent, but simplistic ethos of the '99% against the 1%'.

Yet more dispassionate respecters of Marxism also do not employ its political economy to guide their own proposals. The frissons that greeted Labour Party leadership contender Jeremy Corbyn when he 'praised Marxist ideas' (BBC, 26 July 2015) were not duly reflected in his classic social democratic manifesto of a national education system, targeted money supply increases, more publicly provided housing, with pragmatic nationalisations of market failures among rail and energy retailers. The Syriza coalition in Greece attracted much publicity for a supposed Marxist ethos, such as that espoused by the academic Yanis Varoufakis. Its actual programme, preoccupied with EU-imposed austerity, was more like a paean to Keynesian macroeconomics (Syriza, 2014).

Caught between the anarcho-populism of its erstwhile activist support, and the pull of pragmatic social democracy, Syriza seems unlikely to provide a Marxisant socialist model for others, such as Spain's similarly conflicted Podemos (Stobart, 2015). Without a remarkable adaptation and revival it seems unlikely therefore that classical Marxist ideas have the relevance or support to provide alternative politics and policies to neoliberalism. However, contemporary social movements have developed ideas and practices cognisant of, but outside, Marxist doctrine which often do challenge the logic and injustices of neoliberal globalisation.

Social justice/lifeworld/feminist movements

The 1960s 'new', more fluid and heterogeneous social movements, have begun to consolidate. While, as Chapter Four explains, the roots of erstwhile socialist parties, such as Labour in the UK, in the wider 'old' labour movement, gradually withered. There were differences in beliefs, origins and aims – and affiliations to disparate political-ideological camps (Starr, 2000; Castro Aponte, 2013; Bendell, 2004). Yet by 1999, and the 'Battle of Seattle' protests against the WTO, this shifting but expansive coalition of environmental, human rights, anticorporate, peace and antipoverty movements – sometimes with older church and labour movements – was combining in campaigns with common or overlapping concern. This movement of movements (see Chapter Twelve) developed a discourse of effective critique and clear-cut alternatives to the neoliberal ideologies and globalisation policies.

Two outstanding themes structure these campaigns' discourse: firstly, participative democracy – whether of the direct, anarchistic or deliberative-rational type; and, secondly, an emphasis on irreducible human rights and rights of nature which override market priorities. These two themes are integrated by Coote (Chapter Two) and by O'Donnell (Chapter Four), who go beyond a symbolic invocation of 'participatory democracy' (Hain, 2015, pp 148-149) and identify an overriding right to participate. After the financial crash of 2007-8 and the ensuing public austerity programmes, some of the focus of these movements shifted from the global South to include also the collapse of economic rights and welfare in the advanced economies. For example, Oxfam GB now has a rights-based approach to poverty and inequality in this country, covering women and migrants (see Chapter Twelve). The social democratic thread in these social movement recipes became stronger than those in present mainstream politics. They are also more ambitious in targeting neoliberal corporate strongholds and financial leviathans, on which, for example, recent Labour leaderships have been more circumspect. Could such ideas and campaigning energy help revitalise an ailing social democracy?

Drawing from these movements, Crouch, in Chapter Ten, argues for women's interests as the bedrock of a revived social democracy, which Sylvia Walby has also; argued for:

> the institutionalization of feminism in civil society, including trade unions (where women are now half the members) and in the state, where women are increasingly represented in parliament and in the gender equality policy architecture ... [in] jobs that are disproportionately held by women (in the public services), services (health, education, care-services) that are disproportionately used by women and disproportionately politically supported by women. (Walby, 2015, p 128-130)

This strategic emphasis could link mainstream politics and policy making to the above civil society movements (see Chapter Twelve) and to the more general 'decommodification of labour' principle inherent in some of the social democratic revisions above. A key policy could be the automatic basic income right, finessed by Atkinson so that, for those of working age, this right would be 'conditional, not on citizenship, but on social contribution'. By including 'home care for infant children or frail elderly people' as a social contribution, women's autonomy could increase. Moreover, inclusion of regular voluntary work in a 'recognized association' would also reward activism in community and civil society organisations (Atkinson, 2014, p 633).

Going beyond the widely touted 'citizen's income' (Citizen's Income Trust, http://citizensincome.org/, passim; Green Party, 2015, Standing, 2005), this participation income circumvents the stand-off between neoliberal anti-statism and social democracy's previous reliance on redistributive welfare rights. As 'a variant on the idea of a basic income', participation income would replace the jungle of personal tax allowances, while reducing 'existing state transfers in payment by the same amount'. The participation condition counters allegations that its entitlement as an individual right could be costly and disrupt the solidarity needed to transcend neoliberal market life (Coote, 2015, pp 43-44). By helping to emancipate women and making community activism less costly, such a right could mobilise extra support for a modified social democracy. We expand on this proposition in the Conclusion to this book.

Shades of green

In the worldwide tide of protests against neoliberal economics, governance and social consequences, after 2006, between one-third and a half were composed of 'global justice' events. Of these protests, one-half concerned 'environmental justice' and almost 40% of these took place in high-income countries (Ortiz et al, 2013, pp 15–25). This trend, termed 'social green' by Clapp and Dauvergne (2005), reflected the extension of green movements' focus from strictly natural and biological degradation to social impacts, especially on poverty-stricken communities, initially in the global South but now in the failing economies of countries like the UK (Jones, 2015). As head of Friends of the Earth UK, Craig Bennett, argues about a campaign against open cast mining in South Wales:

> It's an air pollution and a health issue … it's an economic issue because of the jobs needed; it's a social justice issue because all this Welsh community had been offered was more dirty jobs by a bully-boy company. It's completely artificial to think that it's only a climate issue. (Vidal, 2015)

Campaigners' demands for deterrent taxes on environmentally risky business developments (Ortiz et al, 2013, p 40), plus state intervention for low-carbon energy alternatives to fossil fuels, inherently challenge the supremacy of market processes (see Cumbers, 2012; and Chapter Eleven). Through the broadening of the sustainability agenda from natural to social ecologies, today's environmental campaigns play a leading role against corporate and big business hegemony (Jones, 2015, pp 169–175). Craig Bennett diagnoses the Tory government's pro-market, austerity retreat from sustainable energy as part of 'ideological war on all things green', necessitating outright political and ideological opposition (Vidal, 2015).

As Benton explains in Chapter Three, the green movement's more radical wings offer perhaps the most complete, alternative to neoliberalism's 'full spectrum dominance'. 'Social greens' advocate a profound shift in values, decentralised decision making, more participative democracy, and localised instead of corporate and international market economies. Cumbers' chapter gives concrete examples of alternative communal and socially embedded enterprise in societies which have avoided blanket neoliberalism. Anna Coote (Chapter Two) explains the relevance and potential of an environmentally based manifesto which re-centres 'lifeworld' concerns: wellbeing, personal and social security within a different, more democratic and environmentally sustainable 'social settlement'. This idea offers a more profound basis for revamped social democracy proposals. However, its very novelty raises questions about the scale of the cultural–ideological shift needed to popularise it.

Benton's analysis, similar to Jackson (2009), provides further support; arguing that to avoid environmental catastrophe capitalism must abandon continuous material growth. Benton's belief is that such a system needs to transcend its capitalist basis. However, even from within the economic establishment a catastrophe scenario is tacitly acknowledged by warnings that climate change constitutes the biggest threat to financial stability (Carney, 2015). Despite the sidelining of post-Crisis initiatives such as the Green New Deal (see chapters by Coote and Cumbers), our Conclusion affirms the scope for green alternatives to the finance–corporate–market straitjacket.

Summary: towards a 'trilateral rebalancing'

To summarise: neoliberalism has seriously destabilised what we call the 'trilateral balance'. Instead of the state, markets and civil society existing in a balanced and mutually supportive relationship, market institutions have been expanded, penetrating and dominating the two other spheres. Ironically, the neoliberal regime has adopted bureaucratic characteristics of the kind it was founded to curtail. The theme which we extrapolate from the alternatives offered in this book is that the current imbalance should be rectified, primarily by empowering civil society and revitalising democracy at the expense of market, primarily corporate actors', power.

An egalitarian push would then be based on new social rights, rooted in the needs and interests of the 'lifeworld', particularly the promotion of women's interests in both the family/relationship and employment spheres. Neoliberal economics could also be outflanked on the environmental side by demands for curbs on business power to achieve a higher quality of life in the 'natural' dimensions of family and community life. Moreover, as most contributors – especially, Johal et al, O'Donnell, Cumbers, Gilbert, Jones - explain, there is also a strong case for deepening democracy beyond its conventional and stunted parliamentary governance forms to tackle, inter alia, the power bases of corporate neoliberalism.

Three major impediments hinder these alternatives and the kind of societal rebalancing advocated here. Firstly, a defective political democracy has been largely captured by interests with much to lose from any serious change. Secondly, neoliberal ideologies which dominate national and international governance systems, including business regulation, and privilege financial and market forces, are supported by mass media allies. Thirdly, potent and progressive alternative policy sets are either thematically fragmented or unpopular; in part because neoliberalism has either ideologically discredited or infiltrated and corrupted their 'parent' perspectives – socialism, social democracy and so on. These constraints suggest that conventional social democratic paths to greater equality which rely only on redistribution based on higher economic growth are inherently problematic.

Different discourses and models of economic welfare and policy are needed. A synthesis of the contributions in this book suggests that new paradigms should be based on inversions of the intellectually and practically deficient market economics, which privilege individualism over the role of social structures on life chances. We return to these themes in the Conclusion to this book. Neoliberalism's opponents have often argued that the economy should serve the people rather than, as now, people being servants of the market economy and its controllers. Translating this principle into a realisable alternative requires two things: firstly a different, coherent and genuinely social philosophy; secondly, policy ideas consistent with social and political forces that might champion and promote them. A re-envisaged and revitalised socio-political philosophy needs to break with the chaotic, but illusory 'freedoms' of markets and 'rational and free individuals'. To achieve this inversion means locating civil society as both the site of emancipation and the source of political struggles for the changes. This book is a contribution to these ideas and, hopefully, the accompanying political struggles.

References

Amable, B. (2011) 'Morals and politics in the ideology of neo-liberalism', *Socioeconomic Review*, 9 (1): 3–30.

Atkinson, A.B. (2014) 'After Piketty?', *British Journal of Sociology*, 65 (4): 619–638.

Bank for International Settlements (2013) Triennial central bank survey, www.bis.org/publ/rpfx13fx.pdf

Beckett, A. (2016) 'The most potent, permanent and elusive figure in British politics', *The Guardian*, 27 January.

Bendell, J. (2004) *Barricades and boardrooms. A contemporary history of the corporate accountability movement*, Technology, Business and Society Programme, Paper No 13, Geneva: United Nations Research Institute for Social Development.

British Medical Association (2015) *Food for thought: Promoting healthy diets among children and young people*, London: BMA.

Brittan, S. (1975) 'The economic contradictions of democracy', British *Journal of Political Science*, 5 (2): 129-159.

Brown, W. (2003) 'Neo-liberalism and the end of liberal democracy', *Theory & Event*, 7.

Brown, W. (2015) *Undoing the demos: Neoliberalism's stealth revolution*, New York: Zone Books.

Carney, M. (2015) 'Breaking the tragedy of the horizon – climate change and financial stability', speech by Mark Carney, Bank of England, www.bankofengland.co.uk/publications/Pages/speeches/2015/844.aspx

Castro-Aponte, W.V. (2013) *Non-governmental organizations and the sustainability of small and medium-sized enterprises in Peru: an analysis of networks and discourses*, Environmental Policy Series 9. Netherlands: Wageningen Academic.

Clapp, J. and Dauvergne, P. (2005) *Paths to a green world: The political economy of the global environment*, Cambridge, MA: MIT Press.

Coote, A. (2015) *People, planet, power: Towards a new social settlement*, London: New Economics Foundation.

Cumbers, A. (2012) *Reclaiming public ownership: Making space for economic democracy*, London: Zed.

Dart, R. (2004) 'The legitimacy of social enterprise', *Nonprofit Management and Leadership*, 14 (4): 411–424.

Davies, W. (2014) *The limits of liberalism: Authority, sovereignty and the logic of competition*, London: Sage.

Denning, S. (2013) 'The origin of "the world's dumbest idea": Milton Friedman', Forbes, 26 June, www.forbes.com/sites/stevedenning/2013/06/26/the-origin-of-the-worlds-dumbest-idea-milton-friedman/#134469b3214c

Donnan, S. (2016) 'WTO warns on tortuous Brexit trade talks', *Financial Times*, 26 May.

Dore, R. (2008) 'Financialization of the global economy', *Industrial and Corporate Change*, 17 (6): 1097–112.

Elliot, L. (2015) 'Does Doha trade talks' failure suggest second age of globalisation is over?', *The Guardian*, 30 November.

Erturk, I., Froud, J., Johal, S., Leaver, A. and Williams, K. (2008) *Financialization at work*, London: Routledge.

Evans, B., Richmond, T. and Shields, T. (2005) 'Structuring neoliberal governance: The nonprofit sector, emerging new modes of control and the marketisation of service delivery', *Policy and Society*, 24 (1): 73–97.

Evenett, S.J. and Fritz, J. (2015) *The tide turns? Trade, protectionism, and slowing global growth*. The 18th global trade alert report, London: Centre for Economic Policy Research.

Fligstein, N. (1993) *The transformation of corporate control*, Cambridge, MA: Harvard University Press.

Freidman, M. (1977) 'Foreword' in F. Machlup (ed) *Essays on Hayek*, London: Routledge and Kegan Paul.

Friedman, M. and Freidman, R. (1981) *Free to choose*, New York: Avon Books.

Gray, J. (1993) *Post-liberalism: Studies in political thought*, New York and London: Routledge.

Green Party (2015) *General election manifesto 2015*, www.greenparty. org.uk/we-stand-for/2015-manifesto.html

Habermas, J (1981) 'New social movements', *Telos*, 1981 (49): 33–37.

Hain, P. (2015) *Back to the future of socialism*, Bristol: Policy Press.

Hall, S. Massey, D. and Rustin, M. (2015) *After neoliberalism? The Kilburn Manifesto*, London: Lawrence and Wishart.

Harvey, D. (2005) *A brief history of neoliberalism*, Oxford: Oxford University Press.

Hay, C. and Payne, A. (2015) *Civic capitalism*, Cambridge: Polity Press.

Hayek, F. von (1944) *The road to serfdom*, Chicago: Chicago University Press.

Hutton, W. (2015) *How good we can be: Ending the mercenary society and building a great country*, London: Little Brown.

Jackson, T. (2009) *Prosperity without growth? The transition to a sustainable economy*, London: Earthscan.

Jeffries, S. (2012) 'Why Marxism is on the rise again', *The Guardian*, 4 July.

Jones, B. (2007) 'Citizens, partners or patrons? Corporate power and patronage capitalism', *Journal of Civil Society*, 3 (2): 159–177.

Jones, B. (2013) 'Those crazy days of "socialism": The 1970s and the strange death of social democracy', New Left Project, www. newleftproject.org/index.php/site/article_comments/those_crazy_ days_of_socialism_the_1970s_and_the_strange_death_of_social_dem

Jones, B. (2015) *Corporate power and responsible capitalism? Towards social accountability*, Cheltenham: Edward Elgar.

Jones, B. and Nisbet, P. (2011) 'A better model for socio-economic governance?', *Revue de la Régulation*, 9 (Spring).

Lazonick, W. and O'Sullivan, M. (2000) 'Maximizing shareholder value: A new ideology for corporate governance', *Economy and Society*, 29 (1): 13–35.

Liddle, R. (2007) *Creating a culture of fairness. A progressive response to income inequality in Britain*, London: Policy Network, www.policy-network.net/uploadedFiles/Publications/Publications/Creating_a_culture_of_fairness.pdf

Luyendijk, J. (2015) 'How the banks ignored the lessons of the crash', *The Guardian*, 30 September.

Marx, K. (1969) 'The Class struggles in France, 1848 to 1850', in K. Marx and F. Engels, *Selected Works*, Volume 1, Moscow: Progress Publishers.

McKay, S., Moro, D., Teasdale, S. and Clifford, D. (2011) *The marketisation of charities in England and Wales*, Working Paper 69, Third Sector Research Centre.

Mills, T. (2015) The end of social democracy and the rise of neoliberalism at the BBC, University of Bath, PhD Thesis.

Mirowski, M. (2013) *Never let a serious crisis go to waste*, London: Verso.

Monbiot, G. (2000) *Captive state: The corporate takeover of Britain*, London: Macmillan.

Monbiot, G. (2016) *How did we get into this mess? Politics, equality, nature*, London: Verso Books.

Moran, M. (2015) 'It's the democratic politics, stupid!' in C. Hay and A. Payne, *Civic capitalism*, Cambridge: Polity Press.

ONS (Office for National Statistics) (2013) 'UK employment increases by 154,000', Part of Labour Market Statistics, February 2013 Release, www.ons.gov.uk/ons/rel/lms/labour-market-statistics/february-2013/sty-uk-employment-increases-by-154-000.html

ONS (Office for National Statistics) (2014) Self-employed workers in the UK - 2014, www.ons.gov.uk/ons/rel/lmac/self-employed-workers-in-the-uk/2014/rep-self-employed-workers-in-the-uk-2014.html

Ortiz, I., Burke, S., Berrada, M. and Saenz, H.C. (2013) *World protests 2006–2013*, Initiative for Policy Dialogue and Friedrich-Ebert-Stiftung, New York, Working Paper No 2013, http://dx.doi.org/10.2139/ssrn.2374098

Papps, I. (1980) 'For love or money', IEA Hobart Paper, London: Institute of Economic Affairs.

Petsoulas, C. (2001) *Hayek's liberalism and its origins, His idea of spontaneous order and the Scottish Enlightenment*, London: Routledge.

PhilanthropyRoundtable (nd) 'William E. Simon … and the social entrepreneurship awards that honor his legacy', www.philanthropyroundtable.org/topic/excellence_in_philanthropy/william_e_simon

Picketty, T. (2014) *Capital in the twenty-first century*, Cambridge, MA: Harvard University Press.

Poole, S. (2015) '"Offer" – the latest irritating buzzword', *The Guardian*, 12 June, www.theguardian.com/books/2015/jun/12/offer-latest-irritating-buzzword-steven-poole-on-words

Schwartz, J. (2013) *A theory without a movement, a hope without a name: The future of Marxism in a post-Marxist world*, http://papers.ssrn.com/sol3/papers.cfm?abstract_id=2282163

Slee, T. (2016) *What's yours is mine*, New York: OR Books.

Standing, G. (2005) *Promoting income security as a right. Europe and North America*, London: Anthem Press

Starr, A. (2000) *Naming the enemy: Anti-corporate social movements confront globalization*, London: Zed.

Stobart, L. (2015) 'A year of change postponed?', Jacobin, www.jacobinmag.com/2015/12/podemos-iglesias-elections-ciudananos-cup-spain/

Syriza (2014) *The Thessaloniki programme*, www.syriza.gr/article/SYRIZA---THE-THESSALONIKI-PROGRAMME.html#.VrSXqNuLTAU

Talbot, C. (2013) 'Britons say no to smaller state', https://theconversation.com/britons-say-no-to-smaller-state-18020

Telegraph (2015) 'Instead of paying down its debts, the world's gone on another credit binge', www.telegraph.co.uk/finance/economics/11394101/Instead-of-paying-down-its-debts-the-worlds-gone-on-another-credit-binge.html

Tett, G. (2014) 'An unequal world is an uncharted economic threat', *Financial Times*, 4 September.

Thatcher, M. (1982) Letter to Friedrich Hayek, http://delong.typepad.com/sdj/2011/12/letter-from-margaret-thatcher-to-friedrich-hayek.html

Ventura, P. (2012) *Neoliberal culture: Living with American neoliberalism*, Farnham: Ashgate.

Vidal, J. (2015) 'Friends of the Earth CEO Craig Bennett: "Now is the time to listen to ordinary people again"', *The Guardian*, 21 August.

Vogel, S.K. (1996) *Freer markets, more rules: Regulatory reform in advanced industrial countries*, Ithaca, NY: Cornell University Press.

Walby, S. (2015) *Crisis*, Cambridge: Polity Press.

Wilkinson, R. and Pickett, K. (2009) *The spirit level: Why more equal societies almost always do better*, London: Allen Lane.

Wilks, S. (2013) *The political power of the business corporation*, Cheltenham, UK and Northampton, MA: Edward Elgar.

Wolin, S.S. (2008) *Democracy incorporated*, Princeton, NJ: Princeton University Press.

WTO (2014) *International trade statistics*, 2013, https://www.wto.org/english/res_e/statis_e/its2014_e/its2014_e.pdf

Part One
Alternative paradigms and perspectives

Editors' overview

Building on the Introduction's historical and critical review of neoliberalism and of existing proposals to change it, Part One specifies alternative, more radical perspectives to this still dominant, if elusive ideology. Following our proposal in the Preface, of a spectrum of 'regime' and 'system' changes, contributors' political and policy perspectives in this part of the book assume democratic and non-violent, rather than 'revolutionary' change – some modest but strategic, others with broader, societal scope.

Jeremy Gilbert contextualises his recommendations for a renewal of socialist challenges to neoliberalism by distinguishing between critiques and counternarratives as moralistic, pathologising ('neoliberalism makes you ill'), eco-Marxist and Marxist, and his preferred approach of radical democracy. Gilbert describes 'moralistic' approaches as limited to moral stances and exhortations to act differently and 'better', rather than providing specific strategies and programmes of change. Thus the moralism of the left can be as conservative as that of the right and is unlikely to appeal to those voters preoccupied with material hardship. Though impressed by the evidence that neoliberalism can damage people – make them ill – physically and psychologically, Gilbert argues that these perspectives lack a crucial identification of power and material interests in the present system. In an analysis that complements that of Benton in Chapter Three, he finds a lack of convincing solutions in the otherwise devastating demonstrations by Marxists, and particularly eco-Marxists, of the enormous material damage neoliberalism causes. Again Gilbert offers a radical democratic path allied to a modernisation ethos. This would utilise the radical potential inherent in media technologies and new organisational techniques: sophisticated tools to bring the individuals isolated by corporate neoliberalism into 'potent collectives'. The organisational forms to promote these changes would be self-governing alternatives to the corporate model, developed through democratic decision making, rather than top-down, state imposition.

Anna Coote's recommendations cover three overlapping areas: social justice; environmental sustainability and a more equal distribution of power. A key unifying theme is that the distribution and control of resources should be directed towards the needs and potential of all members of society and not, as is currently the case, disproportionately to the few. Accordingly people should 'be able to influence and control decisions that affect their everyday lives'. Her stipulation of a new, society-wide social settlement is similar in several key respects to the changes Ted Benton considers are increasingly urgent for ecological survival. Benton offers a 'red/green' alternative to neoliberalism, combining a sombre and urgent assessment of the impossibility of neoliberal market economics' solution to climatic catastrophe, with a case for reforms for the system change needed to save the planet. He identifies popular and community-based environmental movements as the potential drivers of such changes.

Mike O'Donnell's central argument is that unless democracy is greatly extended and securely institutionalised, it will be difficult, perhaps impossible, to achieve and sustain the various radical and progressive goals proposed as alternatives to neoliberal regimes. Democracy as an essential aspect of liberty has long been a member of the radical trilogy of liberty, equality and solidarity. Arguments for democracy are recurrent prescriptions, both in this part and throughout this book. Several authors make a convincing case for societal rather than merely political democracy, expressing frustration with the inadequacies and limits of Britain's system of parliamentary and local democracy. In this part Gilbert makes clear that the expansion of democracy must also be pursued democratically – there should be a consistency and integrity between means and ends. Addressing the workings of democracy, Coote supports the radical principle of subsidiarity – that decisions should be taken as close as possible to the citizen. In advocating institutional democracy, O'Donnell extends the case for democracy to areas of society in which it is often disregarded or ignored. In their joint chapter in Part Three Jones and O'Donnell substantiate this thread by describing an increasingly potent source of the current democratic surge, in the form of post-war social movements' advancement of an extended range of human and civil rights.

ONE

Modes of anti-neoliberalism: moralism, Marxism and 21st century socialism

Jeremy Gilbert

In this chapter, I will begin by considering a number of different genres of anti-neoliberal discourse and politics, and the implicit or explicit alternatives to neoliberalism which they propose, before fleshing out in more detail what I consider to be the most useful alternative to neoliberalism that contemporary radicals could propose. This first section will not offer an exhaustive typology, but merely an attempt to elaborate on some of the different ways in which neoliberalism is criticised from varying perspectives and what the political implications of those variations are.

Moralism versus neoliberalism

Perhaps the most widely distributed mode of anti-neoliberal discourse in the English-speaking world is that which takes an ethical stance against the moral poverty of neoliberal norms and the perceived injustice of its social effects. Moral appeals to 'social justice' are typical of religious campaigners, the charitable section and mainstream non-government organisations (NGOs). For example, the following comes from
Pope Francis' first 'Apostolic Exhortation' issued in November 2013:

> While the earnings of a minority are growing exponentially, so too is the gap separating the majority from the prosperity enjoyed by those happy few. This imbalance is the result of ideologies which defend the absolute autonomy of the marketplace and financial speculation. Consequently, they reject the right of states, charged with vigilance for the common good, to exercise any form of control. A new tyranny is thus born, invisible and often virtual, which unilaterally and relentlessly imposes its own laws and rules.

Debt and the accumulation of interest also make it difficult for countries to realize the potential of their own economies and keep citizens from enjoying their real purchasing power. To all this we can add widespread corruption and self-serving tax evasion, which have taken on worldwide dimensions. The thirst for power and possessions knows no limits. In this system, which tends to devour everything which stands in the way of increased profits, whatever is fragile, like the environment, is defenseless before the interests of a deified market, which become the only rule.[1]

Such statements have an obvious rhetorical force, but are always subject to an obvious question as to what moral authority or assumptions they are actually based on. The papal critique of neoliberal ideology, unsurprisingly, goes on to assert that 'behind this attitude lurks a rejection of ethics and a rejection of God'. This is perfectly justified in this context, but it is also a reminder that without recourse to some such divine authority, it can be difficult to ground as an essentially moralistic response to neoliberalism in any satisfactory way. Above all, it is worth observing here that this is an essentially conservative response to neoliberalism which judges it for its departure from some perceived set of established moral norms.

The trouble with such a response is that it is quite difficult to imagine it achieving widespread popular currency in a secular culture, especially one wherein the extraordinary capacity of neoliberal capitalism to generate novel modes of being and enjoyment offers very marked compensations to much of the population for abandoning traditional communitarian norms, which are widely perceived as tied closely to the hierarchies and beliefs of a previous epoch. Irrespective of any religious or secularist considerations, it is easy enough to observe that appeals to social justice seem to have had at best a limited effect in mobilising large populations against neoliberalism in countries like the UK in recent years.

The same can be said of various forms of conservative communitarianism, the religious motivation of which is sometimes less explicit, if just as logically necessary to their internal consistency. A very good example in recent British politics was the 'Blue Labour' project, which attempted to articulate communitarianism, social conservatism, anti-immigration policies and localism with a vaguely social democratic politics, on the grounds that both social democracy and social conservatism have a common enemy in neoliberalism, while mass immigration is essentially a neoliberal policy. This synthesis, it was hoped, would enable the Labour Party to connect with white working class voters who had drifted towards the populist right or simply into non-voting apathy.

It didn't work, partly because it was difficult to pretend that an ugly xenophobia was not an element of the structures of feeling to which Blue Labour hoped to appeal, and this was a sentiment which the rest of the Labour movement was unwilling to indulge.[2] More fundamentally, however, there was never any evidence that this was a project which could appeal to anything but the most conservative and residual section of the public. Its most articulate public advocate, Jon Cruddas MP (himself an explicit adherent to 'Catholic Social Teaching'), produced a fascinating and well-researched report into the Labour 2015 electoral defeat, dividing the public into three broad groups of 'pioneers' (modernist metropolitan egalitarians), 'prospectors' (self-interested individualists) and 'settlers' (anxious conservatives) which showed the danger that Labour was in if it could only attract the support of the pioneers.[3] However, the very same data seemed to suggest that Blue Labour, or any comparable conservative communitarianism, could only ever hope to attract the 'settlers', and would alienate the other groups. Arguably, this exemplifies the weakness of all moralistic, conservative and communitarian responses to neoliberalism.

Neoliberalism makes you ill

Another family of anti-neoliberal political discourses which we can identify is those which point to neoliberalism's supposedly objectively deleterious effects on human wellbeing: at a personal, social or even planetary level. Although they may overlap considerably with ethical and communitarian discourses, the difference is that they all make some claim to objective and measurable knowledge of neoliberalism's consequences, and to a set of objective criteria according to which those consequences can be measured and judged.

This isn't a new idea: classical socialism and social democracy, going back to early Fabianism and even some strands of Marxism, have often claimed to be able to administer society according to principles which are not only more just than those informing liberal capitalism, but in some objective sense more efficient, effective and productive. A notable recent variant on this tradition has been the work of Pickett and Wilkinson, authors of the widely read study *The Spirit Level* and founders of the Equality Trust. Epidemiologists by training, Pickett and Wilkinson amass a wealth of evidence that social inequality produces deleterious social and psychological effects (mostly related to various forms of stress) even for the elite beneficiaries. Conversely, they show that higher levels of equality produce concomitant benefits, even in societies as politically and culturally different as Sweden and Japan (Pickett and Wilkinson, 2009). This is extremely interesting so far as it goes, but the lack of any real political or sociological dimension to their analysis leaves Pickett and Wilkinson somewhere short of a political strategy for the actual implementation of equality. Their early hope seems to have been that the sheer objective weight of their evidence would be enough to convince significant sections of the political class to adopt policies with such an objective: a naive hope, to say the least, and not one that has enjoyed any obvious success.

Pickett and Wilkinson's work resembles in some senses that of psychologically oriented writers such as Oliver James and other diagnosticians of 'affluenza' (James, 2008): a set of psychological symptoms supposedly produced by the excessive self-indulgence (psychic as well as material) encouraged by hyper-consumerism and neoliberal individualism. While their methods and diagnoses may vary, all rely on various forms of medical discourse and all try hard to assert that on some fundamental level even finance capitalists suffer from the cultural effects of neoliberalism. This is no doubt true on a certain level, but it is an approach which always risks depoliticising the phenomena which it tries to analyse, to the extent that it occludes any sense that certain material interests are in fact served by the propagation of neoliberalism. James, for example, is at pains to convince us that 'the selfish capitalist' alone in his penthouse with his cocaine and his prostitutes is not really happy. That may well be true, but it is also an approach which tends to occlude the extent to which, whether or not they make him happy, those accoutrements are all evidence for the selfish capitalist having successfully accrued certain significant forms of power which others do not have and which, indeed, he deprives them of. This failure to consider neoliberal society as a field of power relations is entirely typical of other interventions aimed at the general promotion of 'happiness', 'wellbeing' or 'flourishing' (Davies, 2014), such as economist Richard Layard's project to promote Cognitive Behavioural Therapy.

Radical materialism: ecology versus neoliberalism

Perhaps the most powerful analyses of neoliberalism's objectively deleterious effects are those which rely on the most incontrovertibly objective data: not psychological diagnoses or sociological deductions, but physical measurements of carbon, temperature and water flow.

It is interesting to note, therefore, that critics who bring together an understanding of neoliberalism with an interest in topics such as geography and environmental economics also tend to bring to bear a distinctly Marxian analysis of neoliberalism and its motivations. Commentators such as Naomi Klein (2015) explain clearly the close relationship between measurable climate change and neoliberal regimes of governance and intensive marketisation. Put simply, following radical geographer David Harvey (2007), neoliberalism is above all a project to restore the class power of finance capitalism, and the only way to confront it is not with moralising critique, but with projects to build up the collective power of currently subjugated social groups.

However, exactly how to do this is a further question. If such accounts generate analyses of neoliberalism which are both more politically satisfying and more securely evidence-based than either religious communitarianism or psychosocial epidemiology, they are often somewhat lacking in any strong account of why the exploitative relations which neoliberalism facilitates are tolerated in subject populations, or what the political mechanisms might be by which those relations could be changed. We might, therefore, for the sake of schematism, identify both purely Marxist and eco-Marxist accounts of neoliberalism as a third broad family of anti-neoliberal discourse. What characterises this group of analyses and proposals is that they have a clear sense of the material interests supporting and being expressed by neoliberalism, are able to gesture towards systemic alternatives, and do not, like conservative critics, seem to imagine that the entire history of capitalist modernisation could simply be reversed. Programmatically, they would tend to be associated with quite classical projects to build socialist alternatives to capitalism, from Latin America to Northern Europe.

Radical democracy

The final group of anti-neoliberal positions that I will identify here does not sit in any kind of opposition to the former one, but rather exists in a necessary relationship of dialogue with them. These we might call political or radical democratic variants of anti-neoliberalism. They are typically concerned with the anti-democratic consequences of neoliberalism and with attempting to understand the specificities both of its forms of governmentality and of the ways in which its hegemony has been won and secured in various contemporary and historical contexts. My own work clearly falls into this category, as does that of contemporaries like Will Davies (2014), while we have obviously built on the contributions of major thinkers such as Stuart Hall (1988) and Wendy Brown (2015). Perhaps the key observation that unites the different perspective within this family is that neoliberalism has only ever been implemented to the extent that democratic institutions have been weakened, as neoliberalism has never enjoyed an explicit popular mandate anywhere in the world (Gilbert, 2014a). Politically, the logical correlate of this family of anti-neoliberalism would include those political projects which have sought to articulate a critique of neoliberalism with demands for radical democratic institutional reform, as well as major socioeconomic transformation: examples would include, of course, Podemos in Spain, but also Common Weal in Scotland.

Radical modernity

One logical necessity of any such project to link social, political, institutional and economic demands is the need to challenge the institutional nexus which neoliberalism has produced, from international technocratic bodies such as the World Trade Organization (WTO) to the frameworks in place for the monitoring of public services at the level of individual users. An absolute necessity for that is to reject one of neoliberalism's primary ideological claims: that it represents the only viable and logical model of modernity in the world today. If we look back at points in history where the left has achieved real political successes, we can see that progressives have always had to identify the problems which capitalism is creating at any given moment, and respond to them by using new technologies, new forms of government and new types of self-organisation in order to achieve their objectives.

The moment of the socialist left's greatest success – the mid-20th century – was also the moment when it most wholeheartedly embraced what were then the cutting-edge sciences of manufacturing, communication and management. The nationalised industries and universal public services of the post-war welfare states made heavy use of organisational techniques developed by Ford and other pioneers of industry. Lenin had already declared, years earlier, that 'Communism is Soviet power plus the electrification of the whole country'. Gramsci went even further, suggesting in the 1930s that the experience of automated assembly-line factory work might be good for workers – freeing their minds from any necessary engagement with their work and enabling to them think about other matters (revolution, for example), while also inculcating in them the habits of efficiency and sober self-discipline which effective revolutionaries would require (Gramsci, 1971, pp 294–317).

As shocking as this sounds to contemporary ears, we could make a very good case that it was precisely the generation of workers schooled in the factory discipline of the 1930s and 1940s who ultimately won the most significant wave of social reforms in history: those which made possible the New Deal in the US and the post-war welfare states of Western Europe. This all goes to illustrate the fact that socialism has only been able to find the energy and the tools with which to develop a successful political programme when it has understood itself as a modernising project, working with the grain of technological and organisational progress even while it works to dismantle the class relations of capitalism.

Recently we have seen a rash of publications in the UK calling for some kind of left modernisation. The think tank and lobby group Compass published a pamphlet by myself and Mark Fisher (Gilbert and Fisher, 2014) which argues that the embrace of conservative communitarianism by some sections of the Labour Party has been a mistake. It advocated instead the democratisation of public services. Paul Mason's book *PostCapitalism* has recently garnered considerable attention for his claim that capitalism is in the process of mutating into some more democratic and egalitarian form of 'post-capitalism': networked technologies facilitate the development of new economies of free information, collaborative creation and non-hierarchical organisation. Another Compass pamphlet by Indra Adnan and Neal Lawson (2014) explicitly evokes the analysis of '*New Times*' made by *Marxism Today* magazine in the 1980s, while identifying the emergent culture of networks as a major radical resource. The more recent book by Nick Srnicek and Alex Williams (2015) calls on the radical left to abandon any attachment to localism or primitivism and to embrace the dream of a future in which the automation of both manufacturing and many mundane intellectual tasks renders all but the most minimal quantities of human work unnecessary.

Cybernetic revolution

Of course (and ironically), there's nothing new about these sets of claims: radical thinkers have been calling for new technologies to be put to progressive ends at least since the 19th century, and have been discussing the politics of networks at least since the 1950s. Nonetheless, it's striking that across these different contemporary interventions, a common set of themes emerges, focusing on the need to explore the radical potential inherent in the technologies and new organisational techniques which define our time.

That potential is pretty obvious to anyone who recognises the centrality of social media to Jeremy Corbyn's successful campaign to become Labour leader in 2015 or Obama's election in 2009. It should hardly need spelling out why a technology which enables millions of people to communicate with each other at minimal costs should have the potential to facilitate many new forms of democratic social and political organisation. It was obvious, in fact, to Salvador Allende's pioneering democratic socialist government in Chile at the end of the 1960s, when it developed one of the earliest known distributed computer networks – Cybersyn – to facilitate experiments in democratic economic planning: the subject of a brilliant book by Eden Medina (2011). It's surely no coincidence that Chile became the target for the CIA-backed coup in 1973 which created the opportunity for the first full neoliberal economic programme to be imposed upon an unwilling nation.

Of course, there are good reasons as to why claims for the progressive potential of technology are often met with scepticism today. Many of us can remember the wild promises that were made for the democratic impact of the internet in the 1990s, when Californian proselytisers assured us that by now we would be living in a world of perfectly free communication and so of perfectly working democracy. Many of us are also conscious that the everyday reality of the networked world is one of daily exploitation: from the Chinese factories producing iPhones and MacBooks to the call centres of Mumbai and Newcastle. Edward Snowden's revelations about mass state surveillance over the internet have only added to the growing sense shared by many that our entire lives are now monitored and administered by Facebook and Google.

But it would be wrong to see such developments as proof that these technologies lack all progressive potential. In fact they are only proof that such potential cannot be unlocked as long as these technologies are only put at the service of capital accumulation and the exploitation of workers. From this point of view, what ought to become the basis for a powerful popular critique of contemporary capitalism is precisely the gap between the widely shared intuition that these technologies are powerful forces of potential liberation, and the lived reality of them invading our lives, taking over our attention, and giving us relatively little in return.

In fact some theorists would go further, suggesting that the communicative and creative potential which such technologies make possible is precisely what capital needs us to have in order for it successfully to exploit us, but also exactly what we need in order to resist that exploitation. For example, a huge amount of value is produced online today merely by individuals sharing information about themselves and reacting to information shared by others: it's by mining this data and selling it to advertisers that Facebook makes its millions. On the other hand, this just goes to show the real potential of these technologies for communication, social organisation and data gathering. Going even further, we might mirror Gramsci's (1971) observations about the radical potential of Ford's factory workers: today, the contemporary radical may in fact require precisely the skills in complex management of data flows, careful profile management and network agility for which living in a world of social media and ubiquitous computing equips us.

Potent collectivities and neoliberal hegemony

Mason understands this way of being as constituting the 'networked individual', characterised by multiple connections and by weak ties to any specific tradition or community. I look at this slightly differently, however. It is certainly true that networked people today understand themselves primarily as 'individuals' who must weaken their ties to places, people and institutions while staying mobile and maintaining a high profile in order to compete in the labour market. I don't think that's an effect of the technology, however, but rather a consequence of it being deployed under conditions of neoliberal hegemony.

In a culture ruled by neoliberalism and labour market insecurity, the norms of competitive individualism are presented across key social institutions – from TV to schools – as being normal and healthy. Under such circumstances, all other things being equal, people will start to think of themselves in those terms: overlooking the collaborative potential of their networked relations, focussing only on competitive elements of their experience (competing for the most 'likes' and followers, and so on) rather than exploring their potential to facilitate collaboration.

Under these circumstances, the challenge for 21st century socialism is not simply to harness the power of 'network individuals'. Rather, our aim should be to enable networked people to stop thinking of themselves merely as 'individuals' at all. Instead of seeing themselves as being necessarily in competition with each other, the left must find ways to enable networked citizens to realise their potential for collective creativity.

The task is to find new ways of empowering people to coordinate with others, often outside of the traditional contexts of the localised workplace or the immediate neighbourhood, in order to assemble what I call 'potent collectivities': groups on various scales which are actually capable of making some shared decisions and acting on them in a way which changes something. I argue in my book *Common Ground* that this is the basic objective of all democratic politics: to enable 'potent collectivities' to come into existence, whether in workplaces or communities or in any other context (Gilbert, 2014b). There's no question that digital platforms are in some senses the most sophisticated tool for enabling potent collectives that has ever been developed.

Confronting capitalist power

Of course, there's no getting away from the fact that the major global internet platforms are all currently controlled by a handful of huge corporations. More than that, I think it's fair to say that if any group is truly globally 'hegemonic' in the world today, affecting the everyday lives of millions while helping to shape political agendas and cultural norms, it's the 'Big Tech' companies of Silicon Valley, in alliance with the financial institutions, that fund them and profit from them.

This is why the creation of democratic, mutually owned alternative platforms (imagine a free, fully functioning social network), strategically breaking up the power monopoly that that alliance has established, really ought to be a key demand of socialists in the 20th century; and why ultimately any 21st century socialism must have as one of its key global objectives the transformation of Apple and other global tech monopolies into democratic workers' cooperatives. At the same time, any such programme would seek to deploy a range of strategies which all work with the grain of the technological times in positive and egalitarian ways: democratising knowledge, sharing expertise, opening up institutions and empowering workers.

Such a programme would necessarily include measures which place a strong emphasis on introducing democratic governance into all public services – an idea developed further in O'Donnell's chapter. In fact this is a classic historic demand of the New Left, from Raymond Williams (1961) to Hilary Wainwright (2003). In particular, any radical programme for the 21st century would have to bring forward plans to democratise knowledge and learning fundamentally, by converting all schools into democratic community schools, along the lines proposed by reformers calling for 'Citizen Schools' and 'Common Schools'. (Wills et al, 2013; Fielding, 2010).

The principles of network logic, self-organisation and distributed decision making which would inform 21st century socialism could inform policy agendas across a range of different domains. For example, they might inspire government to implement a massive programme of distributed renewable energy generation, through the reinstatement and extension of the feed-in tariffs programme which was scrapped by the last government, and through investment in localised energy production. Something like a Ministry for Mutuality could be set up explicitly to encourage the launch of cooperatives and mutuals and the transition of existing private firms to mutual status wherever possible. At the same time the Ministry of Labour proposed by Corbyn (Labour List, 2015) could seek to explore all possible uses of new technology to facilitate organisation of workers and encourage union membership across the workforce, especially in sectors in which unionisation is currently low. This must include exploring the possibilities of new forms of organisation, online unions for precarious workers in which industries rarely congregate physically, etc. In the UK the proposed Constitutional Convention (Barnett, 2015) should include suggestions for participatory budgeting and participatory democracy in local government, and experimentation with nationwide deliberative mechanisms using web technology.

As the Conclusion chapter to this book explicates, for many people today there's no more pressing issue than the lack of affordable housing. But do we really need more social housing on the old models, or more private housing, encouraging individuals to become small-time property speculators rather than collaborating with their neighbours and communities to solve a shared problem? Surely we need to give people without capital the chance to run their own communities and their own built environments, together. Online technologies, and developments such as generative architecture, could massively facilitate the processes whereby housing co-ops design their living spaces together while making collective decisions across their lifespans.

We all know how dominated the media is by defenders of class privilege. The development of an independent media sector, including social media platforms, would have to be an absolute priority for any seriously progressive government in the 21st century. This might enable a radical government finally to do what everybody knows they should do and everybody assumes that the *Daily Mail* wouldn't stand for: bring forward plans for a Universal Basic Income – as Anna Coote's chapter and the Conclusion to this book argue in more detail. This would both massively simplify the benefits system and begin to prepare people for the automated post-work future dreamed of by radicals since the days of William Morris.

Given how hostile the public currently is to benefits claimants and the welfare system generally, this might be at tricky one to sell. So instead of simply planning to impose it on a reluctant populace, a potential radical government should propose to set up a nationwide process of extensive democratic deliberation reaching into all local communities in order to discuss this and other possible futures for welfare and incomes policies in a democratic and informed fashion. This form of democratic deliberation would be absolutely in the spirit of 21st century socialism.

21st century strategy

It's all very well having a potential radical programme, but it isn't the same thing as having an effective political strategy. So what might actually be distinctive about a strategy for 21st century socialism? The basic class strategy of socialism in the 20th century was to unite the industrial working class with sympathetic members of the professional classes, isolating the traditionally conservative commercial middle classes and forming an effective bloc with which to obstruct the power of capital. However, this strategy was always based on a false assumption, inherited from Marx himself and his 19th century contemporaries: the assumption that the conservative, residual petit-bourgeoisie would disappear soon enough, swallowed up by the big bourgeoisie or the proletariat. But this has not happened. Instead the commercial middle classes – who rely for their incomes and status on commercial activity which does not necessarily escalate into full-scale capital accumulation – have grown in size and importance since the 1970s.

Arguably, in fact, this changing entrepreneurial class is the most creative and dynamic one today – at least in the domains of technology and organisational innovation. It is also very far removed today from its socially conservative antecedents, its members largely seeing themselves as modern, liberal, tolerant and worldly; which is why, for example, the Conservative Party cannot easily rely on their support any more; a point made to me by radical Labour MP Jon Trickett. At the same time, this new entrepreneurial class experiences the reality of precarity on a regular basis, often enjoying uncertain incomes and rewards for large investments of effort and creative ingenuity.

Should it not be possible therefore to imagine new class alliances which would bring together workers, professionals and the entrepreneurial class into a coalition mobilised in support of a 21st century ideal of democratic, distributed decision making in the public sector, government and business? Would it not be easy enough to combine these goals with their natural concomitants: the traditional socialist aims of social equality, strengthened labour organisation and greater democracy? This, I suggest, could be the basis for a new socialist strategy in the 21st century: an active alliance between workers and those creative entrepreneurs who realise that their interests and those of the big financial institutions are from being aligned. If we could achieve that, breaking the historic hold of Big Capital on the imaginations of the entrepreneurial classes, overcoming the left's traditional antipathy to commercial and technological innovation, then many of the suggestions put forward here might really become possibilities.

Notes

[1.] See http://w2.vatican.va/content/francesco/en/apost_exhortations/documents/papa-francesco_esortazione-ap_20131124_evangelii-gaudium.html#No_to_an_economy_of_exclusion

[2.] The best collection of commentaries on Blue Labour, both sympathetic and critical, is to be found at www.opendemocracy.net/ourkingdom/collections/blue-labour

[3.] See http://labourlist.org/2015/08/labour-lost-because-voters-believed-it-was-anti-austerity/; http://labourlist.org/2015/08/labour-has-to-stop-patronising-socially-conservative-voters/; http://www.newstatesman.com/politics/2015/08/why-did-labour-lose

References

Adnan, I. and Lawson, N. (2014) *New times: How a politics of networks and relationships can deliver a good society*, Compass, www.compassonline.org.uk/publications/new-times/

Barnett, A. (2015) 'The Labour leader candidates and the constitution', openDemocracyUK, www.opendemocracy.net/ourkingdom/anthony-barnett/labour-leader-candidates-and-constitution

Brown, W. (2015) *Undoing the demos: Neoliberalism's stealth revolution*, New York: Zone.

Davies, W. (2014) *The limits of neoliberalism*, London: Sage.

Fielding, M. (2010) *Radical education and the common school: A democratic alternative*, London: Routledge.

Gilbert, J. (2014a) 'Populism and the left: Does UKIP matter? Can democracy be saved?', New Left Project, www.newleftproject.org/index.php/site/article_comments/populism_and_the_left_does_ukip_matter_can_democracy_be_saved

Gilbert, J. (2014b) *Common ground*, London: Pluto.

Gilbert, J. and Fisher, M. (2014) 'Reclaim modernity', *Compass*, www.compassonline.org.uk/publications/reclaiming-modernity-beyond-markets-beyond-machines/

Gramsci, A. (1971) *Selections from the prison notebooks*, London: Lawrence and Wishart.

Hall, S. (1988) *The hard road to renewal*, London: Verso.

Harvey, D. (2007) *A brief history of neoliberalism*, Oxford: Oxford University Press.

James, O. (2008) *The selfish capitalist*, London: Vermillion.

Klein, N. (2015) *This changes everything: Capitalism versus the climate*, London: Penguin.

Labour List (2015) Jeremy Corbyn wants to set up a new Ministry of Labour, http://labourlist.org/2015/08/jeremy-corbyn-wants-to-set-up-a-new-ministry-of-labour/

Mason, P. (2015) *PostCapitalism*, London: Allen Lane.

Medina, E. (2011) *Cybernetic revolutionaries: Technology and politics in Allende's Chile*, Cambridge, MA: MIT Press.

Pickett, K. and Wilkinson, R. (2009) *The spirit level: Why more equal societies almost always do better*, London: Allen Lane.

Srnicek, N. and Williams, A. (2015) *Inventing the future*, London: Verso.

Williams, R. (1961) *The long revolution*, London: Chatto & Windus.

Wills, J., Watson, D. M., Chitty, C. and Audsley, J. (2013) *Citizen schools: Learning to rebuild democracy*, IPPR, www.ippr.org/publications/citizen-schools-learning-to-rebuild-democracy

TWO

People, planet, power: toward a new social settlement

Anna Coote

Introduction

As we imagine what life could be like beyond neoliberalism, we must envisage a new social settlement. This would be based on the best elements of the post-war settlement, which was designed to support the market economy and achieve full employment by introducing a welfare state and a degree of governmental macroeconomic management. At the same time it would address contemporary challenges – notably deepening social inequalities, accelerating threats to the natural environment and accumulations of power by wealthy elites.

At the New Economics Foundation (NEF) we have argued the case for a settlement designed around three main goals to address these challenges: social justice, environmental sustainability, and a more equal distribution of power. The goals are interdependent and can be summed up as aiming for 'sustainable social justice', which is taken to require a fair and equitable distribution of social, environmental, economic and political resources between people, places and – where possible – between generations. There are no quick fixes. To build a new social settlement, we need to change systems and structures over the medium and long term, rather than looking for technical solutions to immediate problems within policy silos.

Our framing for a new settlement pays close attention to the assets embedded in people's lives and relationships and to the diverse products and features of the natural environment. In Karl Polanyi's ([1944] 1957) terms, they are 'fictitious commodities' and in Nancy Fraser's (2014) they are 'conditions of possibility' for the functioning of capitalist markets. In conventional economics, they are treated as saleable items, valued only as inputs to production. We maintain that they must be valued and nurtured as shared goods, so that they are able to flourish in the short, medium and long term.

This chapter draws on the main features of a report published by NEF called *People, planet, power: towards a new social settlement*. It is not a definitive plan for policy makers, but a contribution to wider debates, which highlights issues too often overlooked and calls for a radical change of direction. I begin by describing the goals and four distinctive objectives implied by the goals. I then give examples of practical proposals that follow from the goals and objectives.

Goals

We define the first goal, social justice, as an equal chance for all people to enjoy the essentials of a good life, to fulfil their potential and participate in society. Wellbeing, equality and satisfaction of needs are central to this understanding of social justice. Wellbeing means people functioning well, both personally and socially through a sense of competence, meaning and purpose, and connection to others (Abdallah et al, 2009, 2011); based on the satisfaction of physical as well as psychological needs. These in turn depend on external conditions such as income, housing, education, social relationships and connectedness, and personal resources, such as physical health and psychological resilience. All these factors interact dynamically and can reinforce each other. Providing favourable conditions for wellbeing is widely viewed as a responsibility of government – with wellbeing increasingly measured as an official indicator of social progress (Stiglitz et al, 2009; Shelf, 2014).

The pursuit of wellbeing is both ethically and practically desirable. Ethically because it is a good thing in itself and a worthwhile objective in all circumstances; practically because high levels of wellbeing contribute to a flourishing society and economy. But both of these gains depend on equal availability. So equality, like wellbeing, is central to social justice. Equality, in this context, means equal worth before the law and an equal chance to flourish for all. Promoting equality goes well beyond prohibiting unequal and unfair treatment of individuals, promoting antipoverty strategies, or self-reliance among disadvantaged groups – all theoretically consistent with neo-liberalism. It means eliminating conditions that give rise to privilege and unfair advantage.

The second goal, environmental sustainability, is defined here as living within environmental limits and respecting planetary boundaries, ensuring that natural resources that are needed for life to flourish are unimpaired for present and future generations. Remaining within the ecological constraints of a finite planet has been described as 'the single most important challenge facing society today' (Jackson and Victor, 2013, p 9). According to the Stockholm Resilience Centre,

> The exponential growth of human activities is raising concern that further pressure on the Earth System could destabilize critical biophysical systems and trigger abrupt or irreversible environmental changes that would be deleterious or even catastrophic for human well-being. (Rockstrom et al, 2009)

Therefore a new social settlement must take full account of environmental sustainability. Unless we heed scientists' predictions, there will – within a matter of decades – be no recognisable human society for which to plan social policies. So the settlement must be designed to minimise harm to the environment and safeguard natural resources, as an essential precondition for human wellbeing. Neither social justice nor environmental sustainability is attainable through market mechanisms or individual actions alone, but only by pooling resources, recognising shared interests and acting together – both through civil society and through the state. Only the state can promote equality across entire national populations (Coote, 2010)

This brings us to the third goal, a more equal distribution of power. Here, the formal and informal means by which people participate in and influence decisions and actions among local and national populations, and groups where economic, social and cultural factors combine to create inequalities. A new social settlement aims for people to be able to influence and control decisions and actions that affect their everyday lives. It seeks to ensure, as far as possible, a fair balance of power between people, because the dynamics of power determine how far social, environmental, economic and political resources are nurtured or exhausted, sequestered or shared. Wealthy elites accumulate money and power, building influence over policy and the ability to defend and strengthen their positions through donations and lobbying (Stiglitz, 2012). Degrees of power should be determined by the principles of social justice rather than by wealth, connections or privilege.

Individuals should have control over what happens to them personally, but also vital is collective control, through groups and organisations, over access to the means of achieving fair shares of social, environmental, economic and political resources – a theme explored here in the chapters by Johal et al, Cumbers and O'Donnell. The neoliberal momentum toward deregulating markets and privatising services tends to undermine the conditions that make collective control possible. A new social settlement would seek to reverse that tendency, and to reinforce the principle of subsidiarity, so decisions are taken as closely as possible to the citizen. Power is only elevated to higher levels – from neighbourhood to local authority, or from local authority to national government – for overriding reasons in the public interest, for social justice and environmental sustainability, and by public consent.

To realise all three goals, the settlement must be able to meet 'the needs of the present without compromising the ability of future generations to meet their own needs' (World Commission on Environment and Development, 1987, p 41). This formula, from the Brundtland Report on sustainable development in 1987, remains an invaluable guide for policy makers. The essential premise of need theory (Gough, 2014) is that every individual, everywhere in the world, at all times present and future, has certain basic needs – health and autonomy – as the preconditions for participation in society. Health is about physical survival and wellbeing. Autonomy means both autonomy of agency and critical autonomy (Doyal and Gough, 1991). Basic needs apply in all circumstances and to all people. How they are met will vary – often widely – according to people's social, environmental, economic, political and cultural circumstances Nevertheless, certain categories of 'needs satisfiers' are generic because they underpin health and autonomy in all cultures at all times. These include adequate nutritious food, water and protective housing, along with a non-hazardous physical and work environment, appropriate healthcare, security in childhood, significant primary relationships, physical and economic security, safe birth control and childbearing conditions, and basic education.

Needs theory is especially relevant for building a new social settlement because it offers objective, evidence-based and philosophically grounded criteria to guide decisions on future and present generations' needs and the means for meeting those needs. It suggests a moral framework for deciding about tradeoffs. Meeting wants and preferences today cannot be allowed to impair the basic needs – health, autonomy and critical capacity – of poor people and poor countries in the present, or of future generations.

Objectives

Four objectives distinguish this settlement from the post-war settlement and tend to be overlooked in mainstream debates today.

Plan for prosperity without relying on economic growth

The post-war welfare state was built on the premise that the economy would continue to grow, yielding more tax revenues to pay for more and better public services. Despite inconsistencies, continuing high levels of economic growth remained the default expectation for half a century. Now, all sensible forecasts predict significantly slower rates. Furthermore, continuing growth, especially in the economically advantaged world, is now thought to be incompatible with internationally agreed-upon targets to cut greenhouse gas (GHG) emissions. 'Weightless growth' aspirations will fall short, by a wide margin, of the reach and speed required for humanity to live within planetary boundaries, or to keep global warming limits compatible with human wellbeing. As Tim Jackson observes:

> there is as yet no credible, socially-just, ecologically-sustainable scenario of continually growing incomes for a world of nine billion people ... simplistic assumptions that capitalism's propensity for efficiency will allow us to stabilize the climate or protect against resource scarcity are nothing short of delusional. (Jackson, 2009, p 57)

So a new social settlement cannot rely on continuing economic growth to enhance tax revenues. With the right political will public resources could enable public services without growth – for example by raising taxes, closing tax loopholes, or cutting spending on nuclear weaponry. However, once the interdependence of social justice and environmental sustainability is acknowledged, further calls on public funds must be accommodated. Tax revenues are needed urgently for investment in environmentally sustainable infrastructure (such as renewable energy generation and zero-carbon housing and transport systems) and in all possible measures to keep societies and economies within planetary boundaries. At most, any additional public funds will have to be shared between pro-social policies and measures to safeguard the natural environment. Thus a new social settlement must be designed to function well with little or no additional public funds. The next two objectives follow from this.

Shift investment and action 'upstream' to prevent harm

This is probably the best way to improve social outcomes without relying on more tax revenues (Coote, 2012). For example, the National

Health Service costs the taxpayers in England some £96 billion a year, of which a tiny fraction goes toward preventing illness, while £91 billion goes to Clinical Commissioning Groups and National Health England, who spend most of it on treatment and care for people who are ill. Rising demands for healthcare put NHS finances under nearly intolerable pressures. Yet most forms of ill health are avoidable. Michael Marmot's (2010) classic work on health inequalities shows that the primary causes of most social problems, which in turn generate health problems, derive from the same bundle of issues: material poverty combined with a poverty of opportunity and aspiration, locked in by class, culture and location. Investing in measures to tackle these 'upstream' or underlying causes of harm could significantly reduce demand for costly healthcare services.

Preventive strategies not only pre-empt spending in the medium and longer term, they generally cost less than 'downstream' interventions into the consequences of harm (Early Action Task Force, 2011). They can reduce demand for various services, not just healthcare. Unemployment, antisocial behaviour and many forms of crime, for example, have roots in poverty and deprivation. Such conditions are, arguably, best tackled not by the neo-liberal formula of helping individuals to cope with them, but by upstream measures: providing decent jobs, higher wage floors, good education and decent housing for all. Certainly these measures call for public spending, but unlike most 'downstream' services in hospitals, prisons and job centres, they also promote human flourishing and a prosperous economy. I have argued this case for prevention more fully elsewhere (Coote, 2012; see also Southwark and Lambeth Early Action Commission, 2015).

Nurture the 'core economy'

Other resources for a new social settlement, independent of continuing economic growth or increased public spending, consist of uncommodified human and social resources embedded in the lives of every individual. They are rooted in everyday life (for example, time, wisdom, experience, energy, knowledge and skills) and in interpersonal relationships (for example, love, empathy, responsibility, reciprocity, teaching, learning and caring for others). Because they are central and essential to society, these experiences are part of a 'core' belonging to an 'economy' in the sense that they are the objects of human and social production and exchange.

The core economy extends well beyond the domestic sphere: through extended networks, neighbourhoods, and communities of interest and place. Some of its activities are formally organised – for example, through national charities or local authorities; most arise organically from close social relationships. The core economy provides essential underpinnings for the market economy by raising children, caring for people who are ill, frail and disabled, feeding families, maintaining households and building and sustaining intimacies, friendships, social networks and civil society. It is where people learn and share practical skills, such as cooking, gardening, sewing, household repairs and DIY – all of which have been shown to build confidence, connectedness, a sense of self-worth and people's capacity to help themselves and others (Abdallah and Jeffrey, 2014).The core economy has a key role, too, in safeguarding the natural economy, since everyday human activities strongly influence how far environmental resources are used sustainably or squandered. Without the core economy, the formal economy would seize up. Assets and relationships in the core economy are routinely unpriced and exchanged without payment. Though often ignored and exploited, they have enormous value.

The core economy is not inherently good or right, but is profoundly influenced by the rules, protocols and power relations emanating from the state and the market. While it shapes and sustains social and economic life, it also reflects and reproduces social and economic divisions and inequalities. For example, most of its transactions involve unwaged women – a pattern that generates lasting inequalities in job opportunities, income and power between women and men. And time is a vital resource in the core economy. Though everyone's amount of time is notionally the same, some have much more control over how they use their time than others. How paid time versus unpaid time is distributed between men and women and across different social groups can thus exert a strong influence in narrowing or widening inequalities (Coote and Franklin, 2013; Goodwin, 2010). The form of development of the core economy is therefore critical.

For a new social settlement, human and social resources (the 'core economy') must be brought into the centre of policy making, strengthened and given the ability to flourish: shifting the foundations of the settlement from an economy based on scarcity of material resources to one based on an abundance of human resources. It also shifts the focus of the settlement from a deficit model, centred on problems that require fixing, to a systemic approach that starts with people's existing strengths and assets and what it takes to lead a good and satisfying life. The core economy can 'grow' if it is recognised, valued, nurtured and supported in ways that are consistent with – and help to achieve – sustainable social justice. This implies an important role for public institutions, in creating the conditions for equal participation, a vibrant civil society and confident, creative local action.

Strengthen solidarity

This fourth objective – people getting together, pooling resources and acting collectively to support each other – features too rarely in contemporary debates about social policy. In this context, solidarity is understood as feelings of sympathy and responsibility, shared by people within and between groups, encouraging inclusive, supportive action (Wilde, 2013). It rests on an understanding that people's lives and life chances are interconnected. It implies a sense of shared values and purpose, and it often suggests reciprocity (meaning exchanges of similar or equivalent value). Though most easily generated in small groups and among people who share similar interests and identities, it can also apply to relations between groups. For a new social settlement, this kind of inter-group solidarity, what Robert Putnam (2001) calls 'bridging social capital' is especially important. Otherwise groups must fend for themselves, in active competition or conflict with others, or indifferent to how their actions impinge on the capacity of others to fend for themselves.

Historically, solidarity means active mutual support in pursuit of a shared purpose. Typically, it implies concerted action to deal with a common challenge or adversary. But (as with the core economy) it is not intrinsically virtuous. Men can use it to exclude women, or by one gang, class, nationality or ethnic group against others. Nevertheless, there are countless groups, organisations and campaigns where people express sympathy and responsibility for one another, offer active mutual support, and reach out to make common cause with others. Examples in the United Kingdom include the Transition Network, Co-operatives UK, trades union campaigns that reach beyond their members' immediate interests, such as TUC support for campaigns on child poverty and human rights, and social movements connected largely through social media, such as UK Uncut and Occupy.

There isn't a blueprint for solidarity. It's a kind of politics, open to negotiation and subject to change. The aim is to understand how different catalysts can combine to generate the kind of solidarity that will help to achieve the goals of a new social settlement. This solidarity is inclusive, expansive and active, both between groups that are strangers to each other, and across present and future generations. The 'common challenge or adversary' is not specifically other people, but the systems and structures that shore up inequalities, foster short-term greed, plunder the natural environment and blight the prospects of future generations.

Neoliberal ideology weakens solidarity. Promotion of individual choice, competition, consumer sovereignty, and the inherent 'fairness' of free markets widens inequalities which weaken solidarity by interfering with the potentiality for feelings of sympathy and shared responsibility between rich and poor. Measures that should help to strengthen solidarity include narrowing inequalities; devolving power; encouraging dialogue and participation; promoting coproduction; collective forms of ownership and control; an inclusive social security system; and state institutions and actions that encourage collaboration between groups and organisations (Coote and Angel, 2014).

Policy proposals for change

Four linked groups of proposals for practical change would help to realise the goals and objectives of the new social settlement: rebalancing work and time; releasing human resources; strengthening social security; and planning for a sustainable future. Here I will outline just three examples: reducing paid working hours, making coproduction the default model for getting things done, and promoting eco-social policies. Details of the rest are in the NEF's report (Coote, 2015).

Policy one: move toward shorter and more flexible hours of paid work

With little or no economic growth, shorter hours of paid work per person is the surest way to achieve good jobs for all. Lack of growth means more unemployment unless jobs are restructured to spread hours of paid work more evenly across the working-age population. We therefore propose a slow but steady move, over a decade or so, from today's official UK norm of 37.5 to 40 hours (varying according to inclusion of lunch breaks) toward a new standard working week. There are plenty of exceptions to the current 48 hours a week limit. One in five works more than 45 hours per week. The proposal here is for a new norm of 30 hours initially, moving over a longer period toward 21 hours.

Reducing the standard workweek could bring a range of social, environmental and economic benefits (Coote and Franklin, 2013; Coote et al, 2010). Shorter hours of paid work – for men as well as for women – would make it easier to balance employment with family responsibilities. It would help to prevent stress and anxiety, along with the associated risks to health. It would begin to unlock entrenched gender inequalities by freeing up time for men to do more childcare and unpaid domestic work. As a consequence, women could play a more equal role in the labour market and people could spend more time on all those unpaid activities that constitute the core economy: supporting family and social relations while also underpinning the formal economy. It would leave more time for participation in democratic decision making, and in local and political activities. It could make older people's transition from full-time employment to full retirement gentler and more gradual (as we suggest below), rather than the sudden drop from 40 hours to none that many experience today.

Shorter hours would also bring environmental gains. Challenging the prevailing assumption that the main purpose of life is to work more in order to earn more in order to buy more would reduce the amount of resource-intensive consumption associated with being busy and time-poor: eating processed ready-meals, taking flights instead of trains and travelling by car rather than walking, cycling or using public transport. With more time to live sustainably, things could be made and repaired instead of being bought, food could be grown and prepared with more time spent with friends and neighbours, learning new things, and with more creative and rewarding pastimes than shopping. More generally it would help more people to move out of the fast lane and reconsider what really matters in life. Evidence suggests that countries with shorter average working hours per week have smaller ecological footprints than those with longer working hours (Schor, 2013).

Shorter hours of paid work could reduce unemployment in an economy that is not growing, by distributing paid work more evenly. This is not a simple equation, but it would help to create more jobs and keep more people engaged in the labour market, avoiding unemployment's multiple disadvantages: lack of opportunity to improve skills, low self-esteem, a sense of hopelessness and social isolation, and the attendant mental and physical health risks. There is no evidence that shorter hours are bad for a country's economic 'success' as measured by GDP. Indeed, many countries with shorter than average hours have stronger than average economies (NEF, 2012). There is evidence that workers on shorter hours tend to be more productive hour-for-hour (Kunn-Nelen et al, 2013) and those better able to balance paid employment with unpaid responsibilities have higher wellbeing and constitute a more loyal, stable and committed workforce (Golden, 2012). Most people say they would like more time to themselves, but a gradual move to the proposed change would prevent unwelcome cuts in working hours or pay. A supportive regulatory framework and incentives would be needed for employers to take on more workers on shorter hours. Another crucial condition would be a sustained effort to achieve decent hourly rates of pay: no one should have to work long hours just to make ends meet.

Some of the productivity gains which often help to determine annual pay awards could be exchanged for time rather than money. For example, instead of a 3% pay rise, workers could negotiate for a 1.5% increment combined with a commensurate reduction in hours (approximately 30 minutes). This would accumulate over time, without pay reductions or productivity losses. Initially, it may be easier to introduce this change for employees on average or higher earnings, which carries a risk of accelerating inequalities in time as well as money. Nevertheless, this change would begin to undermine the association between long working hours and 'success' at work. An added benefit would be limiting higher income groups' resource-intensive consumption patterns (Schor, 2013; Coote and Franklin, 2013). Working 'part time' would cease to be a mark of low-paid, low-status employment and become instead the new 'full time' and a goal for all workers. Extra time gained cannot be eroded through inflation: an hour remains an hour, while extra pay can lose some of its value over time.

Under these new norms, new labour market entrants – such as young people – could be employed for 30 hours a week. With each new cohort, the numbers working 30 hours would grow until a critical mass was reached, while no one would experience a forced reduction in paid working time. At the other end of the age range, older workers could reduce their hours by one hour a week each year from the age of 50 or 55, facilitating longer labour market participation and the gradual transition to full retirement described above.

Policy two: make coproduction the default model

Under coproduction people routinely described as 'providers' and 'users' of services work together in equal and reciprocal partnerships. They pool different kinds of knowledge and skills, and bring together the formal and commodified resources of professional services with the informal and uncommodified resources of the core economy. This way, people act together to identify needs, design activities to meet those needs and, as far as possible, work together to deliver those activities. Individual and collective control is enhanced.

Coproduction is a set of principles, rather than instructions, used to guide how things are done. People involved in coproduction are recognised as assets, and the process builds on their existing capabilities rather than treating them as problems that need fixing. Coproduction fosters mutually reinforcing relationships, where everyone has something valuable to contribute and is helped by others. It builds supportive networks of equals. It breaks down barriers between professionals and service workers, on the one hand, and laypeople using services on the other. It encourages professionals to act as facilitators and catalysts for change rather than providers of services (Boyle et al, 2011).

On the basis of these principles such coproductive practices could become the mainstream or default approach to meeting needs of all kinds, in third sector and public bodies. For this to happen, those who provide services, in the public sector or in charities and community-based organisations, would need to change how they think about themselves, understand others, and operate on a day-to-day basis. These changes are most feasible if institutional practices change, especially where public authorities commission services.

Coproduction not only taps into human resources, it also encourages people to join forces and make common cause. At its best, it builds local networks and strengthens the capacity of local groups. By drawing upon the direct wisdom and experience that people have about what they need and what they can contribute, it helps improve wellbeing; so that further or more acute needs are less likely to arise. By changing the way people think about and act upon 'needs', coproduction promises more resources, better outcomes and a diminishing volume of demand for services.

Policy three: promote eco-social policies

There is a strong case for promoting, as part of a new social settlement, specific policies (described here as 'eco-social policies') that help to promote both social justice and environmental sustainability, at the same time. This can make good use of public resources by achieving multiple and mutually reinforcing benefits. Five instances of this combination illustrate its potential.

1. Walking and cycling are free or low-cost forms of travel which help reduce living costs and minimise carbon emissions. Resulting reductions in motorised transport improve air quality, and help to make neighbourhoods more congenial and secure. Measures to promote active travel must ensure that conditions are safe and positively encouraging, especially for those in poor neighbourhoods,

where there tends to be more traffic-related injuries and air pollution; and anxiety about walking or cycling alone, especially at night.

2. Access to, and physical exercise in green spaces, such as gardens, parks, verdant playgrounds, and the open countryside, improves mental and emotional wellbeing (Esteban, 2012) and generally produces little or no GHG emissions. Such activities can also raise levels of appreciation and concern for the natural environment. Measures to promote access to green spaces must ensure they are inviting, accessible and safe, especially for those less secure places in disadvantaged areas, for children and women, and for disabled people.

3. Fresh, seasonal, local food is usually more nutritious and its production less energy-intensive than processed food or ingredients transported over long distances. Purchasing local food keeps money circulating within local economies, helping to create and maintain local employment. Learning how to produce and prepare food can raise awareness about the value of land, water, crops, livestock and weather systems, insights about the pros and cons of different agricultural methods, and thus support for pro-environmental policy and practice. However, the picture is complicated by strong vested interests in retailing and agribusiness that are ranged against more local and popular control over food provenance and quality. Measures to encourage local food production should ideally be locally controlled and strong enough to counteract the influence of big business in the food sector. However, many local councils are selling off allotments and other land to make up for shrinking budgets. Institutional structures currently inhibit systemic planning for food, agriculture, health and the environment. Departments of health, environment, agriculture and trade should work together within shared policy frameworks instead of taking partial perspectives (Laing, 2012). NEF has set out more detailed arguments for a sustainable food system, drawing on lessons from other European countries and showing the wider social and economic benefits (Esteban et al, 2014).

4. Programmes to retrofit existing housing stock and to build new, energy-efficient homes can bring multiple benefits. Reducing the impact on natural resources by using renewable materials, insulating walls and roofs and installing solar and PVC panels can make homes more energy-efficient. They reduce high domestic energy bills and the resultant stress and anxiety for low-income households. A combination of ventilation and renewable energy can help to maintain good health by keeping people cool in winter and warm

in summer. Despite recognition and encouragement by a sequence of (albeit inadequate) government programmes, there has not been sufficient investment in the United Kingdom to transform the nation's housing stock or to bring domestic energy consumption down to sustainable levels. National and local government action is urgently needed.

5. 'Collaborative consumption' through community-based initiatives would enable people to share rather than buy things intended for their own use only. Examples include food co-ops (as distinct from food banks); car clubs (car-sharing programmes); centres for repairing and recycling discarded and broken goods; schemes for sharing and exchanging machinery and household equipment to avoid multiple purchasing; community cafés and restaurants run by and for local people; childcare co-ops; intergenerational mutual aid ventures, where younger and older people learn from and help each other – and much more.

Such activities can positively affect health and wellbeing by strengthening local networks; building confidence, social solidarity and local capabilities; and by helping to reduce living costs. Reducing consumption and energy use also has a positive impact on the environment. Initiatives of this kind are on the increase, but many struggle to find and keep affordable premises or to extend and maintain their reach. Local authorities could provide more support by making properties available, providing training and helping with backup functions such as accounting, by spreading information and, more broadly, by helping foster a congenial atmosphere and encouraging conditions. However, as the Airbnb example shows (The Economist, 2013), more thoughtful regulation at national level is needed to safeguard the spirit of the 'sharing economy' and prevent collaborative ventures becoming profit-generating giant corporations.

In conclusion

The goals, objectives and practical proposals set out in this chapter do not add up to a new *Beveridge Report* or a political manifesto. They are a contribution to current thinking about the welfare state and the kind of society we want for the future. They make the case for changing systems and structures over the long term. And they aim to change the ideological weather. In today's climate, we are often told: free markets and small government are the answer to most of our problems; neoliberal economics is an irrefutable science; the only thing that really matters is more economic growth, and inequalities are just collateral damage. The New Economics Foundation has worked hard for more than a quarter of a century to challenge this dominant narrative and to show that economies can be based on other social arrangements. Arguments for a new social settlement are part of an effort to build a new economics based on the premise that markets should serve the interests of people and the planet, not the other way around.

References

Abdallah, S., Michaelson, J., Steuer, N., Marks, N. and Thompson, S. (2009) *National accounts of well-being*, London: New Economics Foundation.

Abdallah, S., Michaelson, J., Seaford, C. and Stoll, L. (2011) *Measuring our progress*, London: New Economics Foundation.

Abdallah, S. and Jeffrey, K. (2014) *Hands-on communities: The community and wellbeing benefits of learning and sharing practical skills*, London: New Economics Foundation.

Boyle. D., Coote, A., Sherwood, C. and Slay, J. (2011) *Right here, right now: Taking co-production into the mainstream*. London: NEF and NESTA, www.neweconomics.org/publications/entry/right-here-right-now

Coote, A. (2010) *Cutting it: The 'Big Society' and the new austerity*, http://b.3cdn.net/nefoundation/fe562b1ef767dac0af_g0m6iykyd.pdf

Coote, A. (2012) *The wisdom of prevention*, http://b.3cdn.net/nefoundation/b8278023a5b025649f_5zm6i2btg.pdf

Coote, A (2015) *People, planet, power: Towards a new social settlement*, London: New Economics Foundation.

Coote, A. and Angel, J. (2014) *Solidarity: Why it matters for a new social settlement*, http://b.3cdn.net/nefoundation/207c255d8a0c04cba0_sum6b1yy7.pdf

Coote, A. and Franklin, J. (eds) (2013) *Time on our side: Why we all need a shorter working week*, London: New Economics Foundation.

Coote, A., Franklin, J. and Simms, A. (2010) *21 hours*, http://b.3cdn.net/nefoundation/f49406d81b9ed9c977_p1m6ibgje.pdf

Doyal, L., and Gough, I. (1991) *A theory of human need*, London: Palgrave Macmillan.

Early Action Task Force (2011) *The triple dividend*, www.community-links.org/uploads/documents/Triple_Dividend.pdf

Economist, The (2013) 'All eyes on the sharing economy', *Technical Quarterly,* Q1, www.economist.com/news/technology-quarterly/21572914-collaborative-consumption-technology-makes-it-easier-people-rent-items

Esteban, A. (2012) *Natural solution,* www.neweconomics.org/publications/entry/natural-solutions

Esteban, A. Devlin, S. and Carpenter, G. (2014) *Urgent recall: Our food system under review,* London: NEF, www.neweconomics.org/publications/entry/urgent-recall

Fraser, N. (2014) 'Behind Marx's hidden abode', *New Left Review,* 86: 63.

Golden, L. (2012) 'The effects of working time on productivity and firm performance: A research synthesis paper', *Conditions of Work and Employment Series No. 33,* Geneva: ILO, www.ilo.org/wcmsp5/groups/public/@ed_protect/@protrav/@travail/documents/publication/wcms_187307.pdf

Goodwin, N. (2010) 'If US consumption declines will the global economy collapse?' in K. Ekström and K. Glans (eds) *Changing consumer roles,* New York: Routledge.

Gough, I. (2014) *Climate change and sustainable welfare: The centrality of human needs,* http://b.3cdn.net/nefoundation/e256633779f47ec4e6_o5m6bexrh.pdf

Jackson, T. (2009) *Prosperity without growth? The transition to a sustainable economy,* www.sd-commission.org.uk/data/files/publications/prosperity_without_growth_report.pdf

Jackson, T. and Victor, P.A. (2013) *Green economy at community scale,* http://metcalffoundation.com/publications-resources/view/green-economy/

Kunn-Nelen, A., De Grip, A. and Fouarge, D. (2013) 'Is part-time employment beneficial for firm productivity?' *Industrial and Labor Relations Review,* 66 (5), http://papers.ssrn.com/sol3/papers.cfm?abstract_id=2368495

Laing, T. (2012) *Food matters: An integrative approach to food policy,* www.oecd.org/site/agrfcn/

Marmot, M. (2010) *Fair society, healthy lives,* www.instituteofhealthequity.org/projects/fair-society-healthy-lives-the-marmot-review

NEF (2012) Analysis by NEF of 10 countries based on data from OECD and World Bank', cited in A. Coote (2015) *People, planet, power: Towards a new social settlement,* London: New Economics Foundation.

Polanyi, K. ([1944] 1957) *The great transformation: The political and economic origins of our time,* 2nd ed, Boston: Beacon Press.

Putnam, R. (2001) *Bowling alone: The collapse and revival of American community*, New York: Simon and Schuster.

Rockstrom, J. and 27 others (2009) 'Planetary boundaries: Exploring the safe space for humanity', *Ecology and Society*, 14 (2): 32, www.ecologyandsociety.org/vol14/iss2/art32/

Schor, J. (2013) 'The triple dividend' in A. Coote and J. Franklin (eds) *Time on our side*, London: New Economics Foundation, pp 3-18.

Shelf, A. (2014) *Measuring national well-being: Insights across society, the economy and the environment*, Office of National Statistics, www.ons.gov.uk/ons/rel/wellbeing/measuring-national-well-being/reflections-on-measuring-national-well-being--may-2014/info-insights-across-society.html

Southwark and Lambeth Early Action Commission (2015) *Local early action: How to make it happen*, www.neweconomics.org/publications/entry/local-early-action-how-to-make-it-happen

Stiglitz, J.E. (2012) *The price of inequality*, New York: W.W. Norton & Company Inc.

Stiglitz, J., Sen, A., and Fitoussie, J.-P. (2009) *Report by the Commission on the Measurement of Economic Performance and Social Progress*, www.stiglitz-sen-fitoussi.fr/en/index.htm

Wilde, L. (2013) *Global solidarity*, Edinburgh: Edinburgh University Press.

World Commission on Environment and Development (Brundtland Commission) (1987) *Towards sustainable development. Our common future*, www.un-documents.net/our-common-future.pdf

THREE

Beyond neoliberalism, or life after capitalism? A red-green debate

Ted Benton

Introduction

The post-war social democratic left had at its core a commitment to socioeconomic equality. At the very least this entailed a publicly provided safety-net to protect the most vulnerable in society, the sick and elderly and those hit by hard times. A legal framework securing the rights of employees (individually or collectively) to counterbalance and restrain the powers of employers, the provision of a secure and healthy place to live and universal free access to education were also indispensable parts of the vision. More contested, even then, was the extent to which the production of goods and services should be allocated either to public or private sectors. The 'mixed economy', in which some basic utilities and 'natural monopolies' remained in the public sector, while a flourishing private sector generated the profits to finance state spending was, until the 1970s, relatively uncontroversial.

Viewed in retrospect, the post-war Labour government was astonishingly successful both in implementing the necessary reforms to achieve much of this and in rendering hegemonic its vision of fundamental entitlements of citizenship. The counterattack by market fundamentalism was already under way at the time the post-war settlement was being put together (e.g. Hayek, 1944), but it took some 30 years of its 'war of position' and the re-emergence of destabilising class conflict for it to be able to present itself as a viable alternative. Even now, despite some 40 years of erosion and systematic attack by the entrenched advocates for 'free markets', it is astonishing how much resilience the values of social democracy still have. For all the continual ferreting out of 'bad news' stories about the NHS, no major political party yet dares to question the universal principle of 'free at the point of need' for basic healthcare. However, until the crash of 2008 public support for the mixed economy had morphed into tacit acceptance of successive waves of privatisation, even where the beneficiaries were the nationalised corporations of foreign governments.

However, earlier generations of socialist thinkers had a still broader vision of the 'good life' than the above version of social democracy. Distributive justice and the recognition of basic rights were supplemented by an alternative vision of human fulfilment. This included creative and convivial relations among people, as well as alternative forms of engagement with (the rest of) nature. Popular practices such as climbing, rambling, gardening, amateur field natural history, bird-watching, angling, as well as just strolling in a park, or breathing in the sea air, were seen as prefiguring a different 'settlement' of our relationship to non-human nature. Although these elements have not been seen as priorities in the social democratic tradition, they did form an important part of the project of the post-war Labour government. It established a locally devolved system of land-use planning in the shape of the Town and Country Planning Act, it set up the Nature Conservancy Council and a network of national parks.

Unfortunately, these nature-friendly intentions were undermined by subsequent publicly subsidised agricultural intensification. Resistance to which, by the 1960s, provided much of the impetus behind a resurgent environmental protest movement, alarmed by the massive loss of wildlife habitat, landscape and historic values and opportunities for rural leisure. A global crisis literature that gained massive public attention in the late 1960s and early 1970s added new energy and perspective: environmental degradation that could be experienced in one's everyday life could now be understood as just the local evidence of a worldwide crisis in humanity's relation to the planet – expanding population, resource-use and pollution were rapidly approaching fixed limits, with dire consequences if urgent action was not forthcoming. Subsequently, a diverse environmental mass movement has found expression, from the local and specialised to the global and general, in a myriad of organisations from the Bumblebee Conservation Trust through the RSPB and National Trust to Friends of the Earth and Greenpeace. Initially these organisations saw themselves as above the divisions of left and right, and even the more radical of them were able to escape condemnation by mainstream media under that interpretation. A memorable example was celebration of the 'trashing' of GM trial crops by Greenpeace as a victory against 'Frankenstein foods' by the *Daily Mail*.

Even as the environmental movement spawned its own 'green' political parties, two critical, oppositional cultures remained at arm's length from one another: on the one hand, feminist, gay rights, welfarist, antiracist and labour activists struggled against injustice, stigmatisation and inequality, while, on the other hand, greens fought to defend 'nature', 'the planet' from potentially catastrophic human destructiveness. However, with growing velocity since the late 1980s, links, alliances and convergences between these two major sources of opposition have formed. Greens and social justice campaigners have found they share common enemies in corporate capital and the state institutions interwoven with their interests. Meanwhile, many on the left, formerly suspicious of the green movement as middle class nimbies, threatening working class jobs, began to see in the environmental critique a potentially powerful ally against the existing order. Where it has not fully capitulated to market fundamentalism, mainstream social democracy has managed at least lip service to environmental concern, most notably to the climate change agenda. The Green parties, meanwhile, have shifted to the left, often to the radical left – in the case of the UK, well to the left of the Labour Party until the election of Jeremy Corbyn to the leadership in September 2015.

As admittedly unsatisfactory catch-all terms I call the struggles for social justice 'Red' and those in defence of the environment 'Green' movements. The rest of this discussion will argue that this dynamic convergence of red and green is well grounded in historic shifts of economy, society and ecology. These diverse forms of suffering, grievance and moral outrage are, arguably, differently placed and differently interpreted responses to a common source of discontent. A developing analysis of the complex historical shifts at work might cement more deeply the connections between these cultures of opposition and critique. To be, perhaps unrealistically, optimistic, it might also be a guide for a strategic orientation to social and political activity, offering some hope of a feasible and desirable alternative future. Two guiding threads might be suggested here. First, that struggles for social justice cannot offer sustainable solutions unless they take into account the nature-given conditions for the flourishing of life, and, indeed, recognise that environmental justice is an essential condition for the achievement of all other dimensions of justice. Second, that no measures to protect non-human nature from destruction can be justified, or are likely to be socially or politically sustainable, unless they are firmly based on the defence or expansion of social justice and human wellbeing. This rules out fighting austerity by unqualified support for economic growth. It rules out protecting tropical forest by driving out its indigenous inhabitants. It rules out addressing climate change without addressing the needs of the world's poor, or the plight of workers in polluting industries.

Contradictions of the present

It is now a commonplace that deep challenges confront not only British or Western capitalist society but our entire civilisation. Critical comments, once uttered only among small groups of radicals, are now openly endorsed and promulgated by the world's economic and political elites and their intellectual allies. The scientific near-consensus on anthropogenic climate change has, as I write, won the commitment of 195 national governments whose representatives have just concluded an unprecedented agreement to move toward a decarbonised world economy in an effort to stabilise the global climate by the end of the present century. This agreement represents the current phase of a long struggle, focused on institutions of the UN, in which attempts mainly by rich countries to impose international constraints on greenhouse gas emissions confronted resistance from mainly poor countries which, rightly, saw the climate threat as a result of the rich countries' past and present mode of development and, rightly, didn't see why they should stay poor to keep gas-guzzling '4 by 4s' on the road in the USA. Geopolitical shifts, most notably promoted by the rapid economic growth of the 'BRIC' countries (Brazil, Russia, India and China), and technical shifts, especially the increasing promise of a range of non-fossil sources of energy, have opened up some new possibilities. These developments, in turn, have underpinned the Paris agreements.

While certainly not wishing to downplay the scale of the Paris achievement, some concerns need to be raised. First, the links between growing emissions of carbon dioxide and other greenhouse gases and potentially catastrophic climate change have been well known for more than 30 years; and arguably go back years before that in global system modelling. The UN-sponsored 'Earth Summit' more than 20 years ago established a legally binding framework convention on climate change, and, more recently, a leading economist, Lord Stern, speaking the language of the powerful, published an internationally praised report showing that the cost of measures taken now to avert climate change would be greatly outweighed by the costs of doing nothing. During that period, losses of ice in the Arctic and mountain glaciers, increases in often devastating extreme weather events, rising global temperatures and changes in the distribution of fauna and flora have added experiential support to the scientific projections, and broadly based social movements have continued to exert pressure on their political leaders.

So, in the face of all that, why has it taken so long? Partly this is because of the resistance offered by powerful interests. Partly because of the geopolitical complexities mentioned above, but also, I think, because of a disjuncture between the nation state as a locus of political power and the flexible global dispersal of economic power. Although some of these obstacles have softened, and their configuration altered, the core obstacles, arguably, remain in place. There is no doubt the Paris agreement expresses a new international political will. However, its terms, its slippery wording, internal tensions and abandonment of the binding Kyoto regime in favour of voluntary aspirations, all signal the effects of continuing difficulties. For example, the voluntary commitments by national governments, even if implemented, would at best amount to a 2.7 degree rise, while the report recognises the need to keep rises to well below 2 degrees by 2100. The agreement itself recognises this inadequacy by promising five-year recalls with increasingly tight emissions targets. However, the current commitments still stand in need of ratification by national legislatures, and there are no sanctions for failure to live up to promises. So far as the UK government is concerned, verbal support for the Paris agreements is belied by cuts to subsidies for renewables, to energy conservation in homes, overriding of local democracy to impose fracking for shale gas and moves to privatise the Green Investment Bank.

If the struggle to avert potentially catastrophic climate change remains in deep trouble, other dimensions of what can be seen as an intensifying crisis in the relationship between contemporary social, economic and political institutions and our underlying naturally given conditions of existence are hardly addressed at all. Perhaps the most threatening of all is the rate of loss of wild and domesticated biodiversity – a rate compared by some scientists to those associated with the major geological transitions of past epochs. One of the successes of the Rio Earth Summit was a legally binding convention on biodiversity, but on close inspection the key aim of that agreement was to provide a framework of property rights to foster the commercial exploitation of biodiversity and derivative biotechnologies. Tropical forests that harbour the greatest diversity of species continue to be lost at an alarming rate, with recent acceleration in the key state - Brazil. But in temperate regions, too, continuing land-use intensification and climate change continue to cause large-scale extinctions as well as simplification and destabilisation of ecosystems. CO_2 emissions and oceanic acidification combined with other sources of pollution are impacting on marine life with reciprocal impacts on atmospheric processes. Again, despite the existence of a scientific consensus, elite political lip service and the invention of concepts such as 'life support systems', and 'ecosystem services' that readily feed into dominant economic paradigms, effective policies to protect biodiversity '*in situ*' are practically non-existent. Again, the UK government looks both ways. While funding a 'pollinator initiative' research programme, it actively lobbies on behalf of the biotech industry against the EU ban on neonicotinoid pesticides, which have known damaging effects on key groups of pollinators.

The diversity of animals and plants has an importance in its own right. However, it is well understood that biospheric processes are also mediators of the water, nitrogen and carbon cycles and maintain soil fertility through the work of decomposer micro-organisms, nitrogen-fixing plants and so on. These processes are crucial to the climate system, to food production and to the distribution of fresh water. For all the importance of addressing climate change, the priority of addressing biodiversity loss is arguably still more fundamental, and, indeed, is a necessary element in tackling climate change itself.

Simultaneously, there is widespread elite concern about accelerating socioeconomic inequalities, both within and between countries and geographical regions. Nobel prize-winning economist, Joseph Stiglitz (2013), has charted a dramatic polarisation of wealth and income in the USA over three decades. He has shown that the top 1% takes 57% of all income from capital and possesses 225 times the wealth of the average American, while just one family owns assets equivalent to that possessed by the lower 30% of the population. The runaway best-seller of 2014, Thomas Piketty's *Capital in the Twenty-First Century* tells a similar story of increasing inequality, conceptualised in terms of the growing global disparity between income from capital and from labour. Interestingly, the dominance of neoliberal ideas is now so pervasive that neither Stiglitz nor Piketty take the mere fact of gross inequality as intrinsically problematic. For Picketty, it might be justified by common utility, or, following Rawls, if it could be shown that the least well-off fare better than they would have under a less unequal regime. For Piketty, it becomes clear, the problem concerns the sustainability of the European social model, and his proposed 'solution' is the taxation of capital wealth. Interestingly, no less a figure than the governor of the Bank of England recently warned of a rather more fundamental risk associated with unrestrained economic inequality: it threatens to undermine the social bonds that are necessary for the conduct of economic activity itself.

Again, however, these elite recognitions have spawned no serious policy initiatives to address either inequality or abject poverty. On the contrary, across the 'rich' world, programmes of austerity in response to the financial crash of 2008 have protected or enhanced the position of the wealthy at the expense of the poorest and most vulnerable in these societies by direct cuts to money income combined with withdrawal or privatisation of public services. Within the EU the most extreme versions of this policy complex have been imposed on the poorest countries – most catastrophically on Greece. Globally, high rates of growth in former countries of the semi-periphery, most notably China and India, have taken large minorities out of poverty. However, they have also vastly increased economic inequalities and generated unprecedented levels of local and regional environmental degradation.

So, there is a widespread recognition among economic and political elites, backed by scientific and mainstream intellectual culture, of current global trends towards increasingly self-destructive levels of socioeconomic inequality at the same time as the world is threatened by a multidimensional crisis in the relation between human activity and the rest of nature. Both elite and oppositional movements in response to these trends have either been repeatedly defeated by the resistance or inertia of the 'system', or have been vilified and repressed as 'extreme' or a threat to 'national security', or ridiculed as absurd, even unhinged. Witness the united media onslaught on Jeremy Corbyn, the twice elected radical leader of the Labour Party – a treatment also meted out to the rebel comedian Russell Brand (and even to Corbyn's much less radical predecessor).

So, why are those in the driving seat, while fully aware of the potentially disastrous route they are following, so determined not to try a different road? One possible answer is to consider deep-rooted features of the present international order, one fostered and imposed by intergovernmental agreements over 40 to 50 years. Interestingly, this international order was set in place by the round of trade and investment negotiations that took place at the same time as, but without connection to, the Rio Earth Summit – the first arguably rendering unrealisable the aspirations of the second.

This new economic and financial order, a distinct, market fundamentalist successor to that prevailing between the end of World War II and the mid-1970s, has four interconnected features that are relevant to this argument. They are:

1. Deregulation of international economic activity.
2. Increased international mobility of capital.
3. Enhanced political and economic power of large transnational corporations vis-à-vis national states.

4. The entrenchment of neoliberal market fundamentalism as hegemonic in policy circles and in the 'common sense' of public discourse.

Three main consequences follow from this combination:

1. A geographical redistribution of costs (including so-called 'externalities') and benefits of economic activity in ways that cut across boundaries of nation states and other loci of political sovereignty.
2. The emergence of forms of ecological degradation at scales which exceed the scope and range of national governments or supranational centres of sovereignty.
3. The frustration of efforts to address these consequences by internationally coordinated action as a result of these very features of the new world order:
   (a) deep geo-political divisions deriving from the past history of Western colonialism and economic imperialism, continuing international inequalities and strategic conflicts at the level of military and security interests of nation states and power blocs;
   (b) the unaccountable power of transnational corporations – most notably financial institutions and energy, pharmaceutical, transport, military and biotech companies;(c) the hegemonic power of neoliberal discourse to rule out a priori all proposed policy responses couched in terms of a common or public interest.

The outcome is a potentially disastrous and unrestrained 'race to the bottom' in terms of individual socioeconomic conditions, employment and reproductive rights, corporate taxation and environmental standards: an outcome recognised by the more intelligent of those with institutional power that threatens to undermine the conditions of existence of the system whose institutions they run.

Alternatives?

The situation looked at from this perspective seems bleak indeed: a system blocked by its own internal contradictions running juggernaut-like to its own destruction. One option is to continue with the twin tracks of technological innovation and international negotiation: GM food, geo-engineering, nuclear power and ecstatic celebration of manifestly fragile achievements such as the Paris agreement. This is the line of least resistance, the one we are most likely to see enacted, and one which, because it deals with issues piecemeal and does not address the fundamental systemic drivers underlying the growing crisis, will certainly fail. For others, those who some might term the 'soft left', remain, understandably, attached to an earlier 'regime of accumulation', including the now fragmented social democratic settlement. Despite the hegemonic status of neoliberalism, the normative elements of social democracy still have a powerful hold over significant majorities in parts of the 'rich' world, especially in Europe. Preserving key elements of the social democratic settlement, as we saw above, seems to be the main priority for Piketty, and similar aspirations are at work in the moderate anti-austerity of the more centrist figures in the UK Labour Party, argued on the basis of neo-Keynesian economic analyses. This approach does have a powerful ideological appeal, and its value orientation is thoroughly defensible.

Unfortunately there are reasons to think that the strategic context is not one in which those aspirations can be realised without more profound transformations than the centrist left will contemplate. *First*, it is arguable that the post-World War II settlement rested on transfers of cheap materials and exploitation of cheap labour from regions of the periphery and semi-periphery. The colonial relations and subsequently relations of asymmetric exchange have been transformed by economic globalisation and the emergence of a new world economic order. *Second*, the legitimation of the post-war settlement depended on the promise of ever-growing material prosperity in the shape of consumer durables, home ownership and leisure pursuits based on car ownership and widening access to cheap air transport. The very success of the concerted promotion of the desire for ever-expanding material affluence turned out to be a significant source of destabilisation of the regime: significant minorities resented their marginal status and exclusion from the consumerist bonanza, while those sufficiently well organised to demand more did so to the point of political crisis. However, it was already clear that the energy, resource and pollution load imposed on global ecosystems by this explosive expansion of material consumption, even if limited to the 'rich' northern countries, was not sustainable in the long term. Even more clearly, to generalise that model of consumer-led affluence as an aspiration for the global population was, and is, to court disaster. Put crudely, the option of universal restoration of the post-war settlement, even if politically feasible, would certainly be ecologically catastrophic. This, of course, does not let neoliberalism off the hook: the shift from Fordism to post-Fordist consumerism carries not less, but more ecological dangers.

Further reasons for thinking the restoration of the post-war welfarist/ consumerist regime is implausible have to do with the dispersal and fragmentation of the major interests that converged to make it possible. First, more limited mobility of capital meant that there was a recognisably national economy, more closely allied with a national state which sought to protect 'British business' internationally, and significant sectors directly under state control. High levels of trade union organisation enabled government to broker settlements between labour and capital that secured relative affluence on the part of 'core' workers and, at the same time, growing domestic markets for big capital. Since that time privatisations and far greater degrees of international mobility of capital have come close to eroding any vestige of a 'national' economy, while protectionist measures and any attempts to resurrect economic nationalism would run counter to the global trading regime and quickly destabilise any national government foolhardy enough to try. At the same time, partly because of economic globalisation, the labour force has become much more fragmented, union membership has declined and the legal powers of the unions have been drastically slashed. Because of the combination of these processes, national government would no longer have the leverage to promote a new settlement, even if the holders of state power wished to do so.

So, 'business as usual' seems to presage a very bleak future, but restoration of what some regard as a golden age of social democratic capitalism appears implausible. What might the alternatives be? Those who take the argument this far can be divided into two broad categories: those who foresee, and perhaps seek to promote, a new 'settlement', a further transmutation of capitalist relations in the direction of sustainability. This is sometimes called ecological modernisation and has its more radical as well as its more conservative, technocratic, advocates. The other group, the red-greens, ecological Marxists and others, see no prospect of a sustainable capitalism, and so posit the necessity of a social and political vision of life beyond the limits imposed by the growth dynamic of global capitalism.

A sustainable capitalism?

Perhaps the most rigorous and sustained presentation of the 'sustainable capitalism' case is that made by Jonathan Porritt in his *Capitalism as if the World Matters* (2005). His argument has two key premises. One is that capitalism is 'the only game in town'. There is no alternative to it, so proposals for a sustainable future must be realisable within a capitalist economic order. Second, however, is his powerful critique of the actually existing phase of capitalist development, in terms of both its socioeconomic injustices and its ecological destructiveness. Porritt's clearer and more eloquent analysis parallels much of what I have argued here:

> fewer people now seriously suppose that this particular model of capitalism (dominated by a small number of hugely powerful interests … a pattern of globalization that alienates millions, impoverishes hundreds of millions, further enriches an already inconceivably wealthy minority, and undermines our life-support systems in the process) can last for very much longer – on ecological grounds alone. (Porritt, 2005, p 104)

Yet Porritt rightly draws on the historical flexibility and adaptability of capitalism to envisage the possibility of transition to a new institutional order of capitalism that would render it both more humane and ecologically sustainable. To characterise this future capitalist order, Porritt first distinguishes five sorts of resource which are indispensable to human wellbeing, designating each one a form of capital. For him, 'capital' is simply the term for any kind of stock from which a benefit can be derived. Following neoclassical environmental economics, he distinguishes 'natural' from human-made capital. Nature is capital in so far as it is a source of benefits, in the shape of materials, energy sources, sinks, ecosystem services and so on. Human-made capital, termed 'manufactured capital', includes tools, technologies, factories and so on, but also money and financial institutions (financial capital). The direct human contribution is split between 'human capital' (physical, intellectual, emotional and spiritual abilities of humans) and 'social capital' (as networks of relations, solidarities, cultures, and so on).

Very simply, a sustainable capitalism would be one so organised and regulated that it lived off the flows, or 'revenues', from these five capitals without depleting them. His ideas about how to do this are familiar and sensible. Long-term planning through government/industry partnerships to develop green technological innovation, alternative measures such as the 'Index of Sustainable Welfare' to replace GDP (gross domestic product), green taxes to redistribute resources to the less well-off and enhancement of 'human capital' through investment in health and education. The overarching argument is that measures such as these are required if we are to halt the growing threat to the viability of natural and human capital. A total of 17 key 'ecosystem services' are valued at $33 billion per annum, so investment to protect such 'critical natural capital' is clearly economically rational, as well as essential to long-term sustainability. Only ignorance or habit prevents the necessary action being taken.

Porritt's argument is persuasive, but not wholly so. I see three sorts of difficulty. First, there are disadvantages implicit in couching the argument in terms of the dominant economic paradigm. Second, would an economic system with the degree of sociopolitical control over investment priorities he envisages still count as capitalist? Third, in case the previous difficulty seems a merely semantic matter, how could the immense networks of power and widespread cultural assumptions that would resist such a change be overcome? How would we get from here to there?

The first set of difficulties arises from what Porritt shares with 'mainstream' environmentalism. The calculation is that to persuade those with power and wealth to change course, it is necessary to persuade them it is in their interest to do so, and for that it is necessary to speak their language. The logic of this is unassailable, and work such as that of Porritt, Stern and the environmental economists has brought the seriousness of our ecological crisis into mainstream discourse. However, it is very doubtful whether it has made much impact on actual policy formation and implementation. For this and other reasons it is essential that it does not displace other sorts of appeal, to other social groups, to other value frames and to other sensibilities. There are several important objections to reliance on the concept of natural capital, as used by Porritt and others. First, there is a normative problem. The concept brackets out nature in so far as it is not a source of benefits to humans. The case for protecting nature rests solely on instrumentality: it exists as a bundle of resources of value only for their utility (utility for whom is a further issue). Unless some other value perspective is introduced, nature, in so far as it has no detectable use for some human purpose, is of no concern. The UK government's pollinator initiative illustrates the problem here. Insect pollination, especially by bees, is important for food production, and declining bee populations threaten a 'pollination crisis'. Yet conservationists who have succeeded in raising the alarm on the basis of the value of the 'pollination services' of bees will be disappointed to find that research points to the possibility that domestication of a small number of wild species could successfully substitute for the lost pollinators. If this outcome were to be adopted, then the remaining 200 and more wild bee species in the UK would remain entirely without protection. Is this what the sincere conservationists who pursued the economistic/ utilitarian argument really wanted?

There are, of course, other problems with the idea of natural capital. There is a serious difficulty not only in assigning monetary value to natural assets, but also in determining just what is, and what is not, a source of benefit to humans. We intervene in highly complex systems and with effects often far removed in time and space from our actions, with scientific methods of measurement and detection that are imperfect, and theoretical understandings that have frequently been shown to be false or misleading. Green thinkers have invented the concept of the 'precautionary principle' to deal with cognitive limitations like these, but where powerful interests are at stake the voice of precaution is generally overridden.

Again, for the neoclassical tradition in economics there is something paradoxical about assigning monetary value to 'natural capital'. For them there is no such thing as objective value, only value as produced by the play of supply and demand through market exchanges. However, for environmentalists who adopt this language the whole point is to show why natural capital should be *excluded* from market transactions. Of course, they can decide to live with the contradiction, and simply assign values by a variety of (often conflicting) non-market methods. The difficulty with this, as illustrated by the failures of carbon trading regimes, green taxation, pollution permits and so on, is that the arbitrariness of the basis of valuation leaves everything up to a process of bargaining in which powerful actors win out. More seriously still, once a part or aspect of nature is given an economic value it is conceptually prepared and packaged for a market transaction. What if it turns out that some market actor is prepared to pay the price for depleting and degrading it? Once protection is made subject to a cost/benefit calculation there is a risk the calculation will go in the opposite direction to the one intended. This is a discursive route to the further commodification of nature – precisely what its promoters sought to prevent.

I'll return later to a further important problem about reducing the environmental argument to one of economic calculation. For now, there is a second difficulty with Porritt's argument. His vision of a future society in which both investment and consumption are restrained by the requirement that they do not deplete the stocks of manufactured, human, social, financial and particularly 'critical' natural capital has much to recommend it from an environmental point of view, but it is hard to see it as implying anything but a highly centralised command economy. Porritt acknowledges that it would require a change of direction from the current pressures for peeling back the economic role of the state. He also seems to imagine a partnership between state and private industry to secure sustainability objectives. However, the degree of public control over the strategic investment priorities of key sectors of industry, motivated by social and environmental objectives, independent of profitability, suggests a transition not to a new phase of capitalist development, but to the transcendence of capitalism as such.

It is possible that Porritt actually had this scenario in mind; that his book was, all along, a disguised attempt to show a way beyond capitalism at a time when capitalism seemed far more secure and unassailable than it does in post-crash 2016. Against that reading is the third difficulty I have with Porritt's argument: the question of what will drive the transition from failing neoliberalism to a sustainable future economy and society. Porritt's answer to this is, essentially, rational persuasion: a transparent case that transition to a sustainable future would be good for all of us. So all that stands in the way of the implementation of the necessary policies is a combination of ignorance, inertia and denial. For Porritt, this could be partly attributed to media bias, and the failure to promulgate attractive alternative visions.

More recent discussions of 'denial' over climate change include a psychoanalytic dimension. Drawing on several contributions – notably Stan Cohen and Paul Hoggett – to her edited collection, Sally Weintrobe (2013) distinguishes three sorts of denial. 'Denialism' refers to the ways in which powerful self-interested lobbies mobilise media bias against the scientific case for action on climate change. Straight denial is likened to the response of someone facing deep personal loss: 'it isn't true'. She argues this can be a transitional phase prior to full acknowledgement, and is less damaging than 'disavowal': both knowing and not knowing at the same time. Unacceptable truths are half-acknowledged but in some sense domesticated by psychological processes that distort, distance and minimise. The multi-level psychological, economic and social ways in which denial, ignorance and inertia reinforce one another as resistances to the challenges of seeking profound social change show the need for something more than rational persuasion or the transparent presentation of a utilitarian calculus. That Porritt now recognises this is evidenced by his recent despair, and abandonment of his efforts to influence the energy oligopolies (Carrington, 2015).

System change and alternatives to capitalism?

Taking the demands of sustainability seriously, as Porritt undoubtedly does, takes him to an account of its necessary conditions that are manifestly incompatible with key system properties of capitalism. That this conclusion runs counter to Porritt's own intentions is a mark of the fearless rigour of his analysis (including his devastating critique of neoliberalism). However, it seems that in avoiding the clear implications of his own analysis, the Porritt of 2005 fails to recognise the immense power of the resistance that any attempt to implement his proposals would unleash. The Porritt of 2015 seems to have a more sober view of this.

So, the question posed by the challenge of 'actually existing unsustainability' is whether such a requirement can be met within the integument of capitalism as the dominant economic system. This is a question that cannot be avoided, since this is the institutional form through which the overwhelming majority of transactions between humans and the rest of nature are conducted. It has its own autonomous dynamics, and generates a specific structure of social, cultural, political and military power as well as forms of resistance to it. To think about large-scale system change involves an assessment of the strategic possibilities of the various forms of endemic opposition that point beyond the present, as well as a sober acknowledgement of the entrenched power of those who will stop at nothing to protect their vested interests.

In recent decades several versions of green left thinking have become influential. They include the view that polarisation of wealth and poverty as well as ecological destructiveness are endemic features of capitalist organisation, rather than only emergent features of the current neoliberal phase. World system theorists see neoliberal globalisation not just as an intensification of these tendencies of the system, but as symptoms of an epochal crisis. Jason Moore has argued that neoliberalism has been primarily a last-ditch means to reappropriate real gains in wealth creation during the Fordist phase from labour and industrial capital to financial capital (for example, Moore, 2015). For Moore the crisis of 2007/8 signifies the limit to that process. In the absence of major new advances in agricultural or industrial technologies to underpin a new phase of expansion of real wealth, capitalism itself may have reached its limit.

Other writers influenced by the convergence between green and left thinking and movement activity have drawn on both the subaltern traditions of socialism mentioned early on in this piece and reworkings of classic Marxian analyses of capitalism (see, for example, Benton, 1996). The concept of a 'treadmill of production' (Schnaiberg, 1980) identified a fundamental source of unsustainability in capitalism as an economic system dependent on ever escalating growth of production and consumption, while depleting resources and degrading the environmental conditions for production. J.B. Foster (2010) and his associates have drawn on Marx's concept of a 'metabolic rift' endemic to the relation between capitalist production and its natural conditions, extending Marx's analysis of the relation between loss of soil fertility and urban pollution to include disruption of other cyclical processes, most notably the carbon cycle, as a general theory of capitalism's ecological unsustainability.

Moore and Foster have relatively little to say in detail about the character of the social and political movements that might arise in response to the combined challenge of social inequality and ecological crisis, and about what alternative forms of socio-ecological relationship might emerge. This limitation is addressed in the work of J. O'Connor and others associated with the journal *Capitalism Nature Socialism*. Taking as given the Marxian notion an inherent contradiction in capitalism between capital and labour, O'Connor (1998) draws on Polanyi's ([1944] 1957) concept of land, labour and money as 'fictitious commodities' to identify a 'second contradiction' of capitalism. For him, both human labour and ecological life-support systems are treated as if they were commodities, but cannot be reproduced as commodities. In fact, of course, some naturally given conditions of production are not even treated as commodities, but as free goods. Either way, the growth dynamic and dominant mode of calculation (monetary) in capitalism result in tendencies to undermine the conditions for the reproduction of labour power and to undermine ecological life-support systems. There is an inherent tendency for capitalism to erode the conditions of its own existence.

But the long history of capitalism as the dominant economic form, despite its inner contradictions, stands in need of some explanation. O'Connor's answer is that the double contradiction spawns social movements of resistance with a potential to challenge the existing order (Polanyi's 'counter-movement'). It is pressure from these movements that provokes the nation state into ameliorative reform. In normal times, extra-economic interventions on the part of the state keep the two contradictions in check: trade union rights, minimum wages, health and safety legislation, welfare provision, public education, infrastructure provision and repair, nature conservation, flood defences and so on all contribute to what we might call the paradoxical unstable stability of capitalist societies.

So long as national states retain the capacity to impose regulations on capital investment and ameliorate the conditions of the labour force they can offset or mitigate the self-destructive tendencies of the system. These conditions were maintained in the richer countries until the rise of neoliberalism and associated economic globalisation, when the power of national states to impose environmental restraints and their will to bolster the social and economic condition of their labour force began to decline. International competition has increasingly undermined the bargaining power of organised labour, and the growing power and mobility of transnational capital has taken environmental regulation out of reach of national governments. Meanwhile a longer-term consequence of globalisation has been the emergence of a fully global ecological crisis, with no global authoritative regime for amelioration comparable with the role of national states in the earlier phase of capitalist development. Neoliberal globalisation and deregulation have set in motion global threats to the survival of the system itself, while depriving it of the necessary means to address them.

So, in the face of such a challenge, what can be done? First, many of the specific policy initiatives advocated by Porritt and many other 'green greens' can be actively supported. The urgency of the threats posed by climate change, biodiversity loss, desertification and oceanic pollution rules out any notion of waiting for a more fundamental social transformation. Even modest demands for amelioration provoke such powerful resistance that high levels of fully evidenced and reasoned argument together with internationally coordinated mass mobilisations are needed to make advances. Witness the global social movement mobilisations leading up to the recent intergovernmental talks in Paris on climate change.

Such mobilisations can bring focused pressure to bear on specific issues, but of themselves they cannot mount a challenge to a whole social and economic order. The above argument carries the implication that nothing less is urgently needed. If thinkers like Moore are right about an imminent terminal phase of what John Barry (2012) calls 'actually existing unsustainability', then democratically acceptable and realistic visions of a better alternative are needed, together with the social and political movements to begin the process of realising them. As to visions of a possible just and sustainable future there is a rich heritage from William Morris' *News from Nowhere*, through to Andre Gorz's 'possible utopia' (1980), Ryle's *Ecology and Socialism* (1988) and more recent work by the Red–Green Study Group (1995 and forthcoming), Derek Wall (2005) and Naomi Klein (2014). How we are to bridge the gulf between the present global disorder and the realisation of such visions of these is a much more demanding question. It is easy to feel hopeless in the face of the enormity of the challenge.

But there are some hopeful signs. First, neoliberal global capitalism looks far less secure and confident post-crash than it did even 10 years ago. Post-crash political polarisations and austerity politics have strengthened right-wing nationalisms and ethnic identity politics. Yet they have simultaneously revitalised the left in many countries: Syriza and Podemos, and the many new activists stimulated by the Corbyn leadership campaign in the UK. Such upsurges signify important shifts in the political culture and have reopened discussion of policy options strictly foreclosed by neoliberal hegemony. Broad coalitions of social movement activists could find expression in the formal political space through electorally successful parties or coalitions. Then pressure from below combined with some capacity to mobilise state power from above could achieve some significant advances. Secondly, the internationalism of these movements, successfully deployed in the climate change campaign, could expand and mobilise around key institutions governing the regulation of global trade and investment; albeit (as at Paris) with international coordination at governmental level. Finally, the many experiments and local projects discussed elsewhere in this book suggest that well thought-through and practicality-tested conceptions of alternative institutional frameworks could emerge.

Of course, change on this scale seems quite unrealistic. Equally, however, continuing for long with 'business as usual' is no less unrealistic. The necessity of fundamental change is at least recognised by a large enough part of the population for serious discussion and movement-building to begin. The breadth of the coalition that is now emerging in the climate mobilisations, involving green parties, traditional parties of the social democratic and radical left, trade unions, development charities, environmental social movements, wildlife conservationists, and a wide range of religious groupings is encouraging – as is the creative imagination on display.

In conclusion, the analysis so far implies that the depth of the current socio-ecological crisis requires fundamental system change, central to which must be a qualitative transformation of the relation between human social and economic practices and the rest of nature. There is no contradiction between recognising this and still fighting for ameliorative reforms, but there are implications for the sorts of reform and the cultural framing through which they are advocated. Even James O'Connor's analysis in terms of the degradation of the conditions of production needs to be broadened to a full acknowledgement that what is at stake is the degradation of the conditions for life itself. The now prevalent practice of making the case for environmental protection in terms of 'natural capital' and cost/benefit analysis fosters ways of thinking that run counter to the changes that are needed. These demand recognition of the deeper meanings and values that bind us to the rest of nature.

The economic reductionism of neoliberal environmentalism fails to acknowledge the everyday, unremarkable, non-instrumental value of nature experienced by the great majority of people. Environmental organisations are by far the largest voluntary associations, a great range of leisure pursuits involve engagement with nature or wildlife in some form or other, while just walking in a local park, picnicking by the river, or feeding the birds in the back garden provide what Marx called 'spiritual nourishment' in the interstices of life's demands and pressures. Although even these innocent activities have been penetrated by consumerism, they still attest to the significance of what Kate Soper (1990) calls 'alternative hedonism'. The everyday non-consumerist pleasures of convivial interactions with other people and fulfilling engagements with non-human nature (often both at the same time) are sources of meaning and satisfaction. They do not depend on destructive exploitation of nature or our fellow humans.

More than that, mobilising popular struggles against threats to the social and physical spaces where these pleasures can be enjoyed can and have moved beyond 'nimbyism' towards a deeper critical perspective on the prevailing commodified vision of the 'good life' and towards alternative, physically located visions of life quality. We might, for example challenge the dominant culture's elision of the need for a secure home to the priority of 'getting onto the housing ladder'. We might question the linguistic equivalence between what someone 'is worth', and how much money they have. We might think of alternative ways of managing water catchments instead of ever more quixotic spending on 'flood defences'. In short, any serious challenge to hegemonic neoliberalism must include reminders and revaluations of non-economic, non-instrumental sources of pleasure and meaning in life. Otherwise the demand to take less of the earth's resources can only be experienced as deprivation, yielding at best reluctant acquiescence. The necessary vital and powerful social movement cannot be built on such a meagre psychological foundation.

Acknowledgements

I am indebted for most of the argument in this paper to discussions over many years with members of the Red-green Study Group. I also wish to acknowledge the careful and helpful comments of the editors on earlier versions.

References

Barry, J. (2012) *The politics of actually existing unsustainability*, Oxford: Oxford University.

Benton, T. (ed) (1996) *The greening of Marxism*, New York and London: Guildford.

Carrington, D. (2015) 'Engaging with oil companies on climate change is futile, admits leading UK environmentalist', *The Guardian*, 15 January.

Foster, J.B., Clark, B. and York, R. (2010) *The ecological rift: Capitalism's war on the earth*, New York: Monthly Review.

Gorz, A. (1980) *Ecology as politics*, London: Pluto.

Hayek, F. (1944) *The road to serfdom*, Chicago: University of Chicago.

Klein, N. (2014) *This changes everything: Capitalism versus the climate*, London: Allen Lane/Penguin.

Moore, J.W. (2015) *Capitalism in the web of life*, London and New York: Verso.

O'Connor, J. (1998) *Natural causes*, New York and London: Guilford.

Picketty, T. (2014) *Capital in the twenty-first century*, Cambridge, MA: Harvard University Press.

Polanyi, K. ([1944] 1957) *The great transformation*, Boston, MA: Beacon.

Porritt, J. (2005) *Capitalism as if the world matters*, London: Earthscan.

Porritt, J. (2015) 'It is impossible for today's big oil companies to adapt to climate change', theguardian.com, 15 January.

Red-Green Study Group (1995) *What on earth is to be done?*, Manchester: RGSG.

Ryle, M. (1988) *Ecology and socialism*, London: Hutchinson.

Schnaiberg, A. (1980) *The environment: From surplus to scarcity*, New York: Oxford University Press.

Soper, K. (1990) *Troubled pleasures,* London and New York: Verso.

Stiglitz, J.F. (2013) *The price of inequality*, London: Allen Lane/Penguin.

Wall, D. (2005) *Babylon and beyond*, London: Pluto.

Weintrobe, S. (ed) (2013) *Engaging with climate change: Psychoanalytic and interdisciplinary perspectives*, London and New York: Routledge.

FOUR

The democratic deficit: institutional democracy

Mike O'Donnell

> No mere declaration of rights can suffice: institutions are
> required to make rights effective. (Karl Polanyi, [1944]
> 2001, p 264)

This chapter argues that the power of the market and private interest
should be better balanced by the democratic institutions representing
the public good. Currently, in Britain the balance of power has shifted
towards the former. However, as Eric Olin Wright (2010, p 6) proposes:

> Social institutions can be designed in ways that eliminate
> forms of oppression that thwart human aspirations towards
> living fulfilling and meaningful lives. The central task of
> emancipatory politics is to create such institutions.

Yet writing in 2009 Gregor McLennan (2009, p 145) regrets that
'[r]adical politics today has no viable institutional programme'. His
observation remains apposite in 2016 and here I apply it to democratic
institutional reform. In his 2015 campaign for Deputy Leader of the
Labour Party, Tom Watson argued the case for 'the empowering state'.
I advocate 'institutional democracy' as a complement, but also as an
antidote to state power: to avoid repeating the failings of previous state-
centred politics. Equally, as well as in the formally political, institutional
democracy is needed in other areas of institutional power/authority,
including the economic and cultural.

The chapter makes two arguments. Firstly, it offers a brief narrative
account from the late 18th century of a grudgingly conceded and
currently troubled British democracy: illustrating that despite its
formidable achievements, the post-war Labour Party largely failed
to build on earlier aspirations to autonomy and democracy of social
movements. During the inter-war and immediate post-war years
socialist as well as communist parties adopted a centralist approach to

reform; partly because of the perceived need to prioritise urgent issues of poverty and inequality over challenging problems of democratic planning and organisation. In contrast to political parties, recent social movements have generally maintained greater continuity with grassroots democratic traditions. However, the further development of democracy in a complex modern society may require the support of a political party, or parties.

My second and related argument is precisely that social democratic and socialist parties must commit to an enlarged democratic vision both to revitalise their popular base and to enhance their prospects of delivering greater equality. Since the debacle of progressive parties at the 2015 election, there are signs that grassroots democratic sentiment has strengthened, impacting particularly on the Labour Party. However, to achieve a cumulative redistribution of power requires democratic institutional consolidation. A crucial consideration is how civil society activism can achieve more sustained effect through democratic institutional reform. The aim of such reform is to facilitate and enhance the flow of democratic power throughout society. This includes national and regional as well as local levels, although different democratic forms and instruments may apply in each. Given the inequalities generated by neoliberalism, intensified by the financial crash of 2008, it is understandable that many on the left have again prioritised the goal of greater economic equality. However, the almost certain resistance of global and national elites to a significant redistribution of their wealth will require substantial and embedded reduction of their power, either prior to or in parallel with wealth redistribution. Democracy, like other political systems, is about power and the argument here is to extend and deepen it by means of institutional reform throughout the public arena. Power is not a limited resource and empowerment can release great individual and collective energy and creativity.

The first section of the chapter locates a desire for autonomy and democracy at the heart of British radicalism. It explores the broad democratic surge of the late eighteenth and early 19th century, which was not confined to politics but had distinctive economic and cultural dimensions. These aspects remain relevant today when democracy is often narrowly conceived in formal political terms, or even equated with parliamentary democracy. The second section analyses democracy with reference to the Labour Party and briefly comments on the impact of Thatcherism on New Labour. It charts a steady decline in the party's democratic practice and imagination. The remaining sections explore and advocate 'institutional democracy'. The terms 'left' and 'progressive' are used interchangeably to indicate both the social democratic and democratic socialist traditions. The term 'radical' is discussed below.

Describing radicalism: early 19th century democratic legacies

Drawing on Edward Thompson's seminal *The Making of the English Working Class* ([1963] 2013), and Craig Calhoun's *The Roots of Radicalism: Tradition, the Public Sphere and Early Nineteenth-Century Social Movements* (2012), this section indicates major characteristics and principles of early 19th century radicalism in Britain. With an eye to our present situation, I highlight the value given to autonomy, particularly in work, and community, and to political rights, including the constitutionalist tradition associated with Tom Paine's *Rights of Man* ([1791 and 1793] 1966). Substantial autonomy was variously sought and experienced in the whole life rather than merely in a political context. The scale of contemporary economic change and social disruption bears comparison to that of the early 19th century. While today people enjoy greater political freedom, they remain constrained and under pressure in many institutional contexts. Further, the widely held perception that an adequately democratic system was achieved with the introduction of universal suffrage, in local and central government elections, was not conducive to the continuing development of democracy.

As Thompson (2013, p 507) observes, 'Radicalism came to include very diverse tendencies as the nineteenth century advanced' and Calhoun (2012, p 12) states that 'early modern thinkers described analyses as radical when they went to the foundations, first principles, or what was essential'. Both historians illustrate a wide range of radical thought and activity in Britain distinct from and predating both modern socialism and liberal reformism; but still relevant to contemporary Britain. This included mass protests at the price of food, communitarian socialist experiments, republicanism often with a citizens' rights dimension, and Chartism. Then, as now, themes of community, morality and fundamental and historic rights recur in protest of various hues, potentially blurring the lines of political identification (Calhoun, 2012, p 19). Thompson refers to the general support for parliamentary reform among radicals and, as the century progressed, Chartism became the main focus of the movement for democracy. As the 20th century approached the socialist challenge to inequality emerged more strongly alongside and overlapping the democracy movement.

In the late 18th and early 19th century, many craft workers, artisans and small-scale farmers, aspired to regain a degree of autonomy lost to industrial and agrarian capital. As Thompson (2013, p 289) observes, '[i]f the agricultural worker pined for land, the artisans pined for an "independence"'. This aspiration colours much of the history of early working class radicalism. With the development of trade unionism, the struggle for independence took on a more collective dimension. However, the desire for autonomy was not limited to the work context but had wider cultural purchase and radical movements 'were … distinctive in the extremes to which they took anti-hierarchical ideology' (Calhoun, 2012, p 269). Similarly, anti-elitism characterises much contemporary social movement radicalism (see Chapter Twelve).

As a major thinker in the 'age of reason' and peripatetic revolutionary, the reputation of Thomas Paine (1737-1809) was international. Thompson emphasises that Paine's impact on English radicalism was programmatic as well as inspirational, referring to *Rights of Man* as a 'foundation text of the English working class movement' (Thompson, 2013, p 99), he comments that

> the main tradition of nineteenth century working class Radicalism took its cast from Paine. There were times, at the Owenite and Chartist climaxes, when other traditions became dominant. But after each relapse, the substratum of Painite assumptions remained intact. The aristocracy were the main target. (Thompson, 2013, p 105)

Paine's target was, indeed, the landed – although increasingly commercially engaged – aristocracy, whom he berated for living corruptly off excessive taxation. His constitutionalist and rights philosophy was based on logical argument and principle, rather than the vagaries of precedent fashioned by the legislative and judicial elites. As he ironically demanded of his conservative antagonist, Burke: '[if Governments … are not founded on the *Rights of Man*, and are founded on *any rights* at all, they consequently must be founded on the right of *something* that is *not man*, What then is that some-thing?' (Paine, 1966, p 194). Paine's constitutionalism reflected his experience in France and America and, as the title of his great work indicates, his reforms transcended class politics. He argued for universal manhood suffrage: that a nation's people were sovereign and equal; that a democratic constitution, subject to regular revision, should define and circumscribe government; and that all inherited distinctions and privileges should be abolished and equal rights for every citizen established (Paine, 1966).

His republican ideas are far more radically democratic than the current British 'system' of government and are well worth revisiting.

In summary, early 19th century social movements contributed to the following strands of the radical tradition: human rights; a commitment to political democracy; a desire for substantial autonomy in work and community life; anti-elitism opposing elites' corrupt self-seeking and abuse of power; and a belief in the efficacy of protest. The struggle for democracy in the form of representative democracy based on universal suffrage was finally successful over 100 years later. However, as both Thompson and Calhoun observe, radicals of this period seldom saw the state as the mechanism through which to achieve social equality. Later this became a goal, perhaps the prime goal, of socialism. Here I argue for a closer integration of radical democratic and socialist egalitarian principles and policies. Greater equality should be achieved democratically, not imposed. Whether people *want* more democracy is therefore a crucial issue. Survey opinion can be cited which is more or less supportive of this proposition (Parker, 2015, p 23). However, the aim of this chapter is to make a convincing argument, not to follow a trend.

From social democracy to neoliberalism

This section gives a brief account of the relative failure of the labour movement in Britain to translate earlier aspirations of autonomy and liberty into strong and sustained participatory democratic institutions. The Labour Party played a prominent part in the development of representative national and local government. However, if socialism also means establishing substantial popular participation and/or control over a wide range of public institutions including public corporations – admittedly a huge challenge given the opposition of powerful elites – this was not achieved. Yet democracy in Britain became widely regarded as a more or less fully accomplished fact – disastrously so from a progressive point of view.

In the latter part of the 19th century into the 20th, the popular struggle for change in Britain gradually shifted from efforts to extend the franchise, cumulatively successful but painfully slow especially in respect to women, to confronting poverty and improving public health and safety. T.H. Marshall (1950) characterised the evolution of citizenship through civil, political to social phases, with the struggle for political citizenship being the main focus in the 19th century and social citizenship in the 20th. The rise of socialism, advocating an interventionist state including nationalisation and wealth redistribution, represented a major shift from earlier communitarian socialism. The Independent Labour Party and Labour Party, with the latter eventually dominant, were at the forefront of this trend. More established parties also responded to the urgent need to deal with the social issues created by industrialisation and urbanisation.

While some measures of social reform were introduced from the centre these were implemented with limited decentralisation other than through state organs of administration. However, ideas of popular participation and control continued to be debated and widely practised in the broad socialist and labour movement. For instance, the constitution of the Co-operative Movement enabled substantial economic and political engagement of its members at the local level and the locally and regionally vibrant Workers Education Association continued to expand. However, the Labour government elected in 1945 adopted a generally centralist approach to policy making. This was not the authoritarianism of Soviet Communism but it did provide some substance for those who argued that social democracy, as well as communism, was prone to bureaucratic and undemocratic solutions and structures. This criticism was made by emergent neoliberals but also later from a different ideological perspective by the New Left and many social movement activists. A rift on the left began to open between the centralist welfare state orientation and various tendencies emphasising democratic participation.

However, contrary to neoliberal critiques, the historical drift of the British labour movement was less towards authoritarianism than accommodation to capitalism. As early as 1961, Raymond Williams expressed unease that capitalist values were beginning to permeate the labour movement. In *The Long Revolution* he comments that, whatever its rhetoric, the socialist movement was becoming more focused on '[s]ectional defence and self-interest' than the: 'discovery of ways of living that could be extended to the whole of society, that could quite reasonably be organized on the basis of collective democratic institutions and the substitution of co-operative equality for competition' (Williams, 1961, p 328). He cited the cooperatives, trade unions and the Labour Party as exemplifying this trend – a comprehensive trio. Williams also voiced concern about burgeoning state bureaucracy, a sentiment echoed almost a quarter of a century later by the more orthodox Marxist historian Eric Hobsbawm (1984, pp 76-77), alarmed that Western, as well as Eastern Europe faced a 'crisis of bureaucratisation' that he regarded as a threat to democracy.

The Wilson and Callaghan administrations of the 1960s and 1970s maintained a broadly centralised approach to governance. Relations between the Labour Party and the trade unions became fraught during the 1970s, with Labour governments preoccupied with controlling inflation and the unions seeking to maintain or improve members' living standards, with a minority set upon more serious industrial-political confrontation. Hobsbawm's seminal *The Forward March of Labour Halted* (1984, based on a speech of 1981) decried 'the illusion of salvation through union militancy' and, thought-provokingly for the contemporary left, comments that this 'has been replaced by ... probably a more dangerous set of illusions, based on the fact that the only dynamic aspect of the movement of late has been the striking advance of the left within the organization of the Labour party' (Hobsbawm, 1984, pp 172–173). Tensions within the labour movement came to a head in the so-called 'winter of discontent' of 1978–9, when the 'social contract' negotiated by the Labour government and the Trade Union Congress finally broke down. This opened the way to the Conservative election victory of 1979 and the introduction into Britain of neoliberalism.

Meanwhile the Bullock Report of 1977 on industrial democracy was effectively abandoned. So a possibility that companies with more than 2000 employees should have worker representation on their boards was lost. If implemented, the Report might have initiated a period of co-determination in British industry similar to the successful German model. In retrospect, the failure of the Labour Party and the trade unions to enact a larger social vision paved the way to a very different philosophy and set of policies: Thatcherism, the original British version of neoliberalism.

The ideological influence of neoliberalism on Blairism is well expressed in Margaret Thatcher's remark to her supporters at a Conservative Party conference: 'Our greatest achievement was Tony Blair. We forced our opponents to change' (quoted in Jones, 2015, p 51). New Labour largely adopted and even extended the lighter regulation, pro free market policies of Thatcherism. New Labour's rationale for this was partly to use some of the economic surplus to fund progressive social policies, some of which were effective – 'the Third Way', expounded by the academic Anthony Giddens (1998). However, as Martin Kettle (2015, p 30) says, 'once the Thatcher and Major governments had brought the unions to heel within a network of law, New Labour had no interest in reopening the subject of workplace democracy, corporate values and industrial co-determination'. By 2010, the creation of a democratic socialist party with mass support of the kind aspired to by activist intellectuals such as Hobsbawn and Williams looked more remote than ever.

The British middle and working classes have struggled for generations to achieve what is a piecemeal and compromise version of a democratic system, albeit qualitatively better than dictatorship or oligarchy. However, under this system the neoliberal settlement has left Britain vulnerable to the self-interested machinations of a global plutocracy, some domiciled in Britain. The next section discusses ideas and policies to revive democratic progress.

Institutional democracy

This section argues that radical and progressive politics, as well as pursuing greater material equality, should urgently address the institutional extension of democracy which itself could be a means of achieving greater material equality. Jodi Dean (2009, p 3) refers to the neoliberal 'reinvention of government as a private contractor and market actor' with the dominant role of capital and diminished involvement of labour and the public this implies. However, there is a strong countertradition on the left supportive of democratic institutional reform (Mills, 1956; McClellan, 2009; Wright, 2010; Jones, 2015). Simon Parker (2015, pp 72-73) has defended the integrity of 'society' from invasion from another direction – the over-controlling central state. However, he distances himself from vague 'big society' notions, stressing the need for fair funding of civil society initiatives and the planned devolution of certain powers to regional and local government. The current revival of Karl Polanyi's thought provides an inspiring perspective on what the politically conscious subordination of the market to a democratic society could achieve (Polanyi, [1944] 2001); our Introduction and Conclusion).

In so far as institutional democracy can be defined in a single sentence it is the maximum practical democratic involvement of people, including in decision making, in the institutions that affect their lives. Direct democracy is the 'ideal' form of institutional democracy but the term also applies to what Sylvia Walby (2015, p 178) refers to as a wider 'deepening' of democratic institutions. Several dictionaries of sociology comment that the use of the term institution within the discipline is routinely similar to lay usage and that is the case here (for instance, *Oxford Dictionary of Sociology*, 2006, p 358). As far as institutional democracy is concerned most institutions are organisations. Thus political organisations extend from party constituency branches to Parliament. Organisations may be part of a common system, the examples in the previous sentence being part of the political system. The main systems under consideration here are cultural, political and economic. Crucial to the approach in this chapter is that agency, and to varying degrees dissent and conflict, play a role in forming and changing institutions. A less obvious institutional form is language, and sufficient competency in language is crucial to understanding political discourse and argument. The particular area under scrutiny here is the interaction between generally less formally institutionalised civil society and the more formally structured sectors. The contention is that civil society activism needs to be more substantially and explicitly directed towards democratic institutional change.

Institutional democracy has several major characteristics. Firstly, it is based on the principle of the maximum practical democratic participation of those involved in the operation and reward distribution of the institutions or systems of which they are members. In terms of decision making, then, subsidiarity applies (see also Chapter Two). Institutional democracy is both a principle of maximal democracy and a concrete practice. Secondly, institutional democracy integrates into a single concept a range of democratic ideas and practices that occur widely if not always systematically in radical, socialist and other progressive traditions; but are routinely neglected in mainstream politics. The term therefore has a holding and consolidating function. Thirdly institutional democracy applies to all major public spheres of society – political, economic and cultural – and internally at every level, with appropriate variation in democratic forms. Fourthly, institutional democracy, as well as empowerment, requires competence, including a practical understanding of rights, duties and responsibilities.

The first point above is fundamental. The principle of maximum democratic participation is mediated by 'practicality' or 'feasibility': recognising that, while the distribution of power determines the degree to which a system is democratic or otherwise, the prime function of power is decision making – power for use. Limitations of scale, time and urgency may make full participatory or direct democracy impossible in some circumstances. Institutional democracy includes Julien Talpin's (2011) description of participatory democracy as the institutionalisation of a space where people can speak and act together, but goes beyond it in embracing all feasible extensions of democracy. Institutional democracy's heuristic edge is that it represents a democratic utopian vision open to gradual but potentially substantial implementation. Britain's currently stunted democratic system demands a counter-concept that offers a wider democratic horizon.

Secondly, as well as recognising the diverse, often hybrid, nature of democratic forms, institutional democracy focuses on their potential for integration rather than presenting them as competing alternatives.

It seeks to facilitate the flow of democratic power, offering a more practically engaged and empowering approach than liberal democracy, particularly in its atrophied neoliberal forms. It draws on *representative* and *direct* democracy and also *associative democracy*. The term 'associative democracy' has come into recent use following the publication of Paul Hirst's *Associative Democracy: New Forms of Economic and Social Governance* (1993). The precise meaning and application of the concept is still evolving but it can usefully be employed to indicate existing or potential collaboration on a basis of equality between groups, formal and less formal, to achieve a mutually desired outcome. Whereas interest groups exist to pursue their own individual or sectional advantage, associative democracy seeks the collective purpose and goals, typically of a diverse range of groups.

An example of an associative network formed to influence government policy is the various businesses, including farms, voluntary organisations, and residents that organised around the Roseacre Anti-fracking Group to oppose fracking in that area. As Olin Wright (2010) suggests, the growing concern about public health and environmental issues lends itself to associative democratic action.

Democratic forms, then, can be complementary and overlapping. For example, the system of participatory budgeting which has spread internationally from the Brazilian city of Porto Alegre combines both direct and representative forms of decision making (Wright, 2010, pp 155-160). Nor, as the Porto Alegre case shows, is the concept of institutional democracy utopian in the negative sense of that word. It focuses on the hard realities of power. As Wright points out, among other successes in Porto Alegre, participation levels have been high and sustained and a substantial shift in spending to the poorest regions of the city has been achieved (see Wright, 2010, pp 155-160).

Thirdly, institutional democracy recognises that power is characteristic of all institutional (as well as interpersonal) relationships and that all actors have an interest in its exercise. To define power exclusively in narrowly political terms distracts from inequalities in other institutional sectors. Acutely hierarchical organisational forms, typical of the corporate model, have been widely imposed beyond business. Accordingly, democracy needs to be established throughout public life. Subject to central government diktat, the public sector is arguably now managed more autocratically even than the corporate sector. For instance, the education system has undergone a metamorphosis from a public service directed profession to a market model of competing executive-led institutions (see next section). Institutional democracy should become the democratic norm across society – the embodiment of a 'common democracy'. It has the potential to empower people in a wide range of roles, such as (co)owners, managers and/or board members, including employees and consumers/service users, through election, role-rotation or, where appropriate, random selection. In some cases it would promote the overlap and integration of roles such as employee and manager through employee membership of boards of management. Industrial democracy is a crucially important form of institutional democracy and public, cooperative, credit union and stakeholder forms of organisation are particularly suited to it (see Chapters Eight and Eleven). Institutional democracy would need to be clarified in law as a general principle and in specific detail in particular instances.

Fourthly, the exercise of institutional power requires competence, including the ability to act responsibly on behalf of others. Participatory democratic approaches, like progressive education, typically demand more engagement and effort than hierarchical ones. Julien Talpin's *Schools of Democracy: How Ordinary Citizens (Sometimes) become Competent in Participative Institutions* (2011) reads as a caution in this respect. Using the ethnographic method, he researched three municipal areas in Southern Europe that practised participatory budgeting. In brief, participation dropped dramatically over time and little discernible effect on social inequality occurred – the opposite of Wright's findings in Porto Alegre. However, participants who persisted often became effectively engaged, some working closely with their communities. Talpin draws a constructive lesson, strongly endorsed here: civic competence requires an understanding of the 'grammar' of the relevant institutions – it has to be explained and learnt. The necessary training to participate in any institutional context might best take place within the given setting, but education about the functioning and distribution of power and rewards in organisations should begin at school along with political education. Schools could become engines of democratic development and experiential learning in a way likely to enhance their other functions, thus preparing young people for a society in which the everyday competent practice of democracy is the norm. A possible model for participatory democracy in Britain is developing in Thanet where the council has devolved a range of decision making on the community.

There are substantial potential benefits to institutional democracy. Firstly, if democratic rights are now considered inherent to modern citizenship, then their practical extension is desirable. Liberal democracy is not the "end of history" (Fukuyama, 1989); in fact in its neoliberal expression it has diminished modern democracy, increasing the need for more diverse sites and flexible flows of power. Secondly, given sufficient education and information, people are best positioned to protect their own interests in the main locations of their lives. In the context of work, people might choose to be represented through their trade union membership. However, the right to participate would extend to the whole workforce – dependent on a minimum period of employment. Liberal individualism and Marxian class theory both recognise that self-interest, whether pursued individually or collectively, is a prime motivator. Institutional democracy embeds this insight, increasing the possibility of a greater equalisation of wealth and resources because a key leverage – the power of members to protect and pursue their own interests – can be routinely exercised as of right. Effective membership acts as a safeguard against the emergence of irresponsible and self-serving elites within the institution. Thirdly, practical experience is important in the acquisition of skills and competencies. John Dewey (1925) conceptualised practical participation in the learning process as part of a general democratic principle that reverses 'top-down', merely didactic approaches. Involvement in the running and reward distribution of organisations could upgrade the skill and competence level of a national labour force. Fourthly, empowerment is likely to have a positive effect on individual and collective confidence and morale, with the practical and the psychological working in synergy.

The scope of institutional democracy: a democratic rebalancing

The limitations of the current British democratic system risk increasing disillusion and disengagement – as is apparent in the rise of populism. Democratic institutional reform has the potential to re-energise public participation and positively transform diffuse sentiments of discontent. It is needed at every level from central government, corporate boards, to local workplaces and educational establishments. In fact these levels are rarely wholly separate and part of the purpose of institutional democracy is to ensure that they engage each other in decision making. In this respect, the internet has already greatly enhanced connectivity. Others refer to its use by political activists, and while the internet should not naively be assumed inherently benign it does lend itself to democratic purposes (Chapters One and Twelve).

Far from conflicting with civil society activity, institutional democracy on any scale depends on the flow of ideas and energy from below. A Ministry of Mutuality, suggested by Jeremy Gilbert (Chapter One), or at least a dedicated subsection of the Department of Local Government and Community should be established to respond to, foster and, in part, fund civil society initiatives. Such support could also ensure that democracy is an effectively functioning reality, not only in the political system but throughout society's major institutional sectors. Some of which currently appear quite remote to the people they should serve.

The main institutions of the central state in Britain – the lower house now elected on a five-year basis, a hereditary monarch in Parliament as sovereign, and an unelected second chamber – are hardly strikingly democratic. Shortly before World War II George Orwell satirised the latter two institutions along with the so-called public schools, suggesting that Britain would be more democratic without them (Orwell, [1937] 2001, ch 10). This remains the case today. Orwell had an acute awareness of how institutions form public culture. The advantages of participatory citizenship are likely to be lost on those whose cognitive and emotional frame of reference is pleasantly stimulated by media images of the monarchy, aristocracy and the 'celebs'. To meet Orwell's criticisms would require establishing a republic, a representative second chamber and perhaps the absorption of fee-paying schools into the state system, so as to maintain and democratise their quality. Such reforms address the residue of Britain's oligarchic past and are consistent with liberal democracy, yet only the reform of the House of Lords is currently in play. Orwell, like Tom Paine, was not only ahead of his time but also of ours. Unsurprisingly, there are several proposals in the public domain to create a more democratic, functional and less expensive second chamber (for example, www.electoral-reform.org. uk/house-of-lords).

The most straightforward way to establish a more comprehensive and vibrant nationwide system of democracy would be through a constitutional convention; although institutional democracy can also be introduced gradually. Such a convention would stimulate debate about fundamental values and citizens' rights and responsibilities with the reality check of the requirement to establish them legally and institutionally. The current fudge of Britain's 'unwritten constitution' has given elites substantial latitude to serve their own interests with inadequate responsibility and accountability. Over 200 years ago Paine contended that Britain should establish a constitution to ensure government accountability to citizens. Just 70 years ago Polanyi ([1944] 2001, p 264) argued that '[h]abeas corpus need not be the last constitutional device by which personal freedom was anchored in law. Rights of the citizen hitherto unacknowledged must be added'. In an echo of Paine he advocates freedom 'not as an appurtenance of privilege, tainted at source, but as a prescriptive right extending far beyond the confines of the political sphere into the intimate organization of society itself' (Polanyi, [1944] 2001, p 265; see also Editors' Conclusion). In similar vein, Johal, Moran and Williams, in Chapter Nine of this book, present the case for a constitutional settlement that would ensure that the basics of 'civilised life' to all. Such ideas challenge current conventional political imagination but, in a period of national soul-searching, they are beginning to get a hearing.

Two particular measures, possibly as part of a written constitution, could revitalise the link between the people and their democracy. Firstly, as in a number of countries, including Australia, voting in national elections should be compulsory, so that it becomes a constitutional responsibility as well as a right. Citizens might choose not to fill in the ballot form but they would still be required to engage with democratic procedure. The requirement to vote in return for the right to participate parallels the idea of a right to a basic income in return for a significant contribution to society (see Introduction and Conclusion). Secondly, and related, political education, providing the necessary technical and substantive information to participate, should be made part of a core curriculum and established as a right. As Anna Coote points out, autonomy requires not only agency but critical autonomy: the capacity to think logically and make judgements as well as to act. Further, a government lead on establishing students' democratic participation at school, such as school councils, with some meaningful decision-making powers, would provide practical experience of democracy. A democracy in which barely two-thirds of those eligible vote in national general elections and less in other elections runs the risk that disengaged groups will be increasingly 'managed' or disregarded by government. To some degree the under -25s have been treated in this way as well as the poor (Savage, 2015). T.H. Marshall (1950) argued that in order to participate in society, citizens require an understanding of its 'common' culture and procedures – regardless of their own particular cultural traditions. Britain is remote from achieving this. Early conceptual and experiential grounding in democracy, as well as access to meaningful institutional power, might well diminish the apparent indifference and alienation of many to the structures of power and decision making.

The case for greater participation is compelling in relation to the economy. As both Bryn Jones and Andrew Cumbers illustrate, there are numerous ways in which business decision making bodies can be democratised and retain efficiency (Chapters Eight and Eleven). Indeed, in Denmark, Sweden and Germany relative institutional corporate democracy appears to correlate with greater efficiency. Power and authority is stratified at interconnected institutional levels, enhancing the prospects for accountability and responsible behaviour. In contrast, the highly centralised institutionalisation of power reduces the opportunity to contribute and risks promoting dependency and sycophancy. The realistic core of institutional democracy is that it reflects that, in general, people are the best advocates of their own interests, while also enabling them to mitigate the power of the business barons. Such a communalisation of power may be more Durkheim than Marx, but is no less practical and potent for that.

With the media, the education system is the main public agency of socialisation and culture. In particular, under neoliberalism higher education has been subjected to an organisational revolution reflecting neoliberal values and aims and undermining traditional collegiate decision making and a shared sense of public responsibility and purpose. Reform is necessary to re-establish substantial staff and student as well as the wider public, rather than pre-eminently managerial and business operation and representation on university bodies. As Peter Scott (2015) argues, the imposition of the ethos and processes of business on a profession that should draw mainly on intrinsic motivation and a sense of public service diminishes all concerned – whatever the league tables and tick boxes say. Efficiency and productivity are quite compatible with a restoration of the sector's humanistic and public culture. As a *Guardian* editorial put it: 'All our lives grow thinner and more flat when governments insist that money alone determines the agenda – and the curriculum – of our universities' (*Guardian*, 28 February 2015, p 34).

Conclusion

Institutional democracy provides a credible direction of 'democratic travel' towards increasing public participation mediated by practical limits. It offers a way of bypassing if not resolving divisive and unproductive disputes about what might be 'the best type' of democracy: representative democracy versus direct democracy – or 'flat democracy', reworked from the anarchist tradition in recent social movements as 'horizontalism'. Such disputes can be subject to pragmatic considerations of what is feasible in a given situation. Their opposition to hierarchy and to the state itself has discouraged some social movement activists from engaging in mainstream politics; even for the purpose of achieving more direct democracy. However, this may be changing with the rise of what some have called 'anarcho-populism' (Gerbaudo, 2013), as illustrated by the successful involvement of Spanish radical party Podemos in electoral politics, and the election of Spanish city mayors from protest movements. In Britain there are signs that ideas of grassroots democracy associated with social movements may be gaining momentum within the Labour Party. The grassroots and the radical centre need each other. However, legislation to substantially democratise the public and private sectors would also need to be implemented with the kinds of innovatory participation and empowerment discussed throughout this book.

Representative democracy can be rendered more accountable through instruments of referenda, recall and popular initiation of legislation via the internet. Proportional representation, inclusive of parties passing a minimum vote-share threshold, would reduce the danger of 'the tyranny of single party rule'. Reform should not be confined to the political system. Participatory democracy could be introduced or increased across a range of institutional sectors including large and medium-sized corporations, banks and regulatory institutions, voluntary organisations, universities and other educational organisations. Further, direct democracy should be considered a norm at smaller scale levels of decision making rather than a rarefied innovation.

The scope of the reforms suggested above and in some instances their radical nature may seem utopian but no doubt the current hegemony of neoliberalism once looked remote even to its supporters. The achievement of a freer and more democratic society requires that the principles and reforms to realise it are widely understood. Otherwise current discontent and protest – seeking uncertainly for solutions – will subside with little effect, or, even worse, the current harnessing of populist unrest by the far right will increase. To reverse this menacing development, radically democratic thinkers and activists must canvass among all the disaffected. They should articulate solutions in terms of freedom and equality refuting authoritarianism and scapegoating of the Other. Democracy offers the better values and arguments if not always the easiest ones.

References

Calhoun, C. (2012) *The roots of radicalism: Tradition, the public sphere and early nineteenth century social movements*, Chicago: University of Chicago Press.

Dean, J. (2009) *Democracy and other neoliberal fantasies: Communicative capitalism and left politics*, Durham, NC: Duke University Press.

Dewey, J. (1925) *Experience and nature*, New York: Dover Publications.

Fukuyama, F. (1989) *The end of history and the last man*, Washington, DC: Irving Kristol.

Gerbaudo, P. (2013) 'When anarchism goes pop', https:www.opendemocracy.net/paolo-gerbaudo/when-anarchism-goes-pop

Giddens, A. (1998) *The third way: The renewal of social democracy*, Cambridge: Polity.

Hirst, P. (1993) *Associative democracy: New forms of economic and associative governance*, Cambridge: Cambridge University Press.

Hobsbawn, E. (1984) *The forward march of labour halted*, London: Verso.

Jones, O. (2015) *The Establishment: And how they get away with it*, London: Penguin Books.

Kettle, M. (2015) 'Wake up, unions: There will be no prime minister Corbyn', *The Guardian*, 1 August, p 31.

Marshall, T.H. (1950) *Citizenship and social class and other essays*, Cambridge: Cambridge University Press.

McLellan, G. (2009) 'Progressivism revisited' in *What is radical politics today*, London: Palgrave Macmillan.

Mills, C.W. (1956) *The power elite*, New York: Oxford University Press.

Orwell, G. ([1937] 2001) *The road to Wigan pier*, London: Penguin.

Oxford Dictionary of Sociology (3rd ed, 2006) Oxford: Oxford University Press.

Paine, T. ([1791 and 1792] 1966) *The rights of man*, London: Everyman's Library.

Parker, S. (2015) *Taking power back: Putting people in charge of politics*, Bristol: Policy Press.

Polanyi, K. ([1944] 1957) *The great transformation*, Boston: Beacon Press.

Savage, M. (2015) *Social class in the 21st century*, London: Pelican.

Scott, P. (2015) *Higher education, the public good and the public interest: Critical perspectives on theory, policy and practice*, New York: Peter Lang.

Talpin, J. (2011) *Schools of democracy: How ordinary citizens (sometimes) become competent in participative budgetary activity*, Colchester: European Consortium for Political Research.

Thompson, E.P. ([1963] 2013) *The making of the English working class*, London: Penguin.

Walby, S. (2015) *Crisis*, Cambridge: Polity.

Williams. R. (1961) *The long revolution*, Harmondsworth: Penguin.

Wright, E.O. (2010) *Envisioning real utopias*, London: Verso.

Part Two
Reform within economic and governance restraints: pushing the boundaries

Editors' overview

The kinds of reforms and transformative changes proposed in Part One would be checked, constrained or shaped by the economic and governmental institutions which currently support the neoliberal regime. The contributions in Part Two of the book assess the current state of some key institutions of this kind: international bodies currently working with neoliberal paradigms to maintain or repress further the role of public expenditure and welfare: para-governmental bodies, such as the central bank, and the business corporations and sectors in which neoliberal market principles have been translated and transmogrified. Some of these institutions are already shifting away from strict neoliberal principles, albeit reluctantly and marginally. Others are attempting to defend the neoliberal regime against economic and sociopolitical pressures for change.

In their chapter Kevin Farnsworth and Zoë Irving place the UK in comparative context. They examine the workings of the austerity frameworks with which neoliberal states and intergovernmental agencies, such as the IMF, have sought to maintain neoliberal economics by undermining the remaining elements of social democratic welfare regimes. Their analysis reveals considerable variation among these welfare states and also division and ambivalence among the governance bodies overseeing austerity. By identifying countries like Iceland, which have successfully resisted and even partially reversed austerity programmes, Farnsworth and Irving suggest that austerity may not be a further entrenchment of neoliberalism but the cusp of a possible shift away from its key principles.

Jones and O'Donnell in Chapter Six, changes the international focus to examine the ways in which the European Union has moved away from the social democratic paradigm of a Social Europe to a more aggressively neoliberal stance which has recently, and famously, clashed with national movements campaigning for abandonment of neoliberal austerity. They argue that the core of the EU has adopted a variant of neoliberalism – 'ordoliberalism'. However, multiple and intersecting crises are still challenging this model. Opposition from what Polanyi described as the anti-market arc of the 'double-movement', are still challenging neoliberalism from both left and right in nearly all EU member countries. This chapter examines how the EU faces potential disruption or even disintegration from nationalistic movements, such as the UK's 'Brexit' challenge, and the political implications for the UK of the referendum result. Notwithstanding the latter development, the EU could still develop a more authentically democratic and socially just form of socioeconomic governance. An alternative which might be assisted by movements such as the DiEM initiative championed by former Greek Syriza minister, Yanis Varoufakis.

At the level of national economies, Grahame F. Thompson probes the shifting role of central banks, particularly the Bank of England, in handling the manifest inadequacies of free market economics in the wake of the 2008 financial crash. Although the Bank has not explicitly disavowed market orthodoxy, Thompson finds that there have been distinct shifts away from the practices initiated by the rise of neoliberal monetary policy 40 years ago. While seeking to pilot the UK's financial system into a leading role in the international economy, the Bank, like its counterparts elsewhere, has also become both the key manager as well as regulator of the national economy. Its championing of 'quantitative easing' to try to stimulate economic growth could, argues Thompson, be compatible with the more radical 'people's QE' advocated by the Corbyn camp in the Labour Party. While such a conversion may currently be beyond the mindset of the mandarin class, its possibility and the newfound pragmatism and powers of the Bank, suggests a non-neoliberal government could pursue a more socially sensitive and progressive path.

The final two chapters in this part of the book drill down into the 'real economy' to examine the present and potential roles of the corporate and business sectors. As the Introduction to this book explained, corporations and their controllers have been the principal organised beneficiaries of neoliberal 'freedoms'. In his chapter, Jones describes the abuses of their enhanced powers and the protest campaigns which this aggrandisement has generated from social movement and civil society organisations. Jones identifies the gradual shift in these campaigns from pressure for corporate social responsibility to more radical demands for corporate accountability. After reviewing the reform proposals of these and other advocates, he isolates the shareholder 'ownership' as the Achilles heel of executive and therefore corporate power, at least in the UK. He identifies relatively modest proposals to adopt Swedish-style accountability to investors, provided these reforms include a guaranteed role for the small investors which could include civil society representatives and 'stakeholders' such as trade unions. Reforms which could concretise the Polanyian forms of social re-embedding set out in O'Donnell's and other chapters, particularly the Conclusion to this book.

A complementary strategic policy for business accountability is outlined by Johal, Moran and Williams in Chapter Nine. Criticising unrealistic ideas for state control of an increasingly nebulous and fragmented 'national economy', they point to the massive potential relevance of a 'foundational economy' of locally based utilities and service provision. These sectors, which range from the 'parastatal' outsourced public services into informal sectors, such as family care, employ up to a third of the UK workforce; often as low-paid – and female – workers. Yet these concerns are mainly sheltered from the major pressures of international markets. Many depend upon approval and quasi-regulation from public and local authorities – for example local council planning permission for retail establishments. So Johal et al recommend a form of re-embedded social accountability for these sectors, through forms of licensing, in which business operation or expansion would be conditional on their meeting key social criteria in community responsibility, such as for sourcing, training and payment of living wages. Echoing the overlapping ideas of Coote in Part One, Johal et al recommend the construction of this foundational compact through a national 'constitutional settlement' involving democratic deliberation and multi-stakeholder participation. Taken together, the chapters in this part of the book identify some of the key economic and public institutions which can either maintain neoliberal practices or by relatively small, but strategic reforms, begin to return benefits and powers to the public and civil society realms.

FIVE

The limits of neoliberalism? Austerity versus social policy in comparative perspective

Kevin Farnsworth and Zoë Irving

Introduction

In 2009, following the meeting in London of the G20 heads of state, the then British Prime Minister Gordon Brown (http://news.bbc.co.uk/1/hi/in_depth/business/2009/g20/7979746.stm) heralded the beginning of a 'new world order' – a more progressive and more citizen-oriented era, less bound by free market fundamentalism. Periods of major economic crisis, especially those on the scale of the 2007-8 crisis, often bring such periods of reflection and have, in the past, driven paradigmatic shifts. In many ways, the Great Depression of the 1930s led to the emergence of the modern welfare state. The US at the time was a social policy pioneer rather than the laggard it subsequently became. The more recent crisis was different, however, and the lessons learned much more quickly forgotten. Any hope that the evolution of progressive social policies would be possible in a less hostile political and economic environment were quickly dashed. The kind of social solidarities within and between states that helped to boost social policies across Europe have been tested to destruction.

If it was questionable before, there is no longer any doubt that the needs of national capitals or, to paraphrase the discourse of international organisations, the needs of the global economy, have come to eclipse the needs of people. Social policy commitments are being stripped back and, in a world in which national economies have failed, alternative justifications for the more marginally productive functions of the welfare state – greater equality, emancipation, anti-poverty – are disparaged as ideas of a settlement inimical to the contemporary conditions of shrinking economies. The post-2008 high levels of national and consumer debt, growing employment instability and low consumption clearly present a challenge to welfare capitalism, but the ascension of austerity as the solution is a challenge in itself. The strategy of austerity, as a means by which governments can cut their way to growth, is undoubtedly leading to perverse economic outcomes and as such is a failing experiment. In the war of position on the welfare state, however, austerity appears to have achieved much greater success, cementing divisions between the secure and the unentitled, reimagining the size and activity of the state and solidifying in policy reform, the privilege of assets.

This chapter examines the role of social policy as the last defence against an increasingly brutal capitalism. It explores our claim that economic policy aims have come to eclipse social policy ambitions in a range of countries post-2008 and it examines the role of international organisations in promoting and managing this shift. The subsequent discussion highlights resistance to the demotion of social policy, and discusses the case of Iceland as an example of an alternative approach to reconciling social goals post-2008. Finally it argues that while austerity may appear to be compatible with a neoliberal vision of the welfare state, the current direction of policy within many countries would be as unlikely to satisfy free marketeers such as Hayek any more than it would satisfy the preferences of interventionists such as Keynes.

The unholy alliance of austerity and neoliberalism

The term neoliberalism is now so widely used in welfare state analyses that it hardly requires an explanation of its meaning (see Harvey, 2007). There is familiarity with neoliberal desires (free markets, individual endeavour and a small state); neoliberal ideologues (Hayek, Friedman); and neoliberal processes (privatisation, marketisation, financialisation). And yet few would describe themselves as 'neoliberal'. It may be that the hegemonic power of neoliberalism is such that these desires and processes have been normalised to the extent that they require no label to contrast them with alternatives because there are none – the ideas are so powerful that they entirely frame the volitions of governments and other key interests, including citizens themselves. From this perspective, the re-ascendance of economic principles and activities implicated in the creation of the 2008 crisis are therefore not surprising despite its severity and aftereffects. Given the history of austerity as a policy response (Blyth, 2013) it is also unsurprising that a scramble to pare back government spending and cut taxes has been presented as the solution to problems of unsustainable public debt, ballooning deficits and low growth.

Austerity appears to symbolise exactly what neoliberals are assumed to desire. However, even if there were a pure form of neoliberalism there is no pure form of austerity. It is as ambiguous and ephemeral as the 'Third Way' and other policy approaches that have been presented as 'pragmatic' and 'un-ideological'. Moreover, austerity is not simply about expenditure cuts – it more accurately describes an intention towards, and reconfiguration of, economies and welfare states that cannot be measured or assessed simply by reference to social spending as a proportion of gross domestic product (GDP). While the intention is to dissolve the bonds of solidarity that characterised the post-war period of welfare state building, because for neoliberalism they have always represented constraints on freedom, it is the reconfiguration of the welfare state that is expected to achieve this outcome. At present the 'austerian' vision of the welfare state necessitates reductions in statutory rights because in the post-war years state expenditure has become increasingly dominated by non-discretionary spending (pensions for example). It also necessitates a rapid disempowerment of labour, whether facilitated through a direct or indirect suspension of democracy or the imposition of world-regional or national fiscal constraints. Reforms towards these aims have seemed relatively easy to undertake in the context of high unemployment and a debt narrative intended to lower welfare expectations reference (see Farnsworth and Irving 2015a).

However, a bigger challenge to neoliberalism emerging from the crisis was that it seriously brought into question the idea that economies would be stronger and more competitive and that corporations would be more entrepreneurial and more profitable if only government 'got out of the way'. Since 2008, the levels of state support for private business, the role of the state in supporting the various forms of loss of income from employment and the identification of needs for 'social' investment have been unprecedented. All of these 'needs' are contrary to the logic of austerity and expose the fallacy of the neoliberal dream of the small state.

Neoliberalism and austerity: always and everywhere?

It might have been assumed that states that were already characterised by liberalism in their economies, welfare and employment regimes would do best in the new flexibilised and liberalised global market of the 1980s, and that social democratic states would struggle to secure a competitive advantage. However, the evidence does not bear this out. Even in the 1980s this was not the case (Katzenstein, 1985) and although in the 1990s the continental European states faced particular challenges in their efforts to engage on neoliberal terms (Palier, 2010), Sweden, the archetype of the social democratic model, remains one of the most competitive economies in the world, ranked equally with the UK.[1]

It is a sign of the present times that the previous period of austerity now resembles a period of relative plenty as far as developed welfare states were concerned. The predicted race to the bottom (see Mishra, 1999) appeared to have been overstated and although neoliberal imperatives (individualisation, marketisation, privatisation and new public management) had influenced change in welfare states, the nature of these changes had largely been assimilated into their essential characters rather than reducing the advanced economies to a mass of low-welfare competitors. Thus global neoliberal economics was more an arena that national economies entered armed with their own models for growth and competitiveness, and clad with their own social models for protection, than a hegemonic force bearing down on all welfare states with equal measure. The national consequences of global pressures were differentiated depending on, for example, the level of corporatism in social bargaining or coordination in the economy (see for example Esping-Andersen, 1999; Hall and Soskice, 2001). More recently, Hay and Wincott (2012) have argued that in the pre-crisis 2000s, welfare state convergence was more intra-regime than inter-regime. Yet the pressures imposed in the age of austerity appear to be of a different order than the pressures imposed in the period of neoliberal globalisation. Notably there is, of course, at least one key difference: periods of economic crisis impose economic structural constraints that are different and, in many ways, more significant than challenges that are altogether more political and ideological in nature. It may be that neither is all-determining, but the room for manoeuvre for states is very much reduced by the former. The question now is whether globalisation was just a precursor, and the alliance of (political) austerity with neoliberal economics enables the authentic imposition of a hegemonic project.

There is a wealth of comparative literature which suggests that national pre-configurations of citizen–state–market relations ought to mediate both the impact of, and fallout from the 2008 crisis. In the early analyses of post-2008 welfare state trajectories, both predictable and more surprising national differences were apparent (see Farnsworth and Irving, 2011; Bermeo and Pontusson, 2012; Starke et al, 2013), but it also became increasingly clear that the financial locus of the first crisis gave rise to a variety of subsequent crises that did not present the same challenges, at the same time and to the same extent. What was often referred to as 'the' crisis in 2008 was in fact a variety of crises that came in waves that continued to change direction and hit states in unpredictable ways (Farnsworth and Irving, 2011). And the crisis is by no means over.

In the earlier phase of economic globalisation, commentators argued that the state-citizen contract would be redrawn as Keynesianism was abandoned; work rather than welfare became the principle of entitlement and interests in national performance in the global market replaced the kinds of national interests that state rebuilding required in the period following the world wars and the decline of colonial powers (Cerny, 1997; Jessop, 1999). A 'period of permanent austerity' (Pierson, 1998) reflected the changing form of state commitments to welfare in the face of pressures to remain competitive and attractive to increasingly mobile capital.

The idea that neoliberalism determined the shape and direction of pre-crisis welfare states had already been challenged by a number of commentators. For Pierson (1994), pressures to drive down social policies met with strong pressures to preserve welfare states which stemmed from the fact that resilient social policies were necessary to mitigate the harsh realities of economic globalisation. For Cerny and Evans (2004), governments did not abandon social policies in the wake of globalisation because certain productive elements of the welfare state were important to maintaining or improving competitiveness in the face of global trade. Hemerijck (2012) similarly argued that states have been forced to shift the emphasis of social policies away from 'inactive' to 'active' forms – increasing social investments in order to boost economic growth and social wellbeing. What these approaches have in common is that they all emphasise the importance of the 'the economy' within social policy decisions. It has always been thus. We argue that in this there is a delicate balancing act. Where social and economic policies are viewed as having compatible goals and ends, there is a symbiotic relationship between the two. The post-2008 crisis has, however, shifted the balance in certain circumstances so that the economy has come to trump the social. This has not occurred uniformly across states.

Different varieties of welfare respond to various pressures in different ways, and 'families' of nations, the literature suggests, tend to respond in similar ways. However, national welfare state change in the years immediately following 2008 has been characterised as much by differentiation as by similarity within 'families' or 'worlds' of welfare. The crisis drew attention to the structural features of national economies, the extent of financialisation – particularly in relation to property markets, for example, in explaining the initial impact, the role of exports in explaining the impact of the subsequent economic slowdown, and membership of the European Union in determining the possibilities for a return to growth. As far as the types of welfare states were concerned, what was most apparent was that the 'automatic stabiliser' function was certainly activated in states with more generous protection systems (Starke et al, 2013) and it was also these states which were under least pressure to make savage long-term cuts to public expenditure to restore the fiscal balance extolled by both the International Monetary Fund (IMF, 2009; Farnsworth and Irving, 2011a) and the Organisation for Economic Co-operation and Development (OECD, 2011a and 2011b). The enormous bailouts to financial institutions and programmes of quantitative easing undertaken by the most liberal, least generous welfare states (the US and UK) account for one dimension of the pressure to cut spending but the actuarial accuracy of this relationship has been very successfully hidden in the wider political agenda fusing neoliberal welfare state intentions and the economic logic of austerity discussed above.

In terms of the responses to the varieties of crisis experienced, the power of 'austerity' as the official panacea to problems of debt and deficits has come to define the terms of debate on welfare states. Although difficult to define, austerity represents the fundamental shift from a public understanding of states' commitment to progressive expansion of social provision, to a public acceptance of reductions in benefits and services, a retreat of the state from its role as guarantor of social rights as the cost of long-term economic security. In economic practice the strategy of austerity, termed 'fiscal consolidation', requires that states reduce public spending and wages in the expectation that economies will thus become more competitive (see Blyth, 2013). Within this overarching theme of austere states, there have been three broad approaches in the responses of individual nations and these do not directly map onto the extent to which the crisis can be regarded as damaging states' economies.

Considering just the richer nations of the global North, we can identify groups of countries affected by the separate waves of crisis: the financial crisis; the 'great recession' and the Eurozone crisis; and three variations of welfare state response to the resulting problems. As already mentioned, there is a group of countries that were implicated in, and shaken by, the initial financial crisis: the US, the UK, Ireland and Iceland. This group of countries hit hardest and most immediately by the collapse of banks and other financial institutions were those most heavily financialised and, except for Iceland (see below), were also those where bank bailouts have contributed most to the subsequent level of government debt and the significance of interest payments in contributing to budget deficits. Most countries suffered the effects of the economic slowdown and what has since been termed the 'great recession'; the economies of Germany and China particularly at risk to stalling export markets; the US and Japan still in anaemic economic recovery in 2015. In relation to the Eurozone crisis, the fortunes of the members continue to depend on their pre-established core-periphery position. Greece has clearly suffered the most in relation to sovereign indebtedness and since 2010 has been unable to resist loan conditions imposed by the European Central Bank (ECB), IMF and European Union. These conditions have defied and compromised the democratic process and, to date, while failing to achieve growth in the Greek economy, have contributed significantly to political destabilisation. Other countries in this group – Italy, Portugal and Spain - have fared little better, with unemployment posing a threat to solidarity and fragile post-2008 economies.

In terms of responses, there is a group of opportunist competition states which even though their economies may not necessarily have slumped to the levels experienced in Greece, for example, have used the crisis and Greece as a stick with which to beat their electorates into believing that austerity is the only logical or rational solution to the problem of 'the deficit'. These countries include Estonia, Germany, the Netherlands, New Zealand and the UK.

At the other end of the spectrum are the reluctant 'austerians'. These countries have felt pressure to introduce austerity measures in order to keep pace with competitors but have found 'austerity' more politically unpopular and so have masked austerity with additional spending or 'social investment' or other state programmes such as QE: France, Japan and the US. The US has, as might have been anticipated given its oft-cited exceptionalism in matters of political economy (see Wilensky, 2002), taken a more unexpectedly Keynesian approach to economic re-flotation. At federal state level there are of course many avid 'austerian' state governors, and the measures implemented across states are subject to variance in the context of subnational intraregime tendencies of welfare model. Austerity is thus far more complex than its manifestation in social expenditure cuts. In considering austerity's character, Bob Jessop (2015) differentiates between policies, politics and polity with only the latter suggestive of an enduring shift in the role of the state. While austerity policies, he suggests, are 'conjunctural' and potentially reversible, austerity politics indicates longer-term 'reorganisation of the balance of forces in favour of capital' (Jessop, 2015, p 97) and the austerity polity, the institutionalisation of this rebalancing. In effect, however, all three of these dimensions represent a serious threat to the welfare state.

What we see across states is a variety of austerities. This variety reflects the particular ways in which the impact of 2008 has reverberated through economies, mediated by the degree to which (neo)liberal tendencies in the domestic economy had become interwoven with the patterns of their pre-existing engagement with the global neoliberal market, and their propensity to being shaped by the international organisations which have discovered new power.

Austerity-lite or not at all: fiscal consolidation and the IMF

Returning to Gordon Brown's vision of a new world order, it is impossible to consider the logic of austerity in the crisis responses of nation states and their location in internationalised neoliberalism without reference to the role of the international financial organisations. Following the 2008 crisis, new life was breathed into the IMF which had, up until the 2009 summit, been undergoing its own existential crisis, as an increasingly uncompetitive and toxic lender with a much more peripheral place in the global financial order than that foreseen by its architects in the 1930s.

As the prime interlocutor of neoliberal interest, it might have been expected that the IMF's position on austerity would be far more coherent than it has appeared. The IMF has given out conflicting messages on how deep and how fast cuts to spending should be made, which countries should and should not be cutting at all, and what the purpose of cuts should be. As we have argued elsewhere (Farnsworth and Irving, 2015b), however, the IMF's seeming inconsistency in approach is actually quite rational in terms of the institutional logic of the organisation. Prior to the crisis the IMF was an organisation that had lost a degree of relevance and authority (Masson, 2007). By the 2000s, many nation states were reluctant to consult with or seek assistance from the IMF. Primarily this was due to the negative perceptions surrounding loan conditionality coupled with the fact that the world was awash with relatively cheap credit in the period leading up the crisis. This in turn meant that relatively wealthy economies with other options had had no need to resort to IMF lending, and all countries were aware that drawing on IMF services sent a much stronger signal to global markets of the fragility of an economy than borrowing from alternative sources. Buoyed by the strength of the global economy, and having experienced an unusually long period of economic growth and stability, governments in the wealthiest economies could not envisage having to approach the IMF for assistance.

This important backdrop feeds into three important points that help to explain the operation of the IMF from 2008 to 2015. First, the IMF was relatively slow to take a coherent position in the immediate aftermath of the crisis, but its role and position was eventually boosted by a large funding injection from its member organisations in 2009.[2] At its most basic, the key priority for the IMF continues to be economic growth through private market development. However, the IMF has also recognised that major cuts in public expenditure across nations has threatened the stability of the global economy. Second, later in 2009, Dominique Strauss Kahn, then President of the IMF, stressed that support to wealthy economies would no longer be underpinned by structural-adjustment-type conditionality. Thus, the IMF has variously pushed or condemned 'austerity' within nations according to the perceived risks regarding the recovery of, in particular, the global economy (Farnsworth and Irving, 2015b). Third, despite its earlier assurances, the length of the crisis, its variability between states and regions, and the fact that the IMF partnered with the European Central Bank and European Commission in the help it offered to Ireland and Greece, meant that the IMF has, paradoxically, been driven back-to-type by the European Union. The Eurozone crisis allowed the IMF a new role representing largely (but not only) US interests in the desperate and ultimately unsuccessful attempts by the Greek people to use democracy to oppose austerity. However, the European Central Bank and the European Union also gained power from Eurozone countries through the mechanisms established ostensibly to deal with debtor members but which lock all members into an 'austerian' fiscal-legal cage (see McBride, 2015). As Schäfer and Streeck (2013) have pointed out, the result of this is the removal of a democratic exit for those 'watching their lives slide out of view'[3] as the resulting policies demolish welfare promises and expectations.

Small acts of resistance: Iceland

In the context of the 2008 crisis, the resilience of neoliberalism in the face of its failures and the part that the strategy of austerity has played in supporting this, instances of resistance have been far less disruptive than might have been expected. Outbreaks of popular and organised protest occur regularly but they are disparate and often disregarded in formal politics. In terms of national resistance, the flouting of the democratic process in Greece is a clear example of how a country has been used by the powerful economic elites to crush the ambitions of critics. Despite the demurrals presented from the perspective of Icelanders themselves, Iceland is the only existing advanced economy counterfactual to the inevitability of neoliberal orthodoxy.

It is commonly assumed that Iceland has always been a member of the Nordic family of nations in terms of its welfare model. In fact, the creation of a Nordic 'welfare society' only became an explicit policy aim in 2009 following the 'pot and pan' revolution deposing the centre-right government, and the subsequent election of the Social Democratic Alliance/Left-Green coalition (see Irving, 2012). Prior to this significant change in Icelandic politics, its welfare state exhibited characteristics much more comfortably associated with the liberal model (Ólafsson, 2003, 2005). The existing individualist tendencies in Icelandic social politics ensured that the explicit project of neoliberalisation pursued under the premiership of David Oddsson (1991–2004) and his successors was as politically painless as it was economically terminal. This period was characterised by the kinds of familiar measures associated with neoliberal reform: privatisation and marketisation of the public sector, huge reductions in corporation tax and privatisation of the banking sector in 2000. With an insubstantial regulatory framework, Iceland's three largest banks embarked on a period of aggressive international expansion exposing the country to impossible liabilities through foreign equity investments financed by dubious interbank and intrabank lending practices. At the same time, however, and despite rising inequality, it seemed that Iceland was living the neoliberal dream, particularly given its relatively recent industrialisation post-independence in 1944. Iceland scored highest on the UN *Human Development Index* in 2007/8 and was among the highest on most other social and economic measures: exceptionally high (and long) labour force participation rates for both women and men, high life expectancy and high incomes, for example, alongside continual GDP growth which peaked at 9.5% in 2000.

The financial euphoria came to an abrupt end in 2008 when the banks failed with net debts equating to 210% of GDP (Sighvatsson et al, 2011), the government failed to deal with the impending national bankruptcy, and the people of Iceland chose to oust the government and elect a coalition whose prime minister presented an alternative vision to the prevailing model of conspicuous consumption. The significant elements of the subsequent Icelandic response comprise, firstly, a refusal to bail out the banks including resistance to considerable international pressure to guarantee foreign investment in Icesave, the online banking arm of the collapsed Landsbanki. Secondly, despite submitting to IMF/bilateral loan arrangements of over US$3.5 billion, the government committed to (successfully) meeting the loan conditions and repayment schedule within a framework of policies that maintained, and in many ways expanded, social protection and provision, particularly those discretionary areas that many other countries have chosen to pare back because of the limited political fallout.[4] Thirdly, neither the challenge to the dictates of international financial capital nor the foregrounding of social over economic policy led to the failure of the state or market exile. Austerity was a feature of the Icelandic recovery but in comparison to the experiences of other advanced economies, it was unquestionably austerity-lite.

In the most recent IMF country report (IMF, 2015) it is clear that Iceland's economic rehabilitation has approval, although with caveats including its 'crisis legacy' of 'lingering vulnerabilities'. The deficit is 0.1%, government debt is down to 80% of GDP, GDP per capita is above pre-crisis levels and unemployment is below 4%. While these and other indicators such as inflation, household debt and the adequacy of reserves have yet to meet their targets, the IMF report opens with the statement that 'Iceland has reached a relatively strong macroeconomic position with good growth prospects' (IMF, 2015, p 1). In the summer of 2015 all of the key ratings agencies upgraded Iceland's rating to their various versions of BBB, suggesting that 'the markets' were also confident that Iceland was a recovered state.

The significance of this is not that Iceland's fortunes should be determined by the whims of international finance, but rather that doubt is necessarily cast on the argument that markets need and want austerity. Nevertheless, although the government's desire to maintain the Nordic welfare model is noted in the IMF report, it also indicates that Iceland is now in a position to scale back the support measures (such as social benefits) which have added to public spending in the post-crisis period. Despite this nudge to further fiscal consolidation, the 2016 Budget proposal indicates increases in spending on housing, healthcare, education and child benefits, and a 9.4% rise in disability and unemployment benefits and old-age pensions.[5] These are cited in addition to cuts in taxes in the lower and middle tax brackets.

The return to power of the centre-right coalition of the Progressive Party and the Independence Party in 2013 challenges the extent to which a nascent Nordic welfare model has been possible in an increasingly neoliberal world, and indicates what the obstacles to further development might be. It has been suggested in media commentary that the perception of collusion between the SDA-Left-Green coalition and the IMF in response to the Icesave issue, combined with continuing hardship for many households as well as the government's pursuit of EU membership, have all contributed to disaffection, or impatience with the 'new' post-crisis politics.[6]

Many public commentators point to the continuing presence of political oligarchy, the fragmentation of the left and the more familiar patterns of voter swings post-crises. The shelving of the so-called 'crowd-sourced' new constitution, which expressed much that could be considered alternative to the neoliberal social and economic vision, appears to symbolise the hopelessness of attempts to challenge the 'power of money',[7] even in the context of a post-revolutionary state. But still, as the budget statement implies, the seeds sown between 2009 and 2013 may yet obstruct a return to business as usual. There is a dichotomy in the presentation of Iceland as a test case. Events can be seen as unique to a small and socially proximate island state where possibilities for communication and mobilisation are more direct.[8] In contrast, we are reminded that the 'New Guinea effect' (Selwyn, 1980) should not prevent us from identifying the structures and processes that are common across states. The Icelandic experience suggests that although a reversion to the political orthodoxy has occurred there is ongoing aversion to austerity and, significantly for the neoliberal dreamers, that this has not prevented a return to economic stability.

Conclusions

The notion that austerity and neoliberalism are not only compatible but pathologically entwined permeates economic and social policy discourse at both the domestic level and in the globosphere of international organisations and their policy advice. The discussion here has indicated that both neoliberalism and austerity are nebulous concepts, amalgams of myths and misrepresentations about the role and size of the state, made even more indeterminable in the 'new world order' given the conflicting needs of economies and people. States have pursued strategies of austerity with varying levels of enthusiasm and coercion only to achieve the same lack of improvement on either economic or social indicators.

A consensus on the application and timeframe of austerity measures continues to escape the international organisations such as the IMF and ECB. The IMF in particular, while clinging to its role as an axiomatic voice of neoliberal economics, is itself unconvinced of a one-size-fits-all austerity solution to the multiple and diverse economic afflictions of advanced economies, individually and by region. Despite this, its policy messages continue to be underpinned by a functional understanding of social policy that fails to comprehend the social impact. Its interactions with Iceland aptly demonstrate this lack of sociological awareness. Iceland may not be the beacon of alternative social progress that many had envisaged but clearly demonstrates that austerity is not a necessary component of competitiveness in the global market – but nor is its absence a guarantee of success for alternatives to neoliberal designs for the state.

We set out in this chapter to ask whether the austerity welfare state is a neoliberal dream come true. Clearly, in some states, political parties that are sympathetic to neoliberal ideas have sought to ensure that, for them, the crisis does not go to waste. However, the more closely we examine social policy debate and direction within nation states and beyond, the more complex the actual politics of welfare appear. The discussion here indicates that it is by no means clear that neoliberals have shared and coherent objectives in terms of the welfare state and, even if they did, it is still less clear that austerity itself is a politically and economically coherent strategy to achieve them.

Notes

[1] According to the World Economic Forum Global Competitiveness Index 2015-16, http://reports.weforum.org/global-competitiveness-report-2015-2016/competitiveness-rankings/

[2] Although this newfound capacity has subsequently been placed under pressure due to US intransigence (see Wade and Vestergaard, 2015).

[3] As Pulp put it in the song 'Common People'.

[4] See Sigurgeirsdottir and Wade (2014) for an account of Iceland's dealings with the IMF.

[5] Ministry of Finance, www.ministryoffinance.is/news/nr/19961.

[6] See for example 'Laurie Penny on Iceland's elections: A shattered fairy tale', New Statesman, 8 May 2013; Alda Sigmundsdóttir, 'Iceland's election: Voters fear the EU more than a return to the bad old days', *The Guardian*, 26 April 2013.

[7] This idea is discussed by an interviewee in the film 'Blueberry Soup' (2012) directed by Eileen Jerret which documents the process of producing the new constitution https://vimeo.com/72931601

[8] Some might argue that the imposition of capital controls after 2009 clearly illustrates this position.

References

Bermeo, N., and Pontusson, J. (eds) (2012) *Coping with crisis: Government reactions to the Great Recession*, New York: Russell Sage Foundation.

Blyth, M. (2013) *Austerity, the history of a dangerous idea*, Oxford: Oxford University Press.

Cerny, P. (1997) 'Paradoxes of the competition state: The dynamics of political globalization', *Government and Opposition*, 32 (2): 251-274.

Cerny, P. and Evans, M. (2004) 'Globalisation and public policy under New Labour', *Policy Studies*, (25): 51-65.

Esping-Andersen, G. (1999) *Welfare states in transition*, London: Sage.

Farnsworth, K. and Irving, Z. (eds) (2011) *Social policy in challenging times: Economic crisis and welfare systems*, Bristol: Policy Press.

Farnsworth, K. and Irving, Z. (2012) 'Varieties of crisis, varieties of austerity: Social policy in challenging times', *Journal of Poverty and Social Justice*, 20 (2): 135-149.

Farnsworth, K. and Irving, Z. (2015a) 'Austerity: More than the sum of its parts' in K. Farnsworth and Z. Irving (eds) *Social policy in times of austerity: Global economic crisis and the new politics of welfare*, Bristol: Policy Press.

Farnsworth, K. and Irving, Z. (2015b) 'Incoherence, indecision and indifference: Unpicking the global politics of austerity', Paper presented at the Annual Social Policy Association Conference, Belfast, 8-10 July.

Hall, P. and Soskice, D. (eds) (2001) *Varieties of capitalism, the institutional foundations of comparative advantage*, Oxford: Oxford University Press.

Harvey, D. (2007) *A brief history of neoliberalism*, Oxford: Oxford University Press.

Hay, C. and Wincott, D. (2012) *The political economy of European welfare capitalism*, Basingstoke: Palgrave Macmillan.

Hemerijck, A. (2012) *Changing welfare states*, Oxford: Oxford University Press.

IMF (2009) *The state of public finances*, Washington, DC: International Monetary Fund.

IMF (2015) *Iceland, Country Report No. 15/72*, March, Washington, DC: International Monetary Fund.

Irving, Z. (2012) 'Seeking refuge in the Nordic model: Social policy in Iceland post 2008' in M. Kilkey, G. Ramia and K. Farnsworth (eds) *Social policy review 24*, Bristol: Policy Press, pp 295-316.

Jessop, B. (1999) 'The changing governance of welfare: Recent trends in its primary functions, scale, and modes of coordination, *Social Policy and Administration*, 33 (4): 348-359.

Jessop, B. (2015) 'Neo-liberalism, finance-dominated accumulation, and enduring austerity: A cultural political economy perspective' in K. Farnsworth and Z. Irving (eds) *Social policy in times of austerity: Global economic crisis and the new politics of welfare*, Bristol: Policy Press.

Katzenstein, P. (1985) *Small states in world markets: Industrial policy in Europe*, Ithaca, NY: Cornell University Press.

Masson, P. (2007) *International Journal, 2006*–7, 17 April, Centre for International Governance and Innovation, Canada, http://economics. ca/2007/papers/0999.pdf_

McBride, S. (2015) 'The economics of austerity' in K. Farnsworth and Z. Irving (eds) *Social policy in times of austerity: Global economic crisis and the new politics of welfare*, Bristol: Policy Press.

Mishra, R. (1999) *Globalization and the welfare state*, Cheltenham: Edward Elgar.

OECD (2011a) Economic policy reforms 2011, Going for growth, Paris: OECD, www.oecd.org/newsroom/46917384.pdf

OECD (2011b) *Restoring public finances*, OECD Working Party of Senior Budget Officials, Public Governance and Territorial Development Directorate, Paris: OECD.

Ólafsson, S. (2003) 'Welfare trends of the 1990s in Iceland', *Scandinavian Journal of Public Health*, 31 (6): 401–404.

Ólafsson, S. (2005) 'Normative foundations of the Icelandic welfare state: On the gradual erosion of citizenship-based welfare rights' in S. Kuhnle and N. Kildal (eds) *Normative foundations of the Nordic welfare states*, London: Routledge.

Palier, B. (2010) *A long goodbye to Bismarck? The politics of welfare reform in continental Europe*, Amsterdam: Amsterdam University Press.

Pierson P. (1994) *Dismantling the welfare state? Reagan, Thatcher and the politics of retrenchment*, Cambridge: Cambridge University Press.

Pierson, P. (1998) 'Irresistible forces, immovable objects: Post-industrial welfare states confront permanent austerity', *Journal of European Public Policy*, 5 (4): 539–560.

Schäfer, A. and Streeck, W. (eds) (2013) *Politics in the age of austerity*, London: Wiley.

Selwyn, P. (1980) 'Smallness and islandness', *World Development*, 8 (12): 945–951.

Sighvatsson, A., Daníelsson, A., Svavarsson, D., Hermannsson, F., Gunnarsson, G., Helgadóttir, H., Bjarnadóttir R. and Ríkarðsson, R.B. (2011) *What does Iceland owe?*, Economic Affairs No 4, February, Reykjavik: The Central Bank of Iceland, www.sedlabanki.is/lisalib/getfile.aspx?itemid=8713

Sigurgeirsdottir, S. and Wade, R. (2014) 'From control by capital to control of capital: Iceland's boom and bust, and the IMF's unorthodox rescue package', *Review of International Political Economy*, 22 (1): 103–133.

Starke, P., Kaasch, A. and van Hooren, F. (2013) *The welfare state as crisis manager: Explaining the diversity of policy responses to economic crisis*, Basingstoke: Palgrave Macmillan.

Wade, R. and Vestergaard, J. (2015) 'Why is the IMF at an impasse, and what can be done about it?', *Global Policy*, 6 (3): 290-296.

Wilensky, H. (2002) *Rich democracies*, Berkeley: University of California Press.

SIX

The European Union and the UK: neoliberalism, nationalist populism, or a cry for democracy?

Bryn Jones and Mike O'Donnell

Introduction

The EU referendum result favouring British exit from the European Union threw up manifold and far-reaching economic and political consequences. The immediate aftermath of the poll does not allow accurate diagnoses of a still unfolding political phenomenon. However, we can examine already apparent aspects of the changing UK-EU relationship for their relevance to the analysis of the neoliberal regime and plausible alternatives to it. The discussion below focuses on three specific questions: (1) What role has the EU so far played in supporting or moderating neoliberalism in the UK? (2) In post-referendum politics which of the politico-ideological movements ignited by the campaigns is likely to be most influential and will lead to the consolidation of either a new, possibly nationalistic populism or a more cosmopolitan and democratic movement? (3) How will these tendencies affect the neoliberal paradigm? They could maintain sufficient support for open markets and big business dominance or favour torsions of, or even transformations of, this paradigm and its institutions. Separation from the core of the EU's economy could push the UK towards an even more open economy and imbrocation in globalised economic relationships. Conversely a nationalistic, sovereignty ethos, or a democratic, cosmopolitan worldview could entail checks and reversals of market corporatism.

The chapter processes these questions in three stages. First we describe the changing character of the EU in relation to neoliberal governance and globalisation processes, as well as the crises in its economy and governance – of which the UK 'Brexit' phenomenon is one symptom. It pays particular attention to the extent to which EU leaders tried, for a while, to provide some social protection from market forces and also to the need for some democratisation of its core institutions. Then we analyse what the referendum campaigns might tell us about support for these contrasting principles. These issues are not merely of historic interest for the UK. As long as it maintains some economic relationship, the EU's institutions and political character will impact the survival, or otherwise of neoliberalism in this country. The third section tries to identify future scenarios for UK–EU relationships. For example, a UK completely detached from the EU and therefore less able to connect to social movements for democratic equality in the Union. Another scenario considered is one in which the UK is semi-detached from Europe, but with little influence at the 'top table'. Finally, we consider briefly the possibility of a restructured EU with less centralisation and more devolved and federal democracy and the implications this might have for a post-referendum UK. The guiding thread for these analyses, revisited in the Conclusion to this book, is the implications for the radical democracy, corporate accountability and lifeworld-focused economics set out in other chapters.

Contradictions in the changing EU project

A belief among sections of the British left, which found a new voice as 'Left leave' in the referendum debates (www.leftleave.org/), is that the EU is an incorrigibly capitalist project. Defined as a capitalist club, dominated by the influence of multinational corporations, the EU is seen as dedicated to exploiting labour and extending the reach of markets at the expense of working class interests and nations' social and public welfare institutions. Incongruously, however, neoliberal economists, such as onetime Thatcherite adviser Patrick Minford, see the EU as a bureaucratic cartel which impedes the efficient workings of both internal markets and a more efficient engagement with the global economy. From this viewpoint, the ultimate folly was the attempt to impose, by bureaucratic diktats, a single currency without a supranational fiscal system and in defiance of international money markets. Another perspective, however, sees the EU as prone to crisis because of its long-standing attempts to combine three different projects: a *political* project aimed at minimising national differences through shared economic interests; an *economic* project creating a single transnational, European market, without national barriers and standards; and a *social* project in which protection from the worst market vicissitudes would be assured by social standards guaranteed at EU levels but defined and implemented by member states.

Inherent contradictions in combining these three projects were manageable up to a point until recent decades. They became unmanageable because the guiding economic philosophy morphed into a neoliberal one and the EU's institutions proved, contrary to original intentions, to be incapable of protecting the continent's weaker economies from the effects of the financial crash of 2008. In this conjuncture, the combination of an external, global, neoliberal economic system and internal neoliberal policies of readjustment through austerity and privatisation has generated a crisis which the EU's present regime seems incapable of resolving. Although detached from the debacle of the Euro currency crisis, the UK has experienced some of the backwash from attempts to solve the Eurozone's crisis with neoliberal policies. The political fallout in the UK has been triggered by the influx of migrant workers from the recession-hit southern economies grappling with the effects of these policies, plus job seekers from less developed new member states such as Poland, Slovakia and Romania. Ironically, it was the neoliberal aspirations of UK governments which precipitated the latter inflow through their promotion of EU enlargement to the east and migration as an answer to perceived rigidities in the UK labour market.

The socially embedded market project

The foundational 1958 Treaty of Rome laid down four market freedoms to operate across the original six, then nine countries of the new European Economic Community: freedom of movement for capital, for goods and services and for labour. The nine included the UK and these were joined by three more Mediterranean states, including Greece, before the collapse of Communism brought in eastern European states after 1990 and, indirectly, changed the political tenor of what had by then become the 'European Union'. The founding Treaty and subsequent decisions pledged social protection as a collective goal. However, actual convergence has not been promoted and the detailed design, and therefore compatibility, of social security and other protections related to labour continue to be the responsibility of each member state (Cornelisse and Goudswaard, 2002). Nevertheless, the paramount condition is that such national, social regulation must be compatible with the foundational principle of free movement. The Commission Presidency of Jacques Delors (1985–95) advanced pan-European social protection; but alongside a parallel intensification of the internal market and its competitive concomitants: the first explicit introjection of neoliberal principles into the tariff zone.

Delors' 1988 speech to the British Trades Union Congress (TUC) was pivotal for converting the bulk of the labour movement to European integration. Using empathic language he argued that 'close co-operation and solidarity as well as competition are the conditions for our common success' (p 87). The real sweetener was, however, the promise of social and labour relations standards and rights. Delors defined these as: maintenance of member states' existing levels of social protection; improvement in workers' living and working conditions and health and safety standards at work; 'every worker's right to be covered by a collective agreement'; and regulation of atypical employment, such as temporary work; as well as a Statute for European Companies. The latter would include 'the participation of workers or their representatives'. In sum, 'social dialogue and collective bargaining are essential pillars of our democratic society and social progress' (Delors, 2002: 89).

The subsequent, Delors-inspired 'Social Chapter' of the 1987 Single European Act (of the Maastricht Treaty), though technically only a 'protocol', was aimed at 'promotion of employment, improving living and working conditions, proper social protection, dialogue between management and labour, the development of human resources with a view to lasting high employment and the combating of exclusion'. The, then Thatcher, government exercised its right to opt out of this anathema to neoliberals. The 1997 Labour government reversed this decision, as it did on the subsequent 1994 Works Council Directive, for workforce consultation in companies, and the 1996 Parental Leave Directive. The 'Chapter' has since facilitated social policy initiatives in other labour and industrial relations issues, equal opportunities, health and safety, public health, protection of children, the disabled and elderly, poverty, migrant workers, education, training and youth (Archer, 2008, pp 82–83).

Relatedly, the Eurosceptic bugbear of the Working Time Directive was meant to limit the extent to which firms in different member countries could get a competitive edge by enforcing unreasonably long working hours. Its patchy national implementation seems to have failed to achieve such harmonisation (but see Coote, Chapter Two), although some of the worst excesses, such as in long-distance haulage, have been curtailed, including in the UK (Barysch, 2013). For all EU-inspired UK legislation it has been estimated that between 1980 to 2009, 'for the most part, the EU element of these Acts is minimal and has been introduced when domestic legislation was amended for other purposes' (House of Commons, 2010, p 42). However, the *economic* intentions of Delors and other architects of the Single European Act have been more obvious.

Residual non-tariff barriers to internal trade, ranging from goods traversing EC borders, public contracts limited to national companies, incompatible product standards and professional qualifications, non-competing service industries, to differential rates of VAT and duty all restricted trade and capital movements. The Single European Act aimed to sweep these away. Significantly the drive to harmonise or standardise all of these factors was promoted largely by Margaret Thatcher's government, to stimulate intra-Union competition. But the Delors Commission sought to safeguard against adverse consequences on working populations and to avoid 'social dumping' – that is, countries gaining an 'unfair' competitive edge by tolerating lower social costs for their workers.

Broad guarantees on employment-related social conditions were to be protected and, where practicable, augmented. However, concrete measures for a European social model waned as commitments to neoliberal economic policy waxed stronger (Zielonka, 2014). Diverse efforts continued to be made to inject social protective measures into the Single Market enterprise. The encouragement of 'social dialogue' – rather than central regulation – involving workforce representatives and management heads of pan-European firms is claimed to have made an impact on health and safety, equal opportunities, training and flexible working, even in the UK (Eurofound, 2008). Similarly, attempts were also made, in the renewed drive for 'competitiveness' following the Lisbon Treaty of 2000, to rely less on central directives and explicit regulation but rather to use 'the Open Method of Coordination'. In this, not so successful process, best practice models for implementing general aims, such as social protection, would be disseminated and differentially adopted without a top-down blueprint from Brussels. However, the OMC seems to have been handicapped by the disproportionate clout of the competitiveness drive and 'lack of bottom-up participation' (Radaelli, 2003).

Monetary Union and the euro crisis

While member states operated with different currencies, distortions and imperfections in trade would continue because of fluctuating exchange rates, payment conversions and incompletely integrated banking systems, as well as susceptibility to currency speculation by global money markets. A common currency would, it was believed, iron out most of these imperfections and risks. However, and to the distaste of Thatcherite UK politics, the governance provisions established by the Maastricht Treaty of 1990 required supranational governance of national fiscal and monetary policy. In particular, it stipulated the permitted rate of inflation, public sector deficits – no more than 3% of GDP - and a limit of gross government debt to 60% of GDP. Furthermore, long-term interest rates were not to be higher than those in the three lowest inflation member states by more than 2 percentage points (Afxentiou, 2000) . Although some countries, including the UK, rejected joining - because of the constraints these conditions would place on national monetary and fiscal policy – 11, and later 19, countries, including the ultimately, hapless Greeks, swapped fiscal autonomy for these EMU restrictions. The majority EU support included a: 'neoliberal ... consensus' which 'traded full employment for price stability as the main goal of macroeconomic policy' (Matthijs and Blyth, 2016: 10).

Social democracy in continental Europe, especially Germany, has traditionally been complemented – or constrained depending on one's view – by an 'ordoliberal' system of economic governance. Unlike neoliberalism, its ordoliberal counterpart prefers a much greater role for the state in overseeing markets and enforcing market 'disciplines' such as competition. It also invests greater faith in public institutions and rule making and enforcing bodies. Germany's willingness to replace national currencies – including the totemic deutschmark – with the euro was therefore, understandably, conditional upon such strong rules and policing mechanisms mentioned above. It is however, debatable – to put it mildly – whether these institutions have contributed to resolving or exacerbating the euro crisis precipitated by the 2008 financial crash.

In March 2011 the European Council (of national ministers) decided to add to Article 136 of the Treaty on the Functioning of the European Union – which was originally a Treaty of Rome agreement updated for the establishment of the Single European Market. This additional paragraph, which establishes a 'financial stability mechanism' for the Eurozone, says that:

> The Member States whose currency is the euro may establish a stability mechanism to be activated if indispensable to safeguard the stability of the euro area as a whole. The granting of any required financial assistance under the mechanism will be made subject to strict conditionality. (European Council, 2011, p 5)

'Conditionality' is a neoliberal concept borrowed from IMF and World Bank policy for marketising the once state-centred economies of the global South and the former communist countries. It means recipient countries get support on condition that they deregulate and privatise.

The 2008 crash revealed that Eurozone rules had been manipulated or fudged by some states. To correct their public sector borrowing levels, Commission and Eurozone authorities urged austerity prescriptions. Unfortunately, Greece and others also owed massive sums to the banks whose reckless lending policies had precipitated the financial crisis, but which were now protected from further losses by governments anxious in case they might fail and therefore intensify the crisis. So Greece and other Southern and peripheral states had not only to clean up their lax fiscal behaviour to satisfy the Eurozone. They also had to swallow austerity medicine to begin paying back, or at least qualify for rescue loans for the stability needed to *begin* repayments. In a more rational and Keynesian world, such deflationary prescriptions would have been rejected as unworkable. But by this time neoliberal thinking had long suffused, not only the monetary guardians such as the International Monetary Fund (IMF), but also Eurozone leaders and officials. Despite mass unemployment, riots, Indignados and Aganaktismenoi occupations, failed governments and mass disaffection, the only solution offered, nay demanded, by the European authorities was fiscal austerity, coupled with the conventional neoliberal devices of privatisation and deregulation. Keynesian and other non-neoliberal economists have ridiculed this deflationary strategy as it can only lead to further falls in both economic activity and the government tax revenues needed to pay back debts. While even the IMF has eventually acknowledged that it would be better for Greece to default on some of its debts, the ordoliberal high command in Berlin and Brussels holds out for its kilogram of flesh.

The most obvious implications of the subsequent, recessionary drift that has destabilised several EU economies relate to neoliberal economics, austerity and labour displacement. As neoliberal policies overshadowed the 'social Europe' model, they facilitated the banking crisis which, for all the rectitude of ordoliberalism, the main countries and the Eurozone authorities were unable to prevent or reverse. Recourse to austerity economics has depressed most of the Eurozone economy and stimulated the migration of younger workers to the more buoyant economies. In a double irony, the UK has experienced a substantial amount of this migration, fuelling xenophobia and the Brexit campaign, largely because former Chancellor George Osborne covertly adopted Keynesian policies: growing the economy by stimulating the housing market and expanding bank funds through quantitative easing (see Chapter Seven). Moreover, as diverse analysts of the euro currency system had pointed out, without more central controls over national fiscal policy making and a full-fledged EU central bank, the only way to compensate weaker economies struggling with uncompetitive euro exchange rates is by substantial EU funding and cheap loans to stimulate investment and demand (Afxentiou, 2000). Such Keynesian has, however, been anathema to the worldview of the EU's current leaders. Indeed, in relation to support for the former Communist bloc member states, they have acted in a more hawkish manner than the IMF (Lütz and Kranke, 2010; also Farnsworth and Irving, Chapter Five). As a result, new entrant states in Eastern Europe experience substantial migration of unemployed and underemployed workers to expanding job markets, like that of the UK.

The EU's stalled democracy

Judged on basic criteria of representativeness, transparency and accountability, the EU seems to score reasonably well on the first but poorly on the second and third. UK Europhobes and Brexit campaigners emphasise the virtues of leaving the bureaucratic and autocratic EU political system for the Shangri-La of UK parliamentary democracy. As the Introduction and Chapter Four explained, the UK's first-past-the-post voting system and the unelected House of Lords discredit this as an electoral institution for representing majority preferences and expectations. In some respects, such as the proportional voting system by which members of the European Parliament are elected, the EU's democracy is superior to that of the UK. However it is less so in terms of *accountability*. The central problem is the unwillingness of the Council of Ministers – composed of national leaders – to cede authority to the Parliament. For a while, the Parliament began to acquire powers to provide a more democratic check on Commission and Council decision making. Regrettably, the election of the current President of the Commission, Jean-Claude Junker, proved to be a limited and temporary advance in this trend. It looks as though the candidature of future presidents will be decided by heads of government in the Council (Muller, 2016).

National parliaments could exercise more scrutiny over Council decision making, but many, for their own, often governing party purposes (especially the UK), choose not to. The power centre of the Council lacks *transparency*. Its meetings are held virtually *in camera* without online or public record of its deliberations (Butt Phillip, 2016).

Nevertheless, as mass, trans-European social movement campaigns like that against the neoliberal Transatlantic Trade and Investment Partnership (TTIP) deal show, the Parliament can check, or at least challenge, Commission policy making; but these are partial successes. On a broader scale, as Zielonka (2004) argued, sheer demographic arithmetic makes participation in decision making by 454 million people in the enlarged EU impossible without radical changes. The only significant reform, apart from reversing the transparency scandal mentioned above, would be greater devolution of the implementation of broad EU policies, perhaps along the lines of the participatory budgeting method described in Chapter Four.

The UK referendum campaign and its implications for political change

The 'In/Out' referendum on European membership of 23 June 2016, by common consent, confronted the British electorate with one of the most serious choices in the post-World War II period. The question was deceptively simple but the answer to it likely to result in fundamental and complex consequences for the country's future, including the possible breakup of the United Kingdom. The immediate aftermath of the clear but narrow win for Leave over Remain of 51.9 to 48.1 was chaos in the two main political parties: Conservative Prime Minister David Cameron, who had led the Remain campaign against massive Eurosceptic sentiment in his party, resigned as party leader. The opposition Parliamentary Labour Party, with the majority already opposed to their leader, Jeremy Corbyn, passed a vote of no confidence in him by 81% to 19%; ostensibly mainly because of his perceived lukewarm performance in support of Remain. However, the party membership and campaign group Momentum continued to back him. The phrase 'existential crisis' was freely used to describe the state of the Labour Party.

Personal fate and conflicts aside, however, the referendum bought more clearly into the open the emerging sociopolitical forces likely to struggle to shape Britain in the coming years. Political turmoil and vendettas signified deeper uncertainty and potential instability in respect to the economic, social and cultural life of the country. Harold Wilson's remark that a week is a long time in politics was amply demonstrated in the week following the referendum. So, to speculate about trends over a period of several years is a clear risk – mainly of being badly mistaken. However, in a policy-oriented book, aimed at facilitating change and at a time of great national uncertainty, some informed speculation from poll data seems justifiable.

The vote itself and the reasons given for it suggest a significant nationalist mood in the turn away from Europe. A highly popular placard of the Leave campaign emblazoned the words 'We want our country back' and polls suggest that the sovereignty issue was the most important to Leavers. The ability of Britain to make its own laws was cited by 53% of Leave campaigners as the most important issue when deciding which way to vote whereas for those voting Remain it was 2% (ComRes poll: *Sunday Mirror*, 26 June 2016, www.comres.co.uk/polls/sunday-mirror-post-referendum-poll/). The Scottish vote to remain, at 62% the highest, was also motivated in part by nationalist sentiment: potentially to leave the United Kingdom but to remain in Europe. Immigration was cited by 34% of Leavers as the most important reason for their vote, whereas for Remain voters it was 4%. However, the sovereignty and immigration issues are related for Leavers in that control of the latter was seen as largely dependent on the former. By far the most important issue cited by Remain voters was the economy at 67%, in sharp contrast to 3% of Leave voters. These differences between the two sets of voters are dramatic and suggest a possible period of political polarisation ahead.

Further to the very different reported reasons between the Leave and Remain camps for their choice of vote, survey data on the sociodemographic background of voters provides substantial evidence, below, that the United Kingdom is a socially and culturally divided and potentially unstable entity. Profound, if possibly fluid, sociopolitical divisions in the United Kingdom might redefine what the two main parties stand for and, possibly, an even wider and more radical political fragmentation and realignment. The importance attached to sovereignty and immigration control indicates a nationalist and broadly right-wing complexion among 'Leavers'; and other surveys provide details of the social, generational, regional and other categorisations of the referendum voting pattern. The main source of data referred to below was published by Dr Robert Ford in the *Observer* (26 June 2016, pp 14–15). Additional data on generation comes from a survey from Lord Ashcroft Polls also published in the *Observer* of the same date (p 11).

Media interpretations have tended to exaggerate the regional nature of the divide. While Scotland, Northern Ireland and London were the only major regions where a majority voted to remain, the respective minorities voting to leave was considerable: at 38%, 44% and 40%. A map highlighting the percentage of both winners and losers in voting constituencies would give a more complex and differentiated picture. A further complexity is that voters from a particular class, generation, or other category were spread albeit unevenly across the whole of the United Kingdom.

The relationship between voting patterns in the referendum and social class gives a different picture than was often presented in the media. Data cited by Danny Dorling (2016) shows that 59% of the Leave vote came from the middle class (A, B and C1) whereas only 24% came from social classes D and E. However, 13 million people were registered to vote but did not do so and 7 million adults were not even registered. Given the total data, it is clear that a substantial majority of the latter groups were working class. The young also made up a relatively large proportion of non-voters. So the Leave win was a victory mainly for the middle class and older or, at least not so young, age groups. There are trends within this broad picture that might give concern to progressive thinkers and activists. The primary worry is that the Remain campaign, to which the Labour Party was formally committed, failed to convince its 'natural' constituency that the EU offered a fairer and more prosperous option for the future than the Brexit leadership. It can be reasonably surmised that a mix of apathy and anger at years of austerity contributed to the low working class turnout. The turnout issue aside, in specific voting constituencies – mainly those where UKIP had already mounted a substantial challenge to Labour – the working class Leave vote was probably influential, if not decisive, for the superior Leave total. Even more marked was a trend among the less well educated to support Brexit. Thus, Brexit support by level of higher education was 62% in local authorities where fewer than 22% had a degree. By contrast, the more graduates in a given area, the larger the percentage for Remain.

Similarly, generation and voting behaviour were strongly correlated. Of those aged 18-24, 73% voted for Remain with 27% voting to leave (Lord Ashcroft Polls, 2016). For those 65+ the split was 60% to 40% in favour of Leave despite the efforts of the Prime Minister and Chancellor of the Exchequer to influence older people to vote Remain by arguing that exit would make their benefit levels unsustainable. Ford's report adds that the young tend to have higher levels of education than older people, and the more educated a person, the more likely they were to vote Remain (Ford, 2016). The Momentum phenomenon and other data (see Savage et al, Table C. 2, p 397; and Chapter One of this book) suggest in addition to latent working class support there is considerable potential among the educated professional young to support a progressive Labour Party. Matthew Goodwin (2016) argues that reconciling the needs and aspirations of these two groups represents a key challenge for the Labour Party in the future.

Prospects for neoliberalism and post-referendum opposition to it

Leavers

At the time of writing it is quite possible that Theresa May's new government may be even more sympathetic to neoliberal tendencies than the Cameron-Osborne led governments of 2010-16. The political dynamic initiated by the Brexit vote – entrusting government with a broadly nationalist and pro-immigration control agenda – points in a more conservative, traditionalist direction. The Brexit vote had a distinct element of sentiment about it, a nostalgic longing for imagined and, no doubt, in certain aspects genuinely better times. If the Conservative Party wants to retain and increase the support of older people and of less educated urban workers, including many UKIP voters, as well as, of course, its core middle class support, it may move towards this more reactionary agenda. However, as Margaret Thatcher demonstrated, nationalist and even retro-imperialist nostalgia is quite compatible with tough neoliberal policies and can even act as a salve to them.

A shrewd reading of the referendum vote by any government could see it partly as a cry of anger against low wages, insecure work and other aspects of persistent and creeping inequality, rather than an excuse to revert to discredited market triumphalism. Leave voters who felt such resentment may have attributed the wrong cause for it, but they showed an awareness of the inequality of which many of them are victims. The blue-collar workers, and for that matter the elderly people who voted in their droves for Brexit, had only one option by which to show anger and discontent with the status quo – to vote against membership of the European Union. This is not to deny that the many Conservative and UKIP voters among them were not ideologically committed to their choice.

However, the EU's several problems, outlined above, will not be resolved by the UK renouncing full membership but then remaining as a semi-dependent trading partner. A UK withdrawal could well make matters worse for both Britain and the EU, and, ironically, for some of the very groups that voted to do so. Had the electorate been asked whether, for example, they favoured a more equal distribution of resources and opportunities in Britain, with a full public debate on the details– they might well have had an answer more to their benefit. Any government would be wise to address the underlying rationale for much of the Brexit vote – inequalities – rather than focusing on immigration and a spurious repatriation of 'democratic sovereignty'.

Remainers

Remain voters were aware of some of the EU's flaws but had an equally strong feeling that the range of rights, protection (including environmental) and regulation the Union provided – social Europe – adds substantially to the material and broadly relational quality of life. Prominent trade unionists, including Len Mcluskey of UNITE, and progressive journalists and academics addressed these matters with as much concern as the anticipated negative economic consequences of Brexit. Nevertheless, some Remain supporters believed that the EU has tended, with the above important qualifications, to facilitate business's own special advantage, rather than constraining the transnational corporations for the common good.

In its more recent, neoliberal phase the 'four freedoms' of the Union and single market – free movement of capital, labour, goods and services – can reasonably be said to have benefited capital - including investments from outside the Union – disproportionately to labour and the general public. These reservations no doubt explain a perceived lack of clarity and enthusiasm in the Labour Party's Remain campaign. However this is not to downplay these campaigners' real fear that Brexit may facilitate, at worst, a free market free-for-all; worsening the social situation of the many who already suffer the effects of austerity (Dorling, 2016). Below we analyse the current, relatively weak or divided, political forces that might be expected to oppose this serious possibility.

Is another EU possible; is another UK possible?

Schematically envisaged, three broad issues and six related scenarios can be extrapolated from the possible UK–EU relationship emerging from the referendum and its political consequences. The issues concern the form any new relationship takes, the impact this has for the structures and policy paradigms of the EU, and the impact on UK politics and economics. For each of these issues it is possible to envisage a dual scenario: the new relationship either strengthens or weakens the political and ideological grip of neoliberalism on the relevant institutions. There is insufficient space here to analyse each of these permutations and key aspects may already be decided by the time that this book is published. So we here focus on three possible and relevant scenarios.

A democratised EU?

The neoliberal and ordoliberal mindset currently running the EU seems unlikely to change in the near future. The prospect of a British resignation looks likely to prompt even more, rather than less, financial dirigisme from the chief heads of government. A related scenario is fiscal integration within the core Eurozone countries, France, Germany and the Benelux states, realising the often mooted 'two-speed Europe'. Such developments would be indifferent, hostile even, to any democratic restructuring of key institutions, or to economic devolution to refloat the Eurozone's recessionary south. Much will depend, however, on political change in the member states. If anti-neoliberal parties were to win government roles in a handful of countries and make gains in the European Parliament, there could be enough leverage to block and change course in both EU economics and decision making.

At the time of writing, these prospects seem improbable. The chief opposition in France is the crypto-Fascist and anti-EU Front National. The most radical challenge in Germany and Austria comes from similar nationalistic parties. Italy remains becalmed between coalitions led by the 'Third Way' Democratic Party on the left and a rightist alliance dominated by the remnants of tycoon Berlusconi's Forza Italia, with the autocratically led Five Star Movement of anti-EU greens – allied in the EU Parliament with the UK Independence Party. Even the rise of Podemos, the descendant of the Indignados/Movimiento 15-M protests of 2011, has failed to break the neoliberal inclined duopoly of the (conservative) Popular Party and centrist Socialist Workers party in Spain. In Greece, Syriza remains in government, but helplessly shackled to European Monetary Union-imposed austerity programmes. And yet there are other straws in the wind.

From the wider centre-left, EU Parliament President Martin Schulz has called for the Commission officials to be elected, for elected representatives, plus a second chamber made up of representatives of member states, like the US Senate or Germany's Bundesrat. More significantly from a British political perspective, Shulz argues for more subsidiarity, so that member states enact more policies than those often decided first at Commission or Council levels. Schulz's pitch may have been influenced both by the Brexit and threats of similar moves by politically volatile EU states, and by the cross-national DiEM25 movement. Under a slogan adapted from the alter-globalisation movements – 'another Europe is possible' – this campaign of greens and leftists, such as ex-Syriza minister Yannis Varoufakis, are demanding transparency, democratic representation and devolved decision making. Their immediate aims are stated as:

> Full transparency in decision-making (e.g. live-streaming of European Council, Ecofin and Eurogroup meetings, full disclosure of trade negotiation documents, publication of ECB minutes etc.) and (B) the urgent redeployment of existing EU institutions in the pursuit of innovative policies that genuinely address the crises of debt, banking, inadequate investment, rising poverty and migration.

After adequate stabilisation of these crises, DiEM25 calls for a multination constitutional assembly, to decide, by 2025, on the provisions for 'a full-fledged European democracy, featuring a sovereign Parliament that respects national self-determination ... sharing power with national Parliaments, regional assemblies and municipal councils' (DiEm Manifesto, 2015, https://diem25.org/manifesto-short-version/).

The UK: semi-detached or castaway?

Economic policy after Brexit could also easily shift into more obviously pro-neoliberal mode. The greater the economic difficulties of the British economy post-referendum, the more a Conservative government is likely to revert to pro-market solutions. If the British economy, which many already see as weak and vulnerable, suffers at least some of the predicted post-referendum problems, a potential recession will have to be tackled. A devalued pound, reduced interest rates and contraction at the high end of the property market could stall the inflow of overseas capital and slow the service sector, by far the biggest economic activity. With Britain as a disadvantaged supplicant, it may take years to renegotiate trading relationships with Europe and the rest of the world. So quick, if temporary 'fixes' will probably be sought to bring in compensating overseas investment; such as George Osborne's post-referendum plan to reduce corporation tax from 20% to 15% by 2020. A comparison with France and Germany, where corporation tax is respectively 33.3% and 29.72%, shows how much this would favour global corporations, and how much public revenue might be lost. The *Evening Standard* reported Osborne's statement under the heading 'Osborne under attack as cuts risk "turning UK into a tax haven"' (Lynch, 2016, p 34). Such a free market approach would be consistent with the Leave campaign's familiar, though much discredited, motif that 'the free market' can produce prosperity for all. It also suggests public investment in infrastructure and the public services would not be enhanced by a Conservative, post-Brexit administration.

The haggling of negotiators over the potentially deal-breaking issue of the 'free movement of labour' will probably determine whether the UK takes a position similar to that of Norway or Iceland, as a trading satellite of the EU which lacks political representation in its institutions. The alternative, much less economically favourable relationship could be similar to that negotiated with South Korea in 2011, even though the latter is 20–40% smaller than the present UK in GDP and population. The 'price' of tariff-free trade between the EU and Korea was adherence to EU requirements on: 'administrative barriers to trade … provision of services, public contracts and investment … competition policy, the transparency of regulatory regimes, and the protection of intellectual property rights' (European Commission, 2016). In other words, EU stipulations on state and public sector roles would still be enforced but, like the Norwegian and Swiss arrangements, the UK would have no presence in the EU forums setting the relevant standards.

Pour encourager les autres, countries such as France and Sweden, with significant ultra-right movements advocating exit, the EU might decide to demand particularly tight conditions on issues such as contracting for UK public services. The prospects of rolling back privatisation and outsourcing by an anti-neoliberal policies could thus be significantly handicapped. On the other hand, UK governments persisting with neoliberalism, but facing reduced advantages in trade with the EU and/ or the almost inevitable fall in economic activity during a transition, would have to seek trade arrangements with equally, or more powerful states such as the USA or China. The example of the faltering EU–US Transatlantic Trade and Investment Partnership (TTIP) suggest that such a bilateral agreement could give multinational corporations and finance capital even greater influence over public services such as the NHS. By contrast the TTIP has been successfully, though only partially, challenged in its EU deliberations by coordinated trans-Europe campaigns by left-wing and civil society groups.

A potentially more progressive policy, which could help fund social and economic stabilisation in countries such as Greece, would be the long-delayed introduction of a 'financial transactions tax' (FTT). By a levy of 0.1% against on exchanges of shares and bonds and

0.01% on 'derivative contracts', it has been estimated that €57 billion per year could be raised if the whole EU participated (Christie and Brunsden, 2011). Perhaps predictably, the UK objected and launched an unsuccessful legal action to block the proposals (Barker, 2014). But this was only a partial defeat as the EU has decided to permit implementation in countries in favour of it, rather than demand an EU-wide application. Of course, if Brexit is realised the lobbying power of the City will probably reduce and the prospects for wider implementation of a FTT increase.

The UK: more intensive neoliberalism or a democratisation upsurge?

The few, but vocal, economist supporters of Brexit were of a fundamentalist neoliberal stamp. They included former Thatcherite adviser and advocate of monetarist policies, Patrick Minford, who opined that outside the EU's economic sphere: 'The structure of production shifts towards non-protected sectors, increasing productivity overall.' The TUC remarked on the similarity between this economic shock treatment and Professor Minford's previous exhortations to ration 'severely and brutally' NHS services 'to the vast majority who ought to be paying for themselves', and to

> remove protection ... particularly to the car industry and other manufacturing industries inside the protective wall, you will have a change in the situation facing that industry, and you are going to have to run it down. It will be in your interests to do it, just as in the same way we ran down the coal and steel industries. (TUC, 2016)

Minford's erstwhile political counterpart, ex-Chancellor Nigel Lawson, similarly opined that Brexit would provide: 'The opportunity to make the United Kingdom the most dynamic and freest country in the whole of Europe, to finish, in a word, the job which Margaret Thatcher started' (BBC, 5 July 2016, www.bbc.co.uk/news/uk-politics-36717050).

Leave campaigners' victory and levels of support within the governing Conservative Party, will give them considerable influence in deciding future relationships with the EU. Liam Fox's appointment as International Trade Minister indicates the kind of trade deals which may succeed the EU agreements. Fox was previously prominent in the Atlantic Bridge 'charity' which had close links to US corporations, neoliberal US politicians and the American Legislative Council –

motto: 'Limited government, free markets, federalism' (Doward, 2011). Much depends on who is in charge of responding to likely recessionary or inflationary consequences of Brexit developments. Despite Conservatives' postponement of overambitious public deficit goals, a more neoliberal Conservative government might defend and intensify austerity as the only way to 'steady the ship'. What matters in the longer term is how changed circumstances and reshaped sociopolitical formations may affect *opposition* to neoliberal hegemony.

Labour is the most likely mainstream conduit for at least some of the reforms put forward in this book to replace neoliberal orthodoxy. If the party can resolve its recent internal divisions it could and should present a coherent alternative to erstwhile working and lower middle class supporters. Anti-austerity is perhaps the most promising policy approach on which some agreement might be found and a common front formed against the prospect of even more free market fundamentalism. As far as the democratic argument against neoliberalism is concerned, the substantial extensions of local and direct forms of democracy suggested in this book are more likely to be supported by the party membership than a Parliamentary Labour Party largely content, like the political elite generally, with the prevailing representative democracy – which may involve even more centralisation of power at Westminster, if Scotland, or even Northern Ireland manage to withdraw from the United Kingdom because of the referendum result.

Austerity has stimulated growth in initiatives for participation across the country, independently of Westminster. One such is the impressive innovation of participatory economic planning by Thanet council: devolving strategic as well as budgetary decisions to the community (see Chapter Four). Despite the depth of the philosophical and policy divide between the parliamentary and activist wings of the party on the issue of democracy, there are areas of common ground. These include support for a democratically reformed upper chamber and devolutionary proposals, which already draw backing from across the party. The spectre of a succession of electoral defeats might also ramp up support for proportional representation, if it were seen as helpful to the Labour cause. Furthermore, future, Brexit-induced renegotiation of trade treaties could offer a progressive government the opportunity to press for agreements requiring companies to operate more democratically in relation to shareholders and employees (see Chapter Eight), and with the sort of social compacts suggested by Johal et al (Chapter Nine). The early aspirations for more 'stakeholder' influence in corporate governance by new Prime Minister Theresa May might create a, possibly wider, political opening for more substantial reforms in this sphere.

Conclusion

To sum up, from one perspective the referendum and its aftermath can be read as a shift to the right, expressed as a combination of nationalism and xenophobia with political elites using economic disarray to reassert neoliberal economics. From a deeper analysis, on the other hand, both the popular Leave and Remain votes seem to combine a protest against the insecurity of market forces and, by at least some 'Remainers', a preference for some sort of embedded markets – within the notional guarantees and protection claimed by the residues of 'Social Europe'.

At the time of writing, some Europhile campaigners believe that the 'leave' decision can be blocked, politically or legally, or even delayed sufficiently to enable a political fix between EU leaders and a more sympathetic UK government. A rising tide of mainly youthful activism in the Labour Party or a regrouped Remain campaign might well favour some of the policy directions indicated in this book. A trend which might be strengthened if, as after Scotland's referendum (McLaverty et al, 2015; Women for Independence, 2016, www. womenforindependence.org), the rash of early protest campaigns against the conduct and outcomes of the EU referendum gels into a broader movement for democratic reforms.

Stretching the speculative view even further: would a reformed EU, minimally more decentralised and democratic and possibly more confederal, make some sort of rapprochement more attractive? Such a change may not take place in time to alter the formal withdrawal of the UK from the EU. However, if the UK economy stagnates and the policies to improve it are based on the already destabilising neoliberal paradigm, it is quite possible to envisage a General Election, or even another referendum which reversed the substance of Brexit. If so, however, the UK could be back in a different Europe from the one it voted to leave. Unfortunately the likelihood of substantial democratic reforms to optimise popular involvement in EU affairs, such as those promoted by the DiEM25, will be all the harder to achieve if the UK's 60 million-plus citizens and thousands of campaign groups are outside its borders.

References

Afxentiou, P.C. (2000) 'Convergence, the Maastricht criteria, and their benefits', *International Review of Economics and Business, RISEC*, 47 (4): 524–540.

Archer, C. (2008) *The European Union*, Abingdon: Taylor & Francis.

Barker, A. (2014) 'UK loses legal challenge to EU financial transaction tax', *Financial Times*, 30 April.

Barysch, K. (2013) *The working time directive: What's the fuss about?*, London: Centre for European Reform.

Butt Philip, A. (2016) 'How democratic is the European Union?', *The Conversation*, 20 May, https://theconversation.com/profiles/alan-butt-philip-267335/articles

Christie, R. and Brunsden, J. (2011) 'EU Transaction Tax debate highlights euro-area disagreement', *Bloomberg Businessweek*, 8 November.

Cornelisse, P.A. and Goudswaard, K. (2002) 'On the convergence of social protection systems in the European Union', *International Social Security Review*, 55: 3–17.

Delors, J. ([1988] 2002) 'Speech to Trades Union Congress', Bournemouth, in *The pro-European reader*, London: Palgrave editions.

Dorling, D. (2016) 'Brexit: The decision of a divided country', *British Medical Journal*, 354: i3697; www.bmj.com/content/354/bmj.i3697

Doward, J. (2011) 'Liam Fox's Atlantic Bridge linked top Tories and Tea Party activists', *Observer*, 16 October.

European Commission (2016) 'Trade boosted by five years of EU–Korea Free Trade Agreement', Press release, Brussels, 1 July.

European Council (2011) *EUCO 30/1/10 Conclusions*, Brussels: General Secretariat of the Council, 25 January.

European Foundation for the Improvement of Living and Working Conditions (Eurofound) (2008) *Working conditions and social dialogue – UK*, Eurofound, http://www.eurofound.europa.eu/observatories/eurwork/comparative-information/national-contributions/united-kingdom/working-conditions-and-social-dialogue-uk

Ford, R. (2016) 'How Britain voted: Analysis by Rob Ford', *Observer*, 26 June, pp 14–15.

Goodwin, M. (2016) 'Labour's core voters no longer share its progressive values', *Guardian*, 24 June, p 36.

House of Commons Library (2010) *How much legislation comes from Europe?*, Research Paper 10/62, 13 October.

Lord Ashcroft Polls (2016) 'Generation gap', *Observer*, 26 June, p 11.

Lütz, S. and Kranke, M. (2010) 'The European rescue of the Washington Consensus? EU and IMF lending to central and eastern European countries', Europe in Question Discussion Paper Series, London: LSE.

Lynch, R. (2016) 'Osborne under attack as cuts risk "turning UK into a tax haven"', *Evening Standard*, 2 July, p 34.

McLaverty, P , Baxter. G, MacLeod, I., Tate, E., Goker, A. and Heron, M. (2015) 'New radicals: Digital political engagement in post-referendum Scotland. Final Report', Working papers of the communities and culture network, 16 (October).

Matthijs, M. and Blyth, M. (2016) 'Ideas that make money: The euro from Maastricht to the Fiscal Compact and beyond', Paper presented at 23rd International Conference of Europeanists, 14–16 June, Philadelphia, PA.

Müller, J.-W. (2016) 'Europe's sullen child', *I*, 38 (11): 3–6, 2 June.

Radaelli, C.M. (2003) 'The Open Method of Coordination: A new governance architecture for the European Union, Stockholm', Rapport No 1, Swedish Institute for European Policy Studies.

Savage, M. (2015) *Social class in the 21st century*, London: Pelican Books.

TUC (2016) 'Minford view on Brexit and exports lacks credibility', www.tuc.org.uk/international-issues/europe/eu-referendum/minford-view-brexit-and-exports-lacks-credibility-says-tuc

Zielonka, J. (2004) 'Challenges of EU enlargement', *Journal of Democracy*, 15 (1): 22–35.

SEVEN

Reform from within? Central banks and the reconfiguration of neoliberal monetary policy

Grahame F. Thompson

Introduction

It is argued in this chapter that the 2008 financial crisis saw the relative demise of the 'science of monetary policy', a policy which embodied all the strongest features of the neoliberal economic policy programme of using market-driven price adjustments as the exclusive mechanism of coordination. Subsequently, it is suggested, the 'art of central banking' became the dominant feature of monetary policy making – a new approach that stresses a range of objectives and instruments which have to be judiciously juggled to maintain financial stability. But does the advent of a period of the 'art of central banking' signal an outright failure of the neoliberal programme and its replacement by another?

Of course this all depends upon what is meant by neoliberalism. There would be a long debate to be had about this but the favoured framework adopted here is to regard neoliberalism as a *regime of governance* rather than a *form of the state* (DuGay and Scott, 2010; Dean, 2014). This is controversial but, at its most general, neoliberalism is considered a regime of governance of the state, where the state is viewed as both an *institutionalised apparatus of rule* and as a *territorial jurisdiction*. So there is some continuity in what would generally be termed the liberal market state running through from the 1930s to the 2010s. But such a liberal market state can be characterised as having several mutations in its logics or rationalities of governance. This chapter explores in more detail the changing role and functions of the Bank of England in the context of these rationalities of governance. Do these changes represent a decisive break with the tenets of neoliberal economic policy, or do they represent just a new logic of this long-standing system of governance?

All change at the Bank of England?

In March 2015 the Bank of England (BoE) launched a rather unusual Discussion Paper (Bank of England, 2015). The Bank introduces the paper by pointing out that 'the Bank of England is one of only a handful of institutions internationally with responsibility for monetary, macroprudential and microprudential policy, and the operation of all of these to achieve policy outcomes' (Bank of England, 2015, p 1). The Bank invites researchers from across the globe to address the issue of the policy relationships between these areas. As the Bank makes clear, this amounts to a call to arms for the academic and economic policy-making community to help it deal with a quite novel institutional position and a new set of operational circumstances. These new circumstances are indicated by the huge increase in its responsibilities following the 2007–8 financial crisis and the novel and innovative policies it has introduced since then. And although this call for assistance was issued by the BoE, a similar set of circumstances and novel activities typify the central banking landscape of those countries in North America, Europe and Asia most acutely affected by the crisis.

As detailed in a moment, central banks (CBs) have been propelled (and propelled themselves) into a central position as managers of their economies as well as regulators of them. While Treasuries and Finance Ministries retreated into an almost single-minded concern with cutting the public deficit and policies for austerity, CBs emerged as the only active policy makers with a mandate to encourage macroeconomic considerations for growth as well as traditional anti-inflationary policy – indeed, as it is turning out, policies to combat deflationary situations. In addition, the BoE was one of the few institutions seriously prepared for the possibility that the UK might withdraw from the EU and for what the consequences of that withdrawal might be. It is both setting out a long-term vision for the international position of the City (and the Bank) but also laying the institutional framework and mechanisms to ensure it could follow through on its vision (Carney, 2013; Bank of England, 2013; Haldane, 2014). The Bank is trying to diversify the City's offerings in order to ensure it plays a leading role in international transactions even if euro-denominated trades were to dramatically decrease as a consequence of the UK's decision to leave the EU or the breakup of the euro area (Rosa, 2014).

The Bank's main initiatives are directed, on the one hand, at securing and increasing business in the Chinese currency, the renminbi, by developing swap agreements with the People's Bank of China and Chinese commercial banks, and giving Chinese banks privileged access to liquidity in London on the other. At the same time the Bank aims to develop the City as an offshore centre for Islamic banking. London has recently seen the emergence of renminbi denominated bonds and Islamic 'sukuk' bonds issued by the UK government – the first outside the Muslim world. The Bank Governor, Mark Carney, has suggested the Bank's assets exceeding eight to ten times UK GDP would not present a problem as long as there is strong macroprudential regulation in place. This is all part of a strategic bid to make the BoE the premier global central bank, a key part of Carney's vision for its future as, and if, the euro zone falters (Carney, 2013; Haldane, 2014). Whether this scenario is feasible – let alone desirable – is not my main concern.[1] It is merely sketched to indicate the vision of the Bank's leadership. My concern is with what the Bank has been doing at the domestic level before and after the financial crisis of 2007-8, which, I would argue, is broadly paralleled by what other CBs have been doing.

The 'science of monetary policy'

The 'Long Moderation' (roughly 1985-2007) was characterised by a cosy consensus among central bankers and their macroeconomic academic mentors about the ability to manage a low inflation rate regime with a steady growth rate economy. This seemed set for the long duration. The economy was characterised by a well understood model – or set of models, see below – that were robust and enduring, and that adequately 'performed' the economy they were tracking.[2]

Figure 7.1 Models for management of the economy

EMH
- Main assumption for a market
  to be efficient:
- A large number of investors analyse and value securities for profit.
- New information comes to the market independent from
  other news and in a random fashion.
- Stock prices adjust quickly to new information.
- Stock prices should reflect all available information.

DSGE models
- For a coherent description of the macroeconomy DSGE models must spell out the following typical economic 'ingredients':
- **Preferences**: households assumed to maximise a utility function over consumption and
  labour effort. Firms assumed to maximise profits.
- **Technology**: firms assumed to have a production function. Technological constraints on agents' decisions include cost of adjusting their capital stocks,
  their employment relations, or the prices of their products.
- **Institutional framework**: the institutional constraints governing economic interactions are specified. Means agents must obey some exogenously imposed budget constraints, and that prices are assumed to adjust until markets clear. It also means specifying the rules of monetary and fiscal policy, and how policy rules and budget constraints change depending on a political process.
- Traditional macroeconomic forecasting models used by central banks since the 1970s estimate the dynamic correlations between prices and quantities in different sectors of the economy, and often included thousands of variables.

Figure 7.1 outlines the features of this 'synthesis', as Woodford (2009) described it.

The synthesis actually combines two types of model. The first represents an abstract theoretical approach known as the Efficient Market Hypothesis (EMH), where markets are thought to generate all relevant information to enable markets to clear smoothly and more or less instantaneously. The second represents the empirical application of this in a macroeconomic policy context – based upon the microeconomic principles embodied in the EMH approach - known as the Dynamic Stochastic General Equilibrium (DSGE) framework. The features of these are outlined in Figure 7.1 and they constituted the core of the 'science of monetary policy'. But they were supplemented by two central modelling approaches that addressed the specificities of the financial markets and their instruments: the way financial derivatives might be priced and the relationships between different instruments and markets.

One formulation, the famous Black–Scholes–Merton (B–S–M) model of option pricing, dealt with the derivatives issue, while the Gaussian copula (G–C) dealt with the relationships between different instruments and markets.[3] A key features of the B–S–M model, shown in note 3, is the volatility coefficient σ. Effectively this becomes the tradable element: derivatives are traded in respect to their volatility and, importantly, volatility in these models is a measure of risk. So derivatives trading becomes an aspect of risk management: the greater the volatility the greater the risk, and vice versa. Volatility becomes the important 'variable'. In the case of the G–C a key element is the correlation coefficient between volatility in respect to different financial instruments and markets, γ. The value of γ indicates the 'spillover' of volatility from one instrument or market to the other. Of course, the B–S–M and the G–C modelling frameworks are closely related – via a probability calculation of risk. This seeming scientific nature of derivative trading led to an overconfidence in the ability of organisations to hedge the risks involved in the huge expansion (indeed, explosion) of these instruments. A correlation coefficient of between 0.2 and 0.3 typically resulting from the use of the G–C (implying low levels of contagion) proved spectacularly wrong when the crisis hit - it was more in the order of 0.8 to 0.9 (MacKenzie, 2009). The overreliance on these two techniques proved fatal.

In the aftermath of the crisis, then, a generalised confidence in the ability of these models to deal with financial risks and sustain the long moderation faded. Hence the BoE Discussion Paper mentioned above. Moreover, without a robust new modelling framework the economics profession is somewhat bewildered and reluctant to offer clear policy advice or, rather, there is no easy consensus associated with this advice. An interesting feature of CB activity over the period of the long moderation and after was the appointment of academic economists to positions as governors or chairpersons. The most conspicuous examples have been Ben Bernanke and Janet Yelland to the US central bank, the FED, Mervyn King to the BoE, Stanley Fischer to the Bank of Israel (now second in command at the FED under Yelland). But there are also academics in charge of the CBs in Switzerland, Turkey and most recently Ireland.[4] The appointment of these academics points to the continuing faith in economic models as the driving force for sorting out monetary policy. Academics know the models and how they work, and they are not beholden to any obvious vested interest. Their pronouncements thus had credibility with the financial community so they appeared as the perfect candidates to run CBs (Braun, 2015).

It is important to note that though confidence in the models was lost, an emphasis on probability and variance as statistical techniques did not diminish. This is illustrated by the graph in Figure 7.2.

In its periodic 'Inflation Report' the BoE produces the kind of 'fan diagrams' shown in Figure 7.2 for its forecasts of inflation – the traditional object of monetary policy – but now, additionally, for growth and employment. All these are based upon a probability calculus illustrated in Figure 7.3, which shows the usual bell-shaped distribution. So analysis based upon a typical probability distribution framework is still alive and well at the BoE (and in other CBs which are increasingly presenting these kinds of fan diagrams in their own monetary policy reports). The B-S-M framework for derivative trading is also still deployed by investment banks, hedge funds and the like. However, as discussed in a moment, this business is under pressure as market volatility has declined.

Thus the argument is not that all confidence in statistical techniques based upon probability distribution, risk analysis, and so on, has disappeared; only that it has gone into a relative decline as faith in the ability to scientifically manage the economy via conventional model building has lost its prime position among regulators and policy makers. Later in the chapter, what has emerged to partly replace this faith will be outlined: it will be suggested that several different rationalities of governance are now in play that do not singularly rely on these techniques. First, however, it is useful to analyse changes in important aspects of the financial system which directly impinge on the ability of CBs to manage their economies.

Figure 7.2: Bank of England inflation forecasts

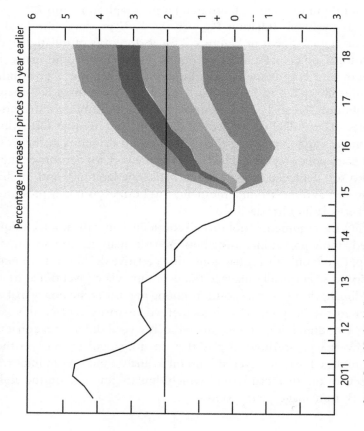

Percentage increase in prices on a year earlier

Source: Bank of England Inflation Report, November 2015, p 31.

Figure 7.3 Bank of England probability distribution of inflation forecasts

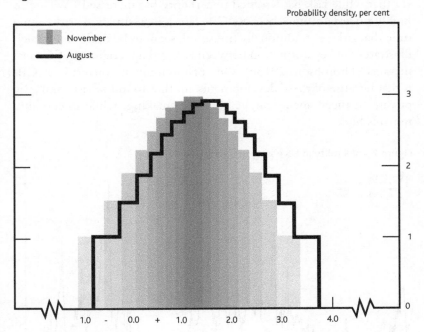

Probability density, per cent

November

August

Source: Bank of England Inflation Report, November 2015, p 49.

What has happened to volatility?

As indicated above, volatility is a major feature of economic activity. During and immediately after the crises volatility escalated, but since 2009 it has fallen significantly and by 2013/14 was back to its historic lower levels. This is shown in Figures 7.4, 7.5 and 7. 6. The US is taken as the example to illustrate the situation in the equity and bond markets (Figures 7.4 and 7.5; though similar trends are found in respect to other stock exchanges: www.forbes.com/sites/jeremyhill/2014/06/06/3-reasons-volatility-might-increase/). Figure 7.6 illustrates volatility in key exchange rates. This recent reduction in volatility increased a little in 2015 for equity and bond markets because of the Greek economic crisis and uncertainty over the future of US monetary policy in particular. However, as volatility is an indicator of risk, the main implication is that 'risk' in the system has significantly fallen. But as risk has lessened the 'appetite for risk' may have increased. This is the inherent paradox of financial matters: as 'stability' (low volatility/ risk) emerges, 'instability' (risk appetite) re-emerges, since taking on risk is a way of making money. Another way of expressing this is to say that while risk has lessened uncertainty has increased.[5] We are in highly uncertain times because CBs face a new situation at the same time that risks, as traditionally measured, seem to be declining which illustrates the key distinction between risk and uncertainty in financial markets (Thompson, 2015b). One of the implicit concerns for CBs is that because of these developments another round of risk taking by private financial agents might be in the making, while uncertainty remains high.

Figure 7.4 Volatility in US equity markets

Note: The VIX measures a weighted average of the implied volatility of a wide range of S&P 500 options with a 30 day maturity.

Source: Derived from Chicago Board Options Exchange (www.cboe.com/micro/volatility/pricecharts. aspx).

Figure 7.5 Volatility in US bond markets

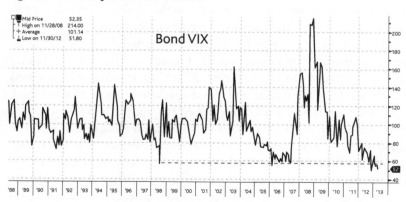

Source: Derived from Chicago Board Options Exchange (www.cboe.com/micro/volatility/pricecharts. aspx).

Figure 7.6 Volatility in foreign exchange markets

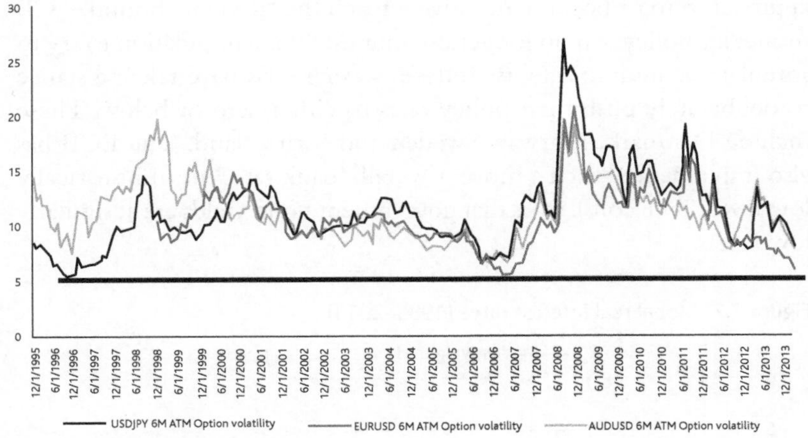

What has happened to interest rates and government bond yields?

We are living in rather unusual times from the point of view of inflation and interest rates. Inflation rates are at historic low levels – almost zero in the UK, and elsewhere they are either zero or negative – and similarly for interest rates. As inflation rates have approached zero CBs have begun to worry since this is below their usual target of 2%. But it has also meant they have relegated 'inflation' – a persistent concern of neoliberal policy makers since the 1970s - to a secondary position in the panoply of monetary targeting. New objectives have emerged. Perhaps it would be better to target nominal gross domestic product (GDP) growth. Perhaps unemployment should be the primary goal. The US FED has always had a dual target - inflation and unemployment – but until recently it was inflation that was of prime concern (see Thompson, 2015a, ch 8). In several smaller European countries, like Denmark, it is the exchange rate that is the prime target. Even in the UK, as indicated above, growth and unemployment now figure among the key concerns of the BoE, as indicated in its Inflation Reports.

Broadly speaking we are witnessing an expansion of CBs' self-declared mandates as they have become the more active agents in managing their economies overall. The exclusive focus on inflation targeting has receded into the background, but the primary focus is still on the operation of monetary policy as this affects these other areas. However, the relaxation of inflation targeting via interest rate policy has raised additional CB concerns in the form of 'quantitative easing' (QE). Figure

7.7 shows the trajectory of global real interest rates. Once interest rates approach zero or become negative – reach the 'zero rate bound' – CB monetary policy can no longer use interest rate manipulation to try to stimulate economic activity. Indeed, several CBs have taken a stance to deliberately push their policy rates to either zero or below. These include Denmark, Norway, Sweden and Switzerland. The ECB has also implemented such a move. Overall, 'bank rates' are at historically low levels. The corollary is that government bond yields are at similarly low levels.

Figure 7.7 Global real interest rates (1985–2013)

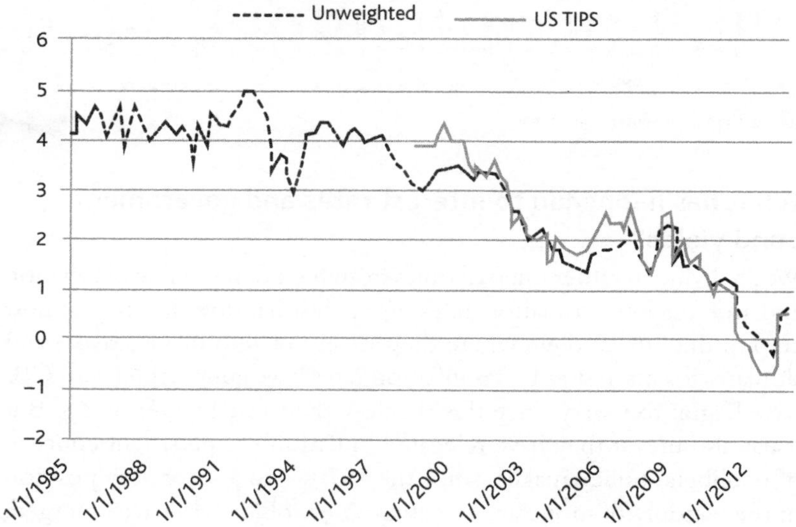

Note: US TIPS = US Treasury inflation proof security.

Source: King and Low (2014, Fig 3, p 21).

In the face of this stalemate CBs have resorted to several novel forms of monetary policy to try to stimulate their economies; the most important and widespread of these is QE. Although the particularities of this differ between CBs (Thompson, 2015a, ch 8), they all involve buying bonds from the private sector so that the payments bond sellers receive inject liquidity into the financial system. It is hoped that this injection will thereby stimulate private financial institutions either to rearrange their own balance sheets or direct lending to firms and households, with the expectation that either or both of these will stimulate economic growth by further spending. The BoE Discussion

Paper referred to above is most concerned with this process because it wants to know more clearly what actual effect it has had in the UK case, and what are the 'transmission mechanisms' between this form of monetary policy and economic growth.

What QE has actually done however is contributed dramatically to the expansion of CBs' balance sheets. The more activist role of CBs stems from their initial bailout of the commercial banks and savings institutions in the immediate crisis period. The expansion of their assets is shown in Figure 7.8.[6] This expansion has exacerbated CBs' present state of uncertainty because the bond purchases further increase their assets. The position of the ECB, as shown in Figure 7.8, has also significantly altered as it embarked on its own €1.1.trillion QE programme in the spring of 2015. One of the problems confronting CBs is how to exit from this situation in an orderly manner. How can they restore their balance sheets to a more sustainable level (reduce assets and liabilities) without this severely disrupting the financial system beyond?

Figure 7.8 Central bank assets 2002–12

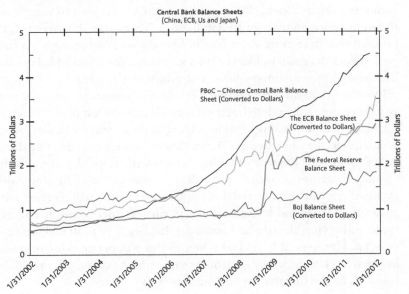

Source: Thompson Reuters, Datastream.

But has this policy programme been successful in encouraging growth via a monetary stimulus? For the UK there was a dramatic decrease in commercial bank lending to the private sector which had not recovered by 2013 despite QE (NEF, 2014, Figure 1, p 6). For the other countries shown in Figure 7.8, although there was a huge increase in liquidity, bank lending to the private sector remained flat (Koo, 2015, ch 2).

Thus the anticipated hope for a recovery in lending to the private sector generated by QE has largely failed to materialise.[7] The commercial banks have mainly 'repaired' their balance sheets and held their newfound liquidity in the form of reserves at the CB, which have mushroomed along with the increase in CBs' assets. These reserves appear on the liability side of the CBs' balance sheet, the counterpart to the increase in their assets. Of course these reserves attract a return. They were paid interest, if at a modest rate: the variation of which represents the manner in which the CB tries to influence interest rates in the economy more generally. So in this way 'idle balances' attracted a return. However, Keynes was at pains to argue against such idle balances receiving a return. Idle balances, he thought, should be taxed not rewarded as Keynes was concerned that such liquidity should be quickly turned into productive investment.[8] Equity and bond prices have recovered because of demand from CBs, commercial banks and other non-bank financial institutions, seeking to rearrange their portfolios following QE stabilisation. Thus what the various QE programmes have done so far is to bolster the stock exchanges. As the well-off are the main holders of such securities, the effect of QE so far has been to increase inequalities, not productive investment.[9]

How long can this situation last? Whatever the answer, this question will determine the underlying trajectory for real interest rates whatever CBs try to do in the short run in respect to their own particular rates. Remember, the objective of QE is to lower interest rates even further. A key element is the role of China, which will eventually move from an excess savings economy towards a consumption economy. And eventually, it can be expected that the US and Europe will reverse their austerity policies and begin to invest in earnest once again. It will be these underlying changes and pressures that begin to push real interest rates up. However, it is unclear when all this will occur, which means low real interest rates may remain for some time to come. All of which just adds to the uncertainty surrounding CB policies.

The emergence of different rationalities of CB management and calculation?

In this section we briefly turn to the reaction to these emergent issues among CB policy makers. As mentioned above, the Bank of England has expanded both its mandate for economic governance and the institutional complex designed to operationalise that mandate. The new institutional complex is shown in Figure 7.9 and managing the concerns embodied in this complex constitutes the 'art of central banking' and preoccupies the BoE Discussion Paper.

Figure 7.9 Bank of England supervisory arrangements

- **Monetary Policy Committee** (setting monetary policy and targets)
- **Financial Policy Committee** (removal or reduction of systemic risks)
- **Prudentail Regulation Authority** (prudential policy and supervision of banks, building societies, credit unions, insurers and najor investment firms)
- **Financial Conduct Authority** (standards and 'culture' of financial institutions)

Buried away in the figure are several rationalities or logics for governance of the new situation being faced by CBs. Two are concentrated upon here: 'macroprudentialism' (the mandate of the Prudential Regulation Authority) and 'evolutionary modelling of systemic interactions' (the way the Financial Policy Committee is framing its activity). Macroprudentialism refers to the attempt to manage the financial system via administrative means in the first instance, not via the 'price mechanism', meaning manipulating interest rates (see Bank of England, 2009, 2011; Schoenmaker, 2014). Thus the emphasis on macroprudentialism represents a partial move away from a strict 'scientific' approach in economic orthodoxy which stressed the complete adequacy and exclusivity of prices and market–driven solutions to monetary policy decisions. It 'supplements' this rationality with one based upon quantities: various quantitative restrictions are placed on financial institutions and their activities. The range of these is summarised in Figure 7.10.

The point here is not to assess the adequacy of these measures or their impacts but to draw attention to the different rationality of

Figure 7.10 Macroprudential policy tools

- Stress testing banks at individual and systemic levels
- Structual capacity adequacy requirements
- Countercyclical capital requirements
- Sectoral-capita requirements/risk weights
- Tools to govern liquidity
- [Mortgage cap: LTV (Loan to value), LTI (Loan to income)]

governance embodied in their characteristics. Something which also goes for the other logic discussed here is the introduction of assessment techniques to analyse the systemic connections between agents, markets and institutions operating in the financial system and particularly the 'globality' of those connections. In the post-crisis period CB regulators were severely criticised for not grasping the extent and complexity of the connectedness between financial activities. The BoE's chief economist Andy Haldane has been at the forefront of trying to meet this criticism with a series of speeches, articles and initiatives designed to analyse the key relationships (for example, Haldane, 2014; and for a readable summary of the state of play, Zigrand, 2014). Central to this 'turn towards complexity' is the treatment of financial networks and the interdependencies between domestic and global markets in relation to the idea of connectedness and contagion between markets (see Thompson, 2015a, 2015b). Networks are one way of operationalising these concerns, set within the contours of dynamic evolutionary models displaying non-linearity in their structure and complex feedback mechanisms. Clearly, this could be viewed as just another ratcheting up of the 'technicist proclivity' embedded in economics but it represents quite a different approach and logic to that advanced under the umbrella of the 'science of monetary policy' revered by neoliberalism.

An alternative central banking world?

None of the above discussion involves a radical alternative vision of the financial system or the role of CBs. But such a vision has arisen in the context of 'people's QE': the idea that there are alternative ways of using monetary policy to stimulate economic activity that bypass the conventional QE policy of buying up already existing government debt. Several possibilities present themselves in this new perspective. It could involve a variant of 'helicopter money': simply sending a cheque to everyone, drawn on the BoE, so that more purchasing power is immediately available to people rather than relying upon the commercial banks to offer this, which they have so far failed to do. But from the point of view of ensuring productive investment this is not a particularly attractive option. It might simply add to a consumption-led boom.

The alternative that has attracted the most attention involves creating a kind of 'infrastructure investment agency' as an adjunct to the BoE which would issue new bonds that the Bank would purchase in a similar manner as it operates with respect to conventional QE. This is the option advanced by Jeremy Corbyn in his successful bid to win the UK Labour Party leadership election in June 2015 (Corbyn, 2015).

Understandably, this suggestion has prompted considerable debate. But it remains a long-term aspiration for a quite different policy environment, one that is unlikely to be opened up before 2020 at the earliest when there might be a change of government. It is yet another in a long line of initiatives that have tried to shift the balance between financial orthodoxy on the one hand and realistic institutional reform for a progressive economy on the other. One suspects its fate rests upon a radical shift in opinion that only a further period of severe economic turmoil might initiate.

Conclusions

What does this all have to say about the fate of neoliberalism in its relationship to the 'art of central banking' as outlined above? Neoliberalism was forged in the context of the turmoil of the 1930s (Mirowski and Plehwe, 2009) so it is reasonable to ask whether we are witnessing a similar turning point in the post-crisis turmoil of the late 2000s. To return to the question raised at the beginning of this chapter: does the advent of a period of the 'art of central banking' signal an outright failure of the neoliberal 'science of monetary policy' and its replacement by another? As suggested above, this all depends on what one means by neoliberalism. If it is regarded as a regime of governance, the liberal market state can be characterised as having several mutations in its logics or rationalities of governance. In light of the analysis conducted above, the main axis around which mutations in the rationalities of neoliberal governance by the BoE have been observed is a move from a regime that rules via prices to one that rules (or attempts to rule) via administrative/quantitative means.

But both of these are still compatible with an emphasis on market-based solutions to social coordination and competition as its mode of operationalisation. So, to be more precise and specific about these regimes as they have emerged in the move from the 'science of monetary policy' to the 'arts of central banking', we have seen three unfolding logics of calculation building one alongside the other. The first is a continuation of the logic of stochastic probability. This is still in play in the context of the arts of central banking, and is articulated around a continued commitment to 'prices'. Secondly, we have a rationality/logic built around quantitative easing and macroprudentialism. This is articulated via the notion of 'quantities' as its operational modality. Finally, there is the rationality/logic of evolutionary dynamics as embodied in 'financial networks'. But this also has a distinctive modality which can be characterised as 'catastrophe'. The field of complex dynamic evolution is haunted by the possibility of catastrophe. It is always on the verge of chaos and this sentiment creeps into the concerns of CBs since there always remains this possibility in respect to the financial system: it is susceptible to a crisis, to a meltdown and a collapse. This is what the examination of complex financial networks is designed to address and avoid via the development of appropriate regulatory mechanisms. But one cannot rely on such technicist mechanisms alone. As always, this needs to be underpinned by a determined alternative politics, something still sadly lacking in current economic contexts.

So, finally, where does this leave the issues of 'alternatives to neoliberalism'? We are facing a period of the rapid potential for the 'pluralisation of monies'. The Central Bank activism discussed in this chapter and technological developments are providing liquidity and incentives for new forms of money and monetary transmission mechanisms to arise, such as virtual monies and crypto-currencies, peer to peer lending, private credit facilitation. Meanwhile low growth is stimulating the emergence of 'local monies' (like the Bristol pound) to try to engineer a growth dynamic outside the ambit of national policy. As a result, a whole host of new financial initiatives are in the offing that, for the most part, bypass the traditional institutions of money creation and financial accumulation, including central banks. This offers a genuine opportunity for a 'bottom-up' reconfiguration of financial activities which could have 'social purposes' as their main objective. If this were to take hold it could radically transform the landscape of neoliberalism and possibly open up a new era for progressive policy making. But it requires an ingenious and innovative political mobilisation that looks determinedly forwards rather than backwards for its inspiration.

Notes

[1] To assess this properly would require a longer analysis of whether an independent monetary policy was at all possible in an interdependent global financial system (see Rey, 2015; Passari and Rey, 2015).

[2] The emphasis on the importance of economic models arises from the way economics itself thinks about economic policy making. Without a clear and well-specified model, economics finds itself wanting. Economists only feel comfortable if they can deploy such a model in any policy-making environment. This is part of the 'culture (indeed, cult) of scientificity' that characterised economics. Without a well-functioning model, economists feel lost and disarmed.

[3] Here is an example of the Black–Scholes–Merton model:

$$\partial w / \partial t = rw - rx \quad \partial w / \partial x - \frac{1}{2} \quad \sigma^2 x^2 \partial^2 w / \partial x^2$$

(Where: w is option price, x is stock price, σ is volatility of stock, r is riskless rate of interest, t is time.) This model has been adapted extensively to deal with different aspects of the derivatives business. It can be rearranged to deal with expectations, to calculate a 'riskless' position, and to deal with various hedging strategies.

$$\partial w / \partial t = rw - rx \quad \partial w / \partial x - \frac{1}{2} \quad \sigma^2 x^2 \partial^2 w / \partial x^2$$

Above is a version of the Gaussian copula (where: Pr is the joint default probability for A and B; TA, TB are survival times between now and when A and B might default; ϕ is the distribution function of a standard normal random variable; F is that which couples the individual probabilities associated with A and B; FA, FB are probability distribution functions for how long A and B are likely to survive; γ is the correlation parameter between A and B defaults.)

4   The current governor at the BoE, Mark Carney, is not an academic but he has a PhD in economics from Oxford University.

5.   Risk is something that can be calculated via a probability analysis based upon past data, while uncertainty is something unexpected that arises uniquely as a consequence of an open future.

6   Note the expansion of the People's Bank of China's balance sheets over this period. These unprecedented increases were not confined just to the advanced capitalist economies. The People's Bank of China is now the largest bank in the world.

7   QE is often argued to be a case of the CBs simply 'printing money'. But this is to misunderstand QE and the way capitalist financial systems work. It is commercial banks that create money in these systems through their activity of extending credit directly to households and firms via their bank accounts. This capacity to 'control the money supply' by the private sector is jealously guarded by orthodox finance, and not even QE could shift this.

8   Note that returns on idle balances have become negative in recent years as CBs resort to zero (or negative) interest rates. Nowadays most depositors receive returns even on current accounts. There is an important corollary to the discussion of the lack of lending from the banking system. It may be that there is just no *demand for such loans* even though there is a ready supply. This is a consideration related to the programme of austerity currently pervading fiscal policy, as discussed below.

9   CBs are also constrained by global trade imbalances. An 'excess of savings' in the international economy creates the current very low real interest rates. China runs a large current account surplus, with a high domestic savings ratio. The USA runs a large current account deficit, with a low domestic savings ratio (the EU is in rough equilibrium on its current account). Austerity in the US and the EU depresses their demand for productive investable funds. So Chinese surpluses are used to

invest in US Treasury bonds and other securities which, felicitously, finances the US current account deficit.

References

Bank of England (2009) *The role of macroprudential policy: A discussion paper*, November.

Bank of England (2011) *Instruments of macroprudential policy: A discussion paper*, December.

Bank of England (2013) *Liquidity insurance at the Bank of England: Developments in the sterling monetary framework*, London: BoE, October.

Bank of England (2015) *One bank research agenda*, London: BoE.

Braun, B. (2015) 'Governing the future: The European Central Bank's' expectation management during the great moderation', *Economy and Society*, 44 (3): 367-391.

Carney, M. (2013) The UK at the heart of a renewed globalization, Speech by the Governor of the Bank of England, 24 October.

Corbyn. J. (2015) *The economy in 2020*, www.solidariteetprogres.org/IMG/pdf/theeconomyin2020_jeremycorbyn-220715.pdf

Dean, M. (2014) 'Rethinking neoliberalism', *Journal of Sociology*, 50 (2): 150-163.

DuGay, P. and Scott, A. (2010) 'State transformation or regime shift?', *Sociologica*, 2.

Haldane, A. (2014) 'Managing global finance as a system', Maxwell Fry Annual Global Finance Lecture, October, University of Birmingham.

King, M. and Low, D. (2014) 'Measuring the "world" real interest rate', NBER Working Paper 19887, Cambridge, MA: NBER, February.

Koo, R.C. (2015) *The escape from balance sheet recession and the QE trap*, Singapore: Wiley.

MacKenzie, D. (2009) 'All those arrows', *London Review of Books*, 32 (12), 25 June, pp. 20–22.

Mirowski, P. and Plehwe, D. (eds) (2009) *The road from Mont Pèlerin: The making of the neoliberal thought collective*, Cambridge, MA: Harvard University Press.

NEF (2014) *Strategic quantitative easing: Stimulating investment to rebalance the economy*, London: New Economics Foundation.

Passari, E. and Rey, H. (2015) 'Financial flows and the international monetary system', NBER Working Paper 21172, May.

Rey, H. (2015) 'Dilemma not trilemma: The global financial cycle and monetary policy independence', NBER Working Paper No 21162, May.

Rosa, B. (2014) 'The City of London in a new geopolitical order', EconoMonitor, 4 November, www.economonitor.com/blog/author/brosa/

Schoenmaker, D. (ed) (2014) *Macroprudentialism*, A VoxEU.org eBook, London: CEPR Press.

Thompson, G.F. (2015a) *Globalization revisited*, London: Routledge.

Thompson, G.F. (2015b) 'Post Katrina and post financial crises: Competing logics of risk, uncertainty and security' in W.M. Taylor, M.P. Levine, O. Rooksby and J-K Sobott (eds) *The Katrina effect: On the nature of catastrophe*, London: Bloomsbury, pp 177–194.

Woodford, M. (2009) 'Convergence in macroeconomics: Elements of the new synthesis', *American Economic Journal: Macroeconomics*, 1 (1): 267–279.

Zigrand, J.-P. (2014) 'Systems and systemic risk in finance and economics', SRC Special Paper No 1, January, London: Systemic Risk Centre, LSE.

EIGHT

The corporate cuckoo in the neoliberal nest: reconnecting civil society with big business

Bryn Jones

The Introduction of this book described how neoliberalism's supposed 'liberation' of markets had in practice empowered large corporations – firms whose accountability to market disciplines is, at best, weak. We described corporations and their executive controllers as the new barons. Elsewhere they have been labelled as oligarchs or power elites (Jones, 2015; Savage and Williams, 2008; Williams, 2006). Neoliberal deregulation, economic policy and political partnerships have gifted corporations and financial business almost unparalleled freedoms. As a consequence, it has furthered their divorce from the status business once had as an integral part of civil society. Big business, together with its sympathisers in the media and academia, masks corporations' current dominance over various sectors of civil society by propagating a narrative of partnership and social citizenship. Relevant details of this hegemony are described in the first section of this chapter

Any alternative to the neoliberal system aiming for reform, or even transformation of this corporate dominance needs to consider the various attempts and proposals made by social movement actors to limit or redistribute the concentration of power. The second part of this chapter therefore examines significant cases of social movement critique and contestation of corporate powers. These efforts are diverse and multifaceted. There are calls for institutional reforms, such as licensing of corporate operations, for more focused changes to their governance, right through to outright abolition or transformation of corporate ownership by abolishing the key legal and political privileges which guarantee corporate power and autonomy.

However, the most pronounced theme of campaigns by civil society organisations (CSOs) is for a sharpening and strengthening of corporate accountability. Its importance is indicated by its ubiquity across social movements; from the more cautious protagonists for Corporate Social Responsibility (CSR) to social and environmental justice campaigns within the heterogeneous sustainability and social justice movements. As well as its target status for social movements, concentration upon this business type, rather than on, say, privately owned or quasi-state enterprises, is warranted by the persistent historic and cultural significance of the share traded, executive managed (ST/EM) corporation in the Anglo-American sphere. After presenting the charge sheet against corporate power, the final three sections of this chapter review the social movement challenges before recommending a limited, but critical focus on reopening the ST/EM firm to civil society influence by changing the balance of control between shareholder-stakeholders and the presently unaccountable executive class. A more in-depth exploration of this case can be found in Jones (2015, pp 224-245).

Why is big business such a social, political and environmental scourge?

Although far from providing convincing solutions, the CSR movement is a useful indicator of the main threats and vices of corporate power. CSR points to the ways in which irresponsible business behaviour damages human rights and well-being through unhealthy products and services and degrades the environment through the creation of waste, toxic emissions and climate-changing fossil fuels. Also on the charge sheet are harmful employment and working practices. Initially these were the injustices suffered by international supply-chain workers in the so-called 'developing' economies of the global South. Increasingly, however, similar criticisms have arisen in Northern metropoles, as social safeguards are eroded there. At a more sociological level, often overlooked by CSR practitioners, power relations bound up with corporate ascendancy have endowed business elites with disproportionate influence on government (and intergovernmental) policy making. At the same time corporations have gained almost unprecedented penetration into the everyday lives of citizens and communities. Consumers have near total dependence on corporate goods and services while charities and community bodies become ever more dependent on corporate donations and patronage (Jones, 2007, 2014, pp 24-28).

As Naomi Klein highlighted some while ago, retail corporations have colonised and often taken over the landscape of civil society (Klein, 1999). Business-owned shopping 'malls' have replaced conventional urban shopping areas. Town high streets are dominated by identical chain stores for almost every type of good, from coffee consumption, to clothing, consumer electronics and foodstuffs. But even these corporate domains are being superseded by more centralised retailing operations as consumer businesses, such as eBay, Amazon and conventional retailers, transfer the high street to the internet. As was indicated in the Introduction to this book, the brave new world of internet freedom has progressively fallen under the dominance of a few giant corporations – Amazon, Microsoft, Google, eBay, Facebook and so on – with increasing powers to monitor, guide and seduce the behaviour of users of their services.

Elsewhere, in the public realm of public utilities and services the neoliberal obsession with market modes of delivery and business forms of organisation has led to sweeping waves of privatisation and contracting out. The earlier Thatcherite privatisations of energy, transport and other utilities now seem almost modest compared to the engorgement of service corporations such as Capita, G4S, Serco and Sodexo, with lucrative contracts in everything from prisons to hospitals, education to benefit controls. Public contracts for these corporations mean that they can at least be cancelled when, as is often the case, their services prove to be substandard or excessively profitable. Public accountability of privatised utilities has proven to be less tractable. An elaborate web of regulation covering transport, water, energy and telecommunications has, effectively, been 'captured' by investor interests which have consistently managed to extract premium profits to reward shareholders' risk-free investments (Jones, 2015; Wilks, 2013). Corporations have become the cuckoos in the market society nest which neoliberals tried to construct. Meanwhile, liberalisation of international trade and investment facilitated the global expansion of existing and would-be multinationals – a process that continues with plans for a Transatlantic Trade and Investment Partnership (TTIP) to open up more public services to corporate takeover and special courts for corporate legal redress (Webb, 2015).

Governments have welcomed some of the gains from this shift: statistical growth records, new employment opportunities, cheaper consumer goods and enhanced living standards. But developed and developing country governments have discovered that corporations can undermine such incidental benefits by relocating business operations, and by tax avoidance through accounting manipulations between national branches and remote tax havens. Nowhere have these transnational powers been more evident than in the financial sector. Deregulation here fostered a mushrooming of financial institutions, products and risk-laden profiteering that culminated in the reckless spread of asset manipulation and trading based on loans to poor homebuyers. The ensuing crash of 2008, of course, prompted some reining in of banking autonomy – even arms-length nationalisations - and re-regulation of trading and investment activities. But these measures have barely touched the financial sector's estrangement from the 'real world' economy of housing, manufacturing and public works. Indeed state refinancing of the wider banking sector has triggered the public debt crisis and resulting austerity which continues to undermine the governance and social stability of many countries - most blatantly for Greece.

The financial sector has severe intrinsic flaws that have attracted considerable political and policy attention, even from ardent neoliberals (Dowd, 2015). However, there has been hardly any focus on the fact that, like other corporations, it is its governance model which facilitates executives' autonomy and irresponsibility. Note just one common, but glaring, flaw in this system: the capacity of executives to exploit allegedly 'independent' pay adjudications to inflate their salaries and bonuses to astronomic heights – a disorder which has spread beyond the corporate sector to infect senior managers in public administration, education and even some charities. As most employees have experienced wage cuts, or stagnation, or small increases which have yet to outpace post-crash inflation (TUC, 2015, p 12), the accompanying income disparities have intensified inequalities in consumption of marketed goods, in housing, social and health care and, indirectly, education.

Social movement challenges: from responsibility to accountability

During the 1970s, large corporations in the English-speaking world were 'on the ropes'. Militant trade unionism was reducing profits through successes in adversarial wage bargaining. At the same time, the vanguards of the new social movements were challenging corporate values and policies in areas such as 'minority' rights in employment, consumer welfare and environmental impacts. The first 'Earth Day', with picketing of corporate head offices and slogans such as 'Stop Pollution' and 'General Motors takes your breath away' (Jones, 2015, pp 165-166). In attempts to transcend inflationary wage settlements and disruptive militancy, progressive employers and governments explored alternative forms of labour relations and wage determination. In 1978/9 the UK came within a political whisker of adopting trade union and employee representation on corporate boards (Jones, 2015, pp 166, 71-73). Relief came from two sources. Firstly, the adoption of neoliberal policies by the Reagan and Thatcher governments diminished the scope for trade union action and made union membership and representation more difficult. Policies also dismantled regulations which had previously circumscribed the range of options for profit making. Particularly in the UK, privatisation of state-owned firms and contracting out of public services converted enterprises into corporations aligned to investor, rather than employee or public interests. Thus began the era of 'financialisation' and 'shareholder value' (Dore, 2008; Lazonick and O'Sullivan, 2000).

Secondly, almost simultaneously – and not unconnectedly – with these developments, big business, prompted by government initiatives, started to redefine its social identity. Existing philanthropic activities in the USA began to be redefined as 'corporate social responsibility', and this new narrative was institutionalised in the UK through joint business–state organisations such as Business in the Community. The latter were partly legitimated in the UK as an emphasis on 'giving something back' to communities devastated by industrial restructuring. But the ethos was expressed more realistically and strategically by the punditry of business school academics in the USA. Freeman and Reed, for example, argued that executives should respond to the 'turbulence' of the late 1960s and 1970s by recognising the more receptive challengers as 'stakeholders', whom managers should win over to a more corporate-friendly relationship by consultation and information sharing (Freeman and Reed, 1983; Freeman, 2010). As one advocate of this approach later argued, such strategies of CSR should aim to 'isolate the radicals, cultivate the idealists and educate them into becoming realists, then co-opt the realists into agreeing with industry' (cited in Rowell, 1999). However, as explained below, CSO opposition means the success of this strategy has not been straightforward.

CSR has had distinct advantages for corporations. Not only does it blunt some of the attacks from campaigners by showing willingness to mitigate negative aspects of business impacts on communities, social groups and environments. It also draws some of these actual and potential adversaries into corporate styles and strategies, through specific 'partnership' projects. Furthermore, it burnishes broader corporate reputations when allied to skilful public relations and marketing strategies. Corporations now compete for customers partly on the strength of their social reputation. It would be a mistake, however, to regard all of this activity as just another corporate *coup de theatre* as a wholly successful bolstering of corporate dominance by propaganda and incorporation. What CSR has undoubtedly done is to extend corporations' business and ideological reach into the more sensitive areas of civil society, enhancing corporate power through patronage (Jones, 2007). In 2015 plans for trade unions to lead the London Gay Pride parade were changed so that corporate sponsors, including Barclays, Citibank and Starbucks, occupied the first ranks instead (Data Lounge, 2016). However the dance between corporations and civil society and social movement organisations (SMOs) has evolved as more of a conflictual tango than an all-embracing waltz.

From the 1990s nongovernmental organisations (NGOs) and social movement campaigns began to switch their focus on environmental and human rights issues from lobbying governments to lobbying corporations. As Peter Melchett, one-time Greenpeace UK director, reasoned: 'there has been a shift in power from politics to business ... asked for by business and given by politicians' (Rowell, 2001). For less cynical campaigners the CSR partnership approach seemed to offer scope for persuading corporations not only to get their own houses in order but to contribute to solving wider problems such as poverty incomes, human rights, carbon emissions and rainforest depletion. As such partnerships and consultations waxed and waned, however, more attention began to be directed to the mechanics and principles of CSR. What exactly were corporations contributing and was their 'responsibility' serious enough? Before long, CSOs' campaigns were being directed not only to substantive causes, but to the wider question of the CSR processes and roles involved. Separate campaigns began to evolve on issues such as transparency and the quality of information disclosure in company reports (Doane, 2005). By 2000 environmental, human rights and labour campaigning was coalescing towards what has been called a 'movement of movements' (Utting, 2005; see also Chapter Two and Chapter Eleven), with common themes of socio-environmental sustainability and social justice. This sharper focus involved CSO campaigns making distinctions between corporate responsibility and corporate accountability. The latter was conceived as obligatory with meaningful arrangements for corporate executives to be held to account for their firm's impact on the wider society.

As Anglo-Saxon corporate law only obliges the directors of a joint-stock firm to be directly accountable to its investors, campaigners' attention honed in more closely on the mechanics of corporate governance. When the last Labour government prepared a new Companies Act in 2006, a coalition of CSOs and NGOs mounted a campaign to broaden the scope of corporate accountability. The proposals of this Coalition for Corporate Responsibility (CORE) included closer regulatory oversight, corporate reporting, directors' duties and foreign direct liability. The coalition got some, but not its most ambitious, governance proposals included in this legislation. However, a subsequent CORE-initiated revision of the Act in 2013 included requirements for corporations to provide a Strategic Report, including corporate human rights performance (Blowfield and Murray, 2014, p 180 et seq; CORE, 2015, p 12). Partly overlapping these movements are a number of smaller but highly active campaigns which target particular companies for their environmental, financial conduct or social justice violations. Manifest, a corporate governance watchdog for concerned institutional investors, provides data and proxy voting advice. Share Action, the 'Campaign for Responsible Investment', whose member organisations include trade unions, Amnesty International, Christian Aid, Citizens UK, Oxfam and Greenpeace, campaigns for pension funds to press companies on issues such as affordable generic medicines, destructive mining practices, human rights, renewable energy and the (UK) Living Wage. Individual networks, like the Living Wage campaign, have also been active, targeting companies through their annual general meetings. Even a financially focused investors' association – ShareSoc – has voiced support for the idea of reforms which would ally its voice with those representing other stakeholders (ShareSoc, nd, p 5).

The fiction of corporate ownership: management versus shareholder interests

The Achilles heel of corporate autonomy is the oxymoron of investor *ownership*. As the juggernaut of political neoliberalism rolled on in the 1970s and 1980s, its economist mechanics busied themselves engineering theories to fit awkward business reality to theoretical purity. Crucial to this task was the development of 'agency theory' (Fama and Jensen, 1983). Essentially this formula aimed to square the circle of corporate executives' independence with investor share ownership rights. Since the 1930s a perennial problem of corporate governance and political regulation was the apparent separation of the investors from the executives' control of the company: the 'separation of ownership from control'. Agency theory argued that executives were allowed some autonomy because they were the 'agents' of the 'principals' - the shareowners. As mere agents, therefore, executives were obliged to cater for the fundamental interest of the shareholders, despite having the discretion to manage the running of the business.

The practical elaboration of this idea – to surmount the ownership control divide – was to align the manager-agents' interests more closely with those of the shareholder-as-principal. Increasingly from the

1980s onwards, therefore, executives' remuneration took the form of awards of shares in their own company; rather than salaried rewards. This development, it was thought, would narrow the shareholder-executive divide because both would benefit from profits which boosted share values and dividends. In practice, it propelled a regime of financialisation, in which financial surplus, the means of corporate growth and innovation, became the over-riding *end*; as Lazonick and O'Sullivan (2000) have shown, this alignment has had disastrous consequences for capital investment, innovation and employment in US corporations. Similar outcomes, abetted by offshoring and globalisation, affected UK corporations.

Unfortunately the alignment of executives' and shareholders' financial interests did not lead to any wider responsibility or accountability by executives. Indeed, if anything they became more irresponsible in the pursuit of ever higher levels of 'shareholder value' in order to satisfy increasingly fickle, volatile and globalised financial markets. Politicians and regulatory authorities were willing to countenance this irresponsibility as long as it brought economic growth, markets boomed and (some) tax revenues rolled in. The 2008 crash, however, refocused concern on what has become known as the 'ownership oxymoron': investors who did not, in the main, act like owners but merely took the money (dividends or higher share prices) and ran, switching their cash to better returns in other investments, at any opportunity – exemplified by speculative hedge fund tactics.

As I have argued elsewhere (Jones, 2015, pp 99–112), corporate executives constitute a new oligarchy which is barely accountable to anyone. With the internationalisation of finance many of the share owners are from overseas and have limited interest in the substance of the business. The general delegitimation of business, with numerous corporate scandals and continuing escalation of executive rewards in the post-crash recession, led both the Conservative-Liberal Democrat coalition government and the Labour Party to examine reforms to governance which would grasp the nettle of the ownership oxymoron. The Conservatives, as might be expected, iterated the need for responsible business in return for 'business as usual': light regulation and low taxation. Liberal Democrats and Labour were more critical. Labour leader Ed Miliband recommended some toughening of shareholder responsibilities to make get-rich-quick takeovers more difficult, (single) employee representation on executive pay committees and making shareholder voting rights conditional on minimum periods of investment, in order to deter speculative investors. The Liberal Democrats voiced similar concerns about the narrow transparency and weak accountability of executive boards; but their Business Minister, Vince Cable, could do little more than endorse the findings of the Kay Review which he set up. That Review only argued for each company to have a non-statutory 'investors forum' to be consulted on strategic issues such as the appointment of new directors.

So the two most critical parties remained stuck in the investor-ownership paradigm, despite the mass of evidence that this was a largely fictitious construct. Neither took into account that corporations' roles now extend beyond the economy into the public sphere and the lifeworlds (see Introduction) and communities of the people. Correspondingly, none acknowledged the need for corporations' social responsibility to be held to account by a wider range of 'stakeholders' from civil society. Miliband and Cable at least recognised that there are different types of investors. So occasional, envious references were made to continental Europe where, in countries like Germany, there is a more numerous class of 'patient' investors willing to hold onto their investments for the long-term development of the business.

Reforms to rein in corporate oligarchies

Many would like to see this 'Rhenish' continental model of corporate governance adopted in the UK (Charkham, 1994; Hutton, 1996; Involvement and Participation Association, 2012). But such reforms face two politico-cultural disadvantages. Firstly, its significant emphasis on worker/trade union representation on companies' supervisory boards prompts unpalatable images of the last major attempt at governance reform by the social democratic Labour government of 1974-9. Neoliberal success in shaping the political memory of that period calls up images of overpowerful and disruptive union militancy and overpowerful union 'barons'. That last pre-neoliberal Labour government was preparing to implement the minority recommendation of the 1977 Bullock Report on industrial democracy when it faltered, then fell in 1979. Under this recommendation there would have been employees - potentially union officers – on the Rhenish-style supervisory boards. (The majority report had argued for unitary boards with equal management and work representation.) The fact that some unions held out for maximum representation, while others opposed their perceived 'incorporation' and emasculation within the managerial system, has contributed to the negative 'memory' of the irrelevance and impracticality of a Rhenish model in the UK.

The second cultural obstacle to a Rhenish model for reform of UK corporate governance is the UK's ideological commitment to unitary boards. These, corporate sympathisers argue, have stood the test of time because they minimise bureaucracy, facilitate rapid decision making and allow flexible, informal dialogue with a range of investors rather than only those with seats on a supervisory board. The fact that most investment bodies, including pension funds and insurance companies, show little interest in abandoning the unitary board system maintains the force of this prejudice. Any political renegotiation of corporate governance would have to overcome, or at least circumvent, this monolithic opposition or indifference. Recasting the main corporate governance principles would also be a major legislative process. The 2006 Companies Act promised much, but it required more than 600 pages of documentation and 1300 sections for a statute which 'essentially confirmed the status quo' (Wilks, 2013, p 224). Major reform would be even more complex politically and legally, offering many opportunities for defeat or disruption by backers of the status quo.

There is, however, another form of corporate governance reform, fully consistent with both unitary boards and with the principles of democratisation alternatives to neoliberalism, proposed elsewhere in this book. This more focused reform could help re-embed corporations in, and make them accountable to, civil society. In Sweden the board of directors, apart from the chief executive officer (CEO), is predominantly composed of non-executive directors (NEDs). UK boards also contain NEDs but these are identified and nominated by the executives and rubber-stamped by the company annual general meeting (AGM). They therefore tend to be drawn from the same elite backgrounds and social networks and hold the same business ideologies – such as financialisation – as the company's existing directors. By contrast Swedish CEOs are prohibited from chairing the board and can be dismissed by the board without stated cause. However, a more important and relevant difference has occurred in a change over the last 10 years to Sweden's system of unitary corporate boards. Reforms consolidated in an Act of Parliament in 2005 require four or five of the largest shareowners, plus the non-executive board chair, to act as the Nomination Committee (NC) for appointing new company directors. This NC is mandated from the shareholder's meeting. By contrast, in the present UK system, the NC is a subcommittee of the board and the board selects its members. The only say which the mass of shareholders have in the UK process is when the Board candidates for the NC are approved – usually automatically – by the company's AGM.

In Sweden, the NC recommends directly to the shareholders' AGM both new appointments to the board and each director's remuneration arrangements. (The remuneration of executive management is handled separately by the board). The NC's commitment to the shareholders' committee is assured by: prohibiting the chair of the board from also chairing the NC; restricting directors to a minority on the committee; limiting director membership from major shareholders to a single seat; and excluding the CEO and other executive managers from being members. NC recommendations to shareholders for appointments have to be justified in terms of strengthening 'diversity and breadth of qualifications, experience and background; and also how the company is striving for equal gender distribution on the board' (Tomorrows Company, 2010, p 19). What if something like this system were to be adopted in the UK, but with shareholders regarded in the widest possible sense as including any stakeholding group taking token shareholdings? In this scenario there could be dramatic changes to the culture and strategies of corporations as they moved away from being vehicles for the aggrandisement of an executive oligarchy.

This Swedish nomination system has already been backed by the UK association representing small and independent shareholders (ShareSoc, nd), which is favourable to the involvement of non-investor stakeholder groups. There would be nothing, in principle, to prevent the current wave of social justice corporate campaigns extending their current practice of buying shares in order to participate in corporate AGMs into active participation in the shareholder forums which would control new, independent NCs. By controlling new appointments to corporate boards, alliances of smaller investors, 'patient' long-term investor institutions such as pension funds and civil society groups could ensure appointment of more socially responsible directors. Such changes could, over time, transform the practices and culture of presently irresponsible corporations by eroding the executive autonomy bestowed by myopic neoliberal market utopianism. There are, of course, complications to the adoption or adaptation of such a model. In Sweden the shareholders' meeting has more status and powers than corporate AGMs in the UK. The shareholders' meeting can, 'if necessary', instruct the board on certain issues. Moreover, under the Swedish legislation, minority shareholders' interests are protected – all shareholdings must be treated equally, unless there is special constitutional provision for alternative arrangements, without special advantage to any group. The, mainly NED members', board can dismiss the CEO, who is not allowed to be its chair, without stated cause. In the UK there is only a 'recommendation', from a non-statutory code of conduct, that CEOs should not also act as the chair.

If the Swedish model were replicated here, there is some risk that the biggest shareholders will dominate the NCs. Usual Swedish practice is to include representatives of the four or five largest shareholders, although this can be varied to involve representatives of smaller shareholders. However, shifting investment patterns mean that the composition of shareholder representatives changes over time, sometimes completely, and the chairman may not be the largest shareholder. Other, non-financial, criteria may be invoked for participation, such as 'geographical proximity to the company'. Taking all of this flexibility into account, it is not unrealistic to imagine that the kind of shareholders' forums envisaged by ShareSoc and, more vaguely, by the last government's Kay Report, could form the source of the membership of NCs in the UK. The main task of such forums would be to decide criteria for board appointments by a process of debate and deliberation among 'patient' institutional investors (a qualifying period of share ownership for voting rights, à la Ed Miliband, would be advisable) like pension funds, small independent investors and civil society stakeholder groups – such as unions, local councils, environmental and social justice campaigns. Inevitably, there would be disagreements and compromises. However, these could be conducted through a process of deliberative debate: a principle shared by a wide social range from ex-Occupy activists to progressive investor groups such as ShareSoc.

Conclusion

This chapter has drawn attention to the growing focus on corporate power and governance coming from the present-day descendants of the 'new social movements' of the last century. Although heterogeneous in composition and activities these can now, as Chapter Twelve shows, be considered as the mass movement vehicles to challenge the institutions which buttress and reproduce neoliberalism. The above analysis has also picked up the case made in the Introduction to this book for the curbing of big business power and particularly its nerve centres in the institutions of corporate governance. As I have argued previously, like Andy Cumbers in Chapter Eleven, reforms in this sphere should not be regarded – as last century's nationalisation model sometimes was – as the ultimate solution to the social evils, welfare deficiencies and injustices of capitalism. As well as the models proposed above and by Cumbers, a useful complement would be the kind of social licensing of 'foundational economy' businesses by local authorities recommended by Johal, Moran and Williams in Chapter Nine.

Nearly four decades of neoliberalism have caused multiple economic and social problems which reforms to corporate power alone cannot resolve. Some features of big corporations, such as international competition and trade regulations, will remain out of reach of popular influence, and beyond some of the several communities that make up a now complex civil society. Pursuing the logic of Polanyi's case for embedding market institutions in civil society, discussed by Benton in Chapter Three and the editors in the Conclusion to this book, more community-based forms of business, such as financial and housing mutuals or the energy cooperatives described by Cumbers, should be promoted. Beyond such longer-term developments, more should be done about the hugely expanded numbers of self-employed and small business enterprises partly derived from corporate offshoring and labour rationalisations. UK regimes, extending back before the neoliberal ascendancy, have paid scant regard to the economic potential and social needs of these sectors. Encouraging these workers and small business owners into the kinds of democratic associations which are common on the continent (see Jones, 2015; Jones and Saren, 1990) could also further the democratic alternative to neoliberalism.

Such developments could be important, but large corporations have too much market power to be easily sidelined or eclipsed by alternative forms of enterprise. Plus, of course, the capacity to mobilise large sums of capital easily and exploit economies of organisational scale should be recognised as important, potential social assets. The fact that mass production/consumption industries damage the national health with torrents of junk food and drink should not obscure the economic and consumer advantages gained from using similar systems to provide products such as cheap bicycles or building products. The point is that in political and economic terms it may be easier to initiate far-reaching change by exploiting the political opportunity presented by widespread anxiety and concern about corporate governance, inside and outside the business world. Some existing business circles could also support reform. Several of the trustees of NGO umbrella group Shareaction are former or current City or big business practitioners. Other respected reformist bodies, such as Pensions & Investment Research Consultants (PIRC) (representing large pension funds, asset managers, faith-based and other 'responsible' investors), Manifest, Tomorrow's Company and ShareSoc might all lend their support and influence. Despite the best efforts of neoliberal apologists and Conservative cheerleaders, the financial and ethical viability of corporate governance remains on the political radar – not least because of the institutionalised scandal of poverty pay accompanied by self-enriching executive pay levels, often in the same company. The whole governance issue may, at least, be opened up for political intervention if Prime Minister Theresa May develops her pre-appointment pledge to put workers and 'consumers' on company boards (*Guardian*, 2016).

Outside the political and business establishment there is an all-important social base to campaign for corporate governance reform. Inside the 'movement of movements', the networks of environmental, human rights, feminist, peace, fair trade, economic rights and (even) trade unionism have been converging towards campaigns aimed not at 'responsible capitalism', the now-tired cliché of Conservative and New Labour politics, but accountable capitalism, The post-war Keynesian welfare state settlement included nationalisation of core industries because the idea was mobilised and supported by trade unions and the wider labour movement. Today's most important and popular campaigns are to be found among the movement of movements' multifarious activists and organisers. As Chapter Twelve argues, their millions of supporters and sympathisers, their legions of young activists and their communication and savvy presence in social media, could play a similar role to that of the 'old movement' trade unions of the mid-20th century. In line with sentiments and ideas expressed elsewhere in this book, if strong democratic outposts can be established in the very citadels of corporate power, its extension to wider reaches of society should be made much easier. The displacement of executive oligarchies would also constitute and symbolise a shift towards substantive equality which could not be ignored by elites and publics alike.

References

Blowfield, M. and Murray, A. (2014) *Corporate responsibility*, Oxford: Oxford University Press.

Charkham, J.P. (1994) *Keeping good company: A study of corporate governance in five countries*, Oxford: Clarendon Press.

CORE/Ceri Hutton (2015) 'The Corporate Responsibility Coalition: Strategic review of its impact, effectiveness and performance', CORE, http://corporate-responsibility.org/wp-content/uploads/2013/06/CORE-Strategic-Review-FINAL_Oct2015.pdf

Data Lounge (2016) 'Pride parade criticised over Red Arrows flypast', www.datalounge.com/thread/16962063-pride-parade-criticised-over-red-arrows-flypast

Doane, D. (2005) 'Beyond corporate social responsibility: Minnows, mammoths and markets', *Futures*, 37: 215–229.

Dore, R. (2008) 'Financialization of the global economy', *Industrial and Corporate Change*, 17 (6): 1097–1112.

Dowd, K. (2015) *No stress – The flaws in the Bank of England's stress testing programme*, London: Adam Smith Institute.

Fama, E.F. and Jensen, M.C. (1983) 'Separation of ownership and control', *Journal of Law and Economics*, 26 (June): 301–25.

Freeman, E. (2010) *Strategic management: A stakeholder approach*, Cambridge: Cambridge University Press.

Freeman, R.E. and Reed, D.L. (1983) 'Stockholders and stakeholders: A new perspective on corporate governance', *California Management Review*, 25 (3): 88-106.

Guardian, The (2016) 'Theresa May's plans to curb boardroom excess receive mixed reaction', 11 July, https://www.theguardian.com/business/2016/jul/11/theresa-mays-plans-curb-boardroom-excess-receive-mixed-reaction

Hutton, W. (1996) *The state we're in*, London: Random House.

Involvement and Participation Association (2012) *The Bullock Report: Thirty-five years old and still relevant today*, 24 March, www.ipa-involve.com/news/the-bullock-report/_

Jones, B. (2007) 'Citizens, partners or patrons? Corporate power and patronage capitalism', *Journal of Civil Society*, 3 (2): 159-177.

Jones, B. (2015) *Corporate power and responsible capitalism? Towards social accountability*, Cheltenham: Edward Elgar.

Jones, B. and Saren, M. (1990) 'Politics and institutions in small business development: Comparing Britain and Italy', *Labour and Society*, 15 (3): 287-300.

Klein, N. (1999) *No logo*, London: Picador.

Lazonick, W. and O'Sullivan, M. (2000) 'Maximizing shareholder value: A new ideology for corporate governance', *Economy and Society*, 29 (1): 13-35.

Rowell, A. (1999) 'Greenwash goes legit', *The Guardian*, 21 July.

Rowell, A. (2001) 'Corporations get engaged to the environmental movement', *PR Watch*, 8 (3): 6, http://www.prwatch.org/files/pdfs/prwatch/prwv8n3.pdf

ShareSoc (UK Individual Shareholders Society) (n.d.) *Shareholder committees a way to improve shareholder engagement*, www.sharesoc.org/Shareholder%20Committees.pdf_

Tomorrow's Company (2010) *Tomorrow's corporate governance: Bridging the UK engagement gap through Swedish-style Nomination Committees*, London: Tomorrow's Company.

TUC (2015) IDS and TUC pay forum 2015, www.tuc.org.uk/sites/default/files/IDS%20Presentation%20Reel%20Final%20310315%20updated%20to%20upload.pdf

Utting, P. (2005) 'Corporate responsibility and the movement of business', *Development in Practice*, 15 (3-4): 375-388.

Webb, D. (2015) 'The Transatlantic Trade and Investment Partnership', Briefing Paper, No 06688, House of Commons, 4 December.

Wilks, S. (2013) *The political power of the business corporation*, Cheltenham: Edward Elgar.

Williams, H. (2006) *Britain's power elites. The rebirth of a ruling class*, London: Constable.

NINE

Avoiding 'back to the future' policies by reforming the 'foundational economy'

Sukhdev Johal, Michael Moran and Karel Williams

The most striking feature of the political economy of Western Europe since the great financial crisis is, simply, the continuing ascendancy of neoliberal policies, practices and priorities. The term neoliberalism is more convenient shorthand than precise concept but, in this case, it serves to identify an important continuity. The doctrine of the superiority of market intelligence, and the cult of light touch regulation gave us the crisis, and we might have expected the cataclysm of 2007–9 to have damaged it irreparably. On the contrary: in the Eurozone we have had nearly a decade more of austerity pursued in the name of the neoliberal project of creating a single currency within a unified market; and in the United Kingdom the general election result of May 2015, in returning a majority Conservative government, intensified the austerity policies pursued since 2010 in the name of shrinking the state.

Faced with the resilience of neoliberalism its opponents have been like rabbits before stoats – paralysed into immobility and ineffectiveness. In the nations of the Eurozone subjected to the most severe neoliberal policies – Ireland, Portugal, Greece – opposition has been either weak or, as in the case of Greece, brutally pushed aside. In the United Kingdom the Labour opposition has been deeply divided. On the one hand, the parliamentary inheritors of New Labour defend post-1997 Blairite achievements, accept the austerity implications of the neoliberal case and wish only to moderate its most savage consequences. Against this, a resurgent 'retro left' in the country (by which we mean a left still wedded to policies pursued before the neoliberal revolution) hankers after reversal of the post-1979 changes and defends the forms of an earlier settlement, including the centrally controlled, hierarchical nationalised corporation - something that, of course, suits the interests of its allies at the head of centrally organised trade unions. At the time of writing, in the immediate aftermath of Jeremy Corbyn's unexpected victory in the Labour leadership campaign in 2015, it still remains uncertain how these internal divisions in the party will be resolved.

Nevertheless, a striking common assumption unites these very different visions of economic life. It might be summarised as the assumption of a mono economy – an image of economic life reduced to one set of relations summarised in a single set of whole system indicators, like the rate of growth in GDP. It is a view characteristic of a metropolitan elite used to viewing the economy from a central, elevated position and used to measuring its conditions by centrally created indicators. 'Steering the economy' evokes an economy and a society where an officer class controls the power and direction of the vessel from a metaphorical bridge at the centre. A new kind of steering, but still central steering, is offered by Jeremy Corbyn and his allies who are struggling to reshape Labour policy following unexpected victory: a re-empowered Keynesianism incorporating a National Investment Bank to fund infrastructure, and a vision of an entrepreneurial state such as that developed by Mazzucato (see Corbyn, 2015; Mazzucato, 2013).

There is a different way of conceiving of the economy, and it is one that guides this chapter. It has been succinctly expressed by Braudel: that there are not one but several economies. The schema outlined by Braudel of course had its origins in his great historical inquiry into civilisation and capitalism. But his key notion – that there is no one economy but several distinct zones of economic life – still resonates. Even the most important zones identified by Braudel – material life, market exchange and high capitalism – have modern echoes. 'There were not one but several economies' in the early modern period, says Braudel (1981, p 29). Likewise we may say that there are not one but several economies in our time. This simple insight provides the starting point for an alternative to the orthodoxies termed neoliberalism, one that is developed in this chapter. Our insight borrowed from Braudel illuminates the way contemporary apologists for the status quo equate the economy with only one zone – that of market exchange and its competitive logics. Here, for example, is a prominent British politician expressing precisely such a conception in one of the great annual celebrations of neoliberal triumphalism, the Margaret Thatcher Annual Lecture: 'Like it or not the free market economy is the only show in town. Britain is competing in an increasingly impatient and globalised economy, in which the competition is getting ever stiffer' (Johnson, 2013). This is, appropriately, a modernised version of the Thatcherite mantra that dominated British economic debate for much of the 1980s and 1990s: TINA (there is no alternative).

Boris Johnson is right insofar as retro leftism will never resurrect the institutions and practices destroyed by the policy experiment that began at the end of the 1970s. The past as our guide to the future is irrelevant for several reasons. In everything from railways to health and care, centralised, hierarchical organisation would not be greeted as the solution but would be scapegoated for problems about managing demand and containing costs. And 'retro' policies would not engage with how to manage the structural and ideological transformation of the UK private sector. The productive, tradeable core has shrunk so that British manufacturing now employs just 8% of the workforce and there are fewer than 2000 factories employing more than 200 workers. Across the service economy, shareholder value and private equity have legitimated the devices of cash extraction. Finance, which brought the crash, has not been diminished and caged but continues to drive the economy through housing equity withdrawal; and a huge para state of private firms extracts tax revenue to provide outsourced services.

But Johnson and others are wrong in claiming that there is no alternative. We can begin to put together an effective resistance to neoliberalism by building on Braudel's insight that, on the contrary, 'the free market economy' is not the only show in town. There are a variety of 'shows' or, to put it more formally, alternative zones of economic life with their alternative logics of organisation. This chapter is about one of the most important of those alternatives, and we demonstrate below that it is far from being a sideshow. There is a large zone of economic life – ironically one whose expansion has been stimulated by neoliberal policies – where competition is far from 'stiff' and which is not subject to the 'impatience' of global rivals. We show that this zone is not only quantitatively big but is in every sense of the word the foundation of economic – indeed of civilised – life in a country like Britain. We demonstrate that it runs to a rhythm very different from that of free market capitalism. We argue that, as presently organised, it is often highly damaging to the public interest. But we also show that its sheer importance, and the fact that it is entangled with the state as a provider and regulator, provides a golden opportunity to begin to rewrite the script of economic life.

The proposal we outline below is modest, but it is also radical, because it is a proposal for a fresh constitutional settlement. The language of constitutional settlements is rarely applied to economic life. But the point of constitutional practice in a country that claims to be democratic is to fashion morally defensible arrangements for the exercise of powers by institutions. Neoliberalism offered an economic constitution which empowers owners of (often un)productive property and organised money. Some of the retro left want to return to an old world where centrally organised trade unions and nationalised corporations are re-empowered. By contrast, we try to think out what obligations are owed by institutions that are privileged to operate in the foundational economy, and begin the task of writing the economic constitution accordingly.

The foundational economy: another show in town

The foundations of a civilised life include some very obvious things: good personal care for the young, the infirm old and the sick; the provision of education, at a minimum for the young; the provision of an infrastructure devoted to public health, including the networked infrastructure necessary to deliver clean water and effective sanitation; infrastructure networks that deliver cable utilities, ranging from energy to telephone systems to, increasingly, broadband; transport networks that range from road to public transport systems; and a complex network joining production and retail systems for food allocation. They are all foundational because to be excluded from these is to be excluded from participation in civilised life in Britain now. They amount to a kind of operationalisation of the ideal conditions for the realisation of human capability spelled out in the work of moral theorists like Sen (1985) and Nussbaum (2000). And the failure to organise the foundational efficiently soon leads – as the example of many less fortunate economies across the globe shows – to the collapse of the conditions of tolerable human existence.

The provision of many of these services is organised in a kind of infra-economy below the radar of market competition. Many foundational services are not only beyond market forces; they are not even within the domain of commercial monetary relations at all. For instance, much personal social care, especially of the young and of the old, is done by carers within families without thought of monetary reward, mostly by women. In this short chapter we do not have space to cover this vast area of non-commercial care - also discussed in the Introduction and Conclusion chapters and Chapter Two. However, we can note its importance and how attempts to value it in monetary terms soon show that it is a major part of economic life, and if it were systematically organised in commercial exchange it would dramatically change our view of the character of economic activity (for an overview, National Audit Office, 2014). Our more limited concern here is with that important part of the foundational economy which is indeed monetised.

These mundane and often taken for granted goods and services are necessary to lead a tolerable life in Britain today, are as a result consumed by all regardless of income, and are typically distributed according to population through branches and networks. The foundational is a kind of infra-economy in the sense that for much of the time it is invisible – sometimes literally so, as in the drainage infrastructure that supports public sanitation created by the heroic Victorians, and more often metaphorically so, in the sense that we only start to worry about it when it goes wrong – for example, when droughts or flooding occur; or, more trivially, when the broadband connection breaks down, or when some part of the public transport network is disrupted. But this infra-economy is not the result of the workings of impersonal economic laws. It is politically constructed, and by the same token, as our final section will show, it can be politically reconstructed.

These signifiers of the importance of the foundational economy – its scale, and the fact that this scale is substantially a product of political choice – can be straightforwardly demonstrated. Table 9.1 summarises our evidence on the significance for employment of the foundational economy in the UK.

The figures show that one-third of the UK's workforce is employed in the foundational economy as we have identified it above, with nearly 10% in private and privatised activities and twice that number in state-provided and state-funded activities. The number working in capital-intensive pipe and cable utilities is small, but retailing remains labour-intensive, with some 440,000 employed in retail banking, a million in supermarkets and some 323,000 in food processing. But by far the largest number of foundational workers are to be found in the state or para-state sectors of health, education and welfare/social care which, in total, employ 4.6 million. In the UK, such services (which have in the past been delivered locally by the state) are now increasingly delivered by the para-state (including private sector firms, charities and social enterprises), where some or all of the funding comes from government. We use the term 'para-state' to emphasise that numerous, nominally private sector providers – for instance of care for the very young in nurseries and of the old in residential care homes – are partners of the state in the delivery of public services. The existence of this para-state sector, and its expansion, is the result of political choice – for instance, the political choice to outsource service delivery to a private contractor. This turns corporate actors in the foundational sector into governing institutions joined in relations of co-dependence with the state. Table 9.1 also includes, as a comparator, the numbers employed in manufacturing – the sector usually invoked by the 'global capitalist competition is the only show in town' school – and shows that it is dwarfed by the foundational economy.

Table 9.1 Private sector, state and state-supported employment in foundational economy activities

		England		Wales	
		Employees	Share of total employment	Employees	Share of total employment
		No.	%	No.	%
Private, state and state-supported foundational economy activities	Private sector activities	2,256,674	9.4	122,772	9.8
	State and state-supported activities	5,744,372	23.8	353,247	28.1
	Total foundational economy activities	8,001,046	33.2	476,019	37.8
Comparators	Total employees	24,104,050		1,259,038	
	Manufacturing	2,066,567	8.6	129,680	10.3

Source: Bowman et al (2014, p 120).

The foundational economy rests to a substantial degree on the power of the state, for it is plain that it is, in part, financed by tax revenues. That happens even when it is privately delivered by a franchised firm, because the state uses its authority to provide the money, or to mandate the commercial exchange. But there is also a more subtle sense in which the foundational economy is, for all households, an offer they can't refuse: it is a significant, and unavoidable, lien on household budgets. Households cannot live a tolerable life without access to foundational goods and services, and to a substantial degree they cannot get this access unless they commit a substantial part of their budgets. Table 9.2 assembles in summary form the scale of these commitments. The detail of the table drives home our argument about the significance of the foundational. For the items covered there are essential if an individual is to live according to the standards of civilised life in 21st century Britain. Even the lack of access to a car, which looks at first like a luxury, is a serious source of social exclusion over large parts of rural and suburban Britain.

Table 9.2 shows that in 2011, £141 or nearly 30% of all weekly household expenditure went on foundational activities, with the big ticket items being £55 on groceries (excluding alcoholic drink), £42 on pipe and cable utilities and £34 mainly on car fuel. And while expenditure on these objects varies with income, *all households are foundational consumers*. So, for instance, food and non–alcoholic drink accounts for 15.9% of total expenditure in the poorest Q1 households and 9% in the richest Q5 households. Foundational activities are therefore both *distributed* and sheltered: they are distributed across the UK because schooling or retailing follow populations; and they are *sheltered* because they are either directly provided by the public bodies, are franchised by the state, or are protected from direct, non–territorial competition.

The sheltered, politically negotiated character of these economic activities has been magnified by a development which is hinted at in Figures 9.1 and 9.2: the extraordinary scale of outsourcing of services hitherto delivered by state institutions. Figure 9.1 highlights the picture in central government; Figure 9.2 widens the picture to domains – healthcare, local government – where there has been a huge boom in outsourcing since the onset of the new age of austerity. The exhibits also identify the big corporate players in this outsourcing industry. Behind these exhibits lies a key constitutional development. Firms like ATOS, Serco, Capita and G4S are in effect governing institutions. They only exist because they are deliverers of services which lie at the heart of the state – from incarceration to security to healthcare. They are largely the creation of the age of the outsourcing boom, and they are recipients of contracts which make them monopoly holders of valuable franchises. Because of all this they are bound to the state in relations of co-dependence, much as the nationalised corporations were in the post-war settlement. That is why we describe the significance of all this as constitutional: the state increasingly relies on these institutions to carry out core public services, and the firms rely on the state for business.

Table 9.2 Weekly family expenditure by UK households on foundational economy goods and services in 2011

	Quintile group					
	Q1	Q2	Q3	Q4	Q5	All/average
Persons per household	1.4	2.1	2.4	2.8	3.1	2.4
TOTAL EXPENDITURE	£198.20	£323.85	£444.65	£573.60	£878.35	£483.60
Food and non-alcoholic drink	£31.60	£44.95	£54.80	£63.50	£79.10	£54.70
Percentage share of total expenditure	15.9%	13.9%	12.3%	11.1%	9.0%	11.3%
Expenditure per person in household	£22.57	£21.40	£22.83	£23.09	£25.93	£22.79
Electricity, gas, other fuels and water	£18.20	£24.85	£29.50	£34.05	£42.10	£29.80
Percentage share of total expenditure	9.2%	7.7%	6.6%	5.9%	4.8%	6.2%
Expenditure per person in household	£13.00	£11.83	£12.29	£12.38	£13.80	£12.42
Telephony, internet and postal services	£6.85	£10.00	£12.60	£15.15	£19.00	£12.70
Percentage share of total expenditure	3.5%	3.1%	2.8%	2.6%	2.2%	2.6%
Expenditure per person in household	£4.89	£4.76	£5.25	£5.51	£6.23	£5.29
Rail, bus and other fares (excluding cars)	£3.60	£5.60	£8.20	£12.30	£21.50	£10.10
Percentage share of total expenditure	1.8%	1.7%	1.8%	2.1%	2.4%	2.1%
Expenditure per person in household	£2.57	£2.67	£3.42	£4.47	£7.05	£4.21
Car spares, patrol, diesel and repairs and servicing	£8.50	£20.00	£31.05	£44.85	£65.95	£34.10
Percentage share of total expenditure	4.3%	6.2%	7.0%	7.8%	7.5%	7.1%
Expenditure per person in household	£6.07	£9.52	£12.94	£16.31	£21.62	£14.21
Spending on foundational economy activities	£68.75	£105.40	£136.15	£169.85	£227.65	£141.40
Percentage share of total expenditure	34.7%	32.5%	30.6%	29.6%	25.9%	29.2%
Expenditure per person in household	£49.11	£50.19	£56.73	£61.76	£74.64	£58.92

Source: Bowman et al (2014, p 122).

Note: UK households are arranged by quintile group as measured by income: Q1 are the poorest fifth and Q5 are the richest fifth.

Figure 9.1 Estimated spend with third parties across central government, showing spend on ATOS, Capita, G4S and Serco 2012–13

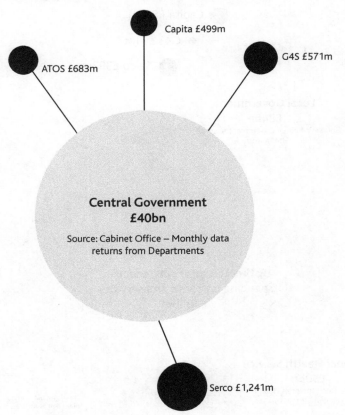

Capita £499m

ATOS £683m

G4S £571m

Central Government £40bn

Source: Cabinet Office – Monthly data returns from Departments

Serco £1,241m

Source: National Audit Office (2013, p 7).

Figure 9.2 Estimated spend with third parties across the public sector, showing spend on Capita, G4S and Serco 2012–13

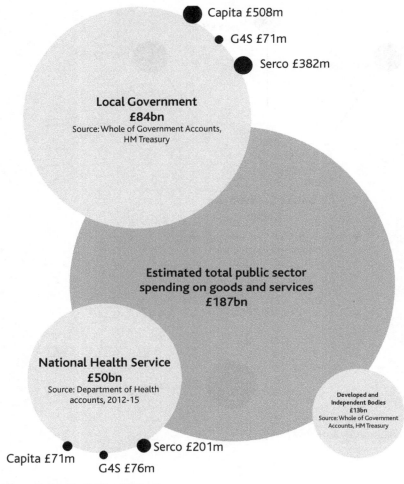

Source: National Audit Office (2013, p 6).

In the outsourcing sector, which is central to the range of services which we identify with the foundational economy, we see most visibly the truth of the claim that this is a politically constructed domain of economic activity. The outsourcing boom is the result of a conscious political choice that, in the last generation, has reshaped the landscape of the foundational economy. The choice is that franchising to a private sector operator is a better way of delivering goods and services than delivery by a publicly owned institution – an argument elaborated elsewhere (Bowman et al, 2015). That strategy explains, obviously, key changes of recent decades: the demise of the nationalised corporation and its replacement by regulated privatised utilities and other privatised providers, and the boom in outsourcing right across all parts of the public sector. But this has not abolished the question of what constitutes the appropriate level of state intervention. Rather, it has replaced crude issues about the amount of public ownership with more subtle and hard to solve problems: in essence, about the terms of what is essentially a contract, under which a set of sheltered franchises are guaranteed by state resources and state authority. That is why we insist on the argument that a fresh economic constitution is needed as the alternative to both what we call neoliberalism and the 'retro' fantasies of parts of the left.

All economic classifications, including measures like GDP, are constructs and the notion of the foundational economy is no exception. It is neither a 'natural' nor a privileged 'scientific' measure. Like 'manufacturing', it is a bracketing category or tool that may do useful economic and political work (Mitchell, 2002, 2008). It is also a political construction – the result of a long chain of decision about how to organise the provision of the goods and services necessary for civilised life. The principles that should guide its organisation are therefore different from those advocated by the 'global competition is the only show in town' school. Because it so intimately linked to the development of the most basic human capabilities – health, nourishment, learning – it needs to be judged by its potential to provide for the development of those capabilities. The relevant criteria are, for instance, discussed in the work of moral theorists referred to earlier (Sen, 1985, Nussbaum, 2000). Their concept of human capability highlights how people need the support of a well-functioning foundational economy if they are to flourish and develop their capabilities.

It is precisely this factor which is neglected when representatives of the officer class express their vision of the economy, pontificate on the bridge at metropolitan ceremonies – like Mr Johnson at the Thatcher Memorial Lecture. They prefer to work with the abstractions of competition and markets which assume that what is appropriate to tradeable goods and services is similarly appropriate to sheltered parts of the economy. Moreover, in terms of everyday policy language, the foundational economy is an unglamorous economic domain. When politicians talk excitedly about the organisation and reorganisation of the British economy they speak about advanced manufacturing and knowledge-based industries. Yet, as our evidence about the sheer scale of the foundational shows, something as immediate and pressing as the puzzle of stagnating British productivity must originate in what is happening within the low wage, low skill occupations so common in the delivery of foundational activities. Rewriting the script for this 'other show in town' is a vital matter, and one to which we next turn.

Rewriting the script for the other show: rejecting utopianism

Two utopian ideals presently influence thinking about the organisation of the foundational economy. The first, dominant now for nearly 40 years, insists that it must be subject to the workings of 'the only show in town' - free market competition. Every catastrophic failure in privatised service delivery or in outsourcing is followed by a renewed attempt to reconfigure economic structures so that they fit a model of competitive economics – a process which we have documented in detail in our study of the successive failings of the outsourcing system (see Bowman et al, 2015.) This is utopianism because it chases a will o' the wisp – free market competition in an economic domain which in reality is a set of overlapping sectors that operate in the shelter of state franchises. The foundational economy is a state-licensed economy; the key task is not the insertion of an abstract model of market competition but the determination of what the terms of that licence should be.

A less influential utopianism – because it has mostly been on the losing side in the last generation – is associated with critics of the new order from the left. It partly explains the striking upsurge of support for Jeremy Corbyn in the Labour Party leadership election of 2015 – an election that was as much an inquest on Blair's policy legacy as a competition for the party leadership. This view is utopian because it hankers after a lost (indeed in part an imaginary) past, of monopoly public service providers, centrally controlled public corporations on a Morrisonian model, and empowerment of centrally controlled trade unions. In its way it offers another 'view from the bridge' because it conceives the economy as a single system which can be steered from a re-empowered centre. The view ignores the fact that the kind of privatised and outsourced foundational economy profiled above is now embedded not only in Britain but across a wide range of other advanced capitalist economies. Precisely because it is embedded, any policy prescriptions have to accommodate this fact. The revolutionary changes over the last generation have irrevocably altered the capacities and structures of the public sector. The public sector that existed before the Thatcher revolution has largely disappeared. Even to think of direct labour in local authorities, or the vast public corporations that existed in the 1970s, is to see the problem. The renationalisation of rail, through taking back expired franchises, would be no more than a gesture.

More fundamentally, to attempt to go back to these once viable institutional forms is to engage in backward looking utopianism. It is the institutional equivalent of bringing back the horse drawn carriage because we dislike the motor car. There are reasons why the old public sector was swept away, and they amount to more than ideological delusion or the malign influence of free market lobbying: the old command public sector in the UK had serious problems in delivering efficient and responsive services to citizens. The command and control health service built in the late 1940s and 1950s cannot be recreated for the second decade of the 21st century – a decade when deferential, isolated patients have been replaced by questioning patients underpinned by a dense network of civil society advocacy groups.

Our proposals do not have the emotional attractions of right or left utopianism which dream of a mono-economy constructed around a single principle. They accept that outsourcing on a large scale, a big privatised sector and a food distribution system with giant corporate actors, like supermarkets, are not going to disappear, or even significantly diminish. They do not imagine an economy reconfigured around either pure market competition or command and control. They accept what we have now, recognise that the foundational is organised into a set of sheltered, licensed parts, and turn to the task of rewriting the script for 'the other show in town' – the foundational economy. But they are radical because they reimagine economic life in an altogether fresh way: in the language of a morally defensible constitutional settlement.

We begin with an important constitutional and economic reality: the foundational economy, as presently organised, is a system of licences. Some of these are elaborately negotiated and publicised: for instance in the franchises that govern the privatised rail system. Some are embedded in systems of corporate regulation: for instance in the regulatory systems that govern the operation of privatised energy, cable and water utilities. Some are governed by contracts framed in commercial language: for instance in the huge and expanding world of outsourcing. And some, though vital to corporate actors, are barely noticed in public debates: out-of-town supermarket branches are socially licensed de facto because British planning regulations limit direct competition between superstores and effectively give the successful pioneering applicant a licence to take money from households in the surrounding area. Planning regulation PPS 6 makes out of town centre development subject to a test of 'need', so that one or two successful applications to build stores effectively close the door to competitors which cannot subsequently obtain permission because the need has already been met (Friends of the Earth, 2005).

The foundational economy is already a licensed economy; the problem is that the licences are not governed by the essential purpose of that economy – which is to secure the conditions of civilised life. Actors in the foundational economy have public functions; private and public are necessarily joined in relations of co-dependence. A defensible system of licensing has to be governed by the need to hold business to account in fulfilling those public functions. The central principle was expressed over 50 years ago by one of the greatest of all 20th century American observers of the market economy, Adolf Berle: a man whose views exerted a profound influence on Roosevelt's New Deal. Big business, Berle (1962, p 2) observed:

> exists and derives its right to exist under, and only under, a tacit social contract. This social contract requires management of big business to assume certain responsibilities. Assumption and fulfillment of them entitles big business to the privileges it receives from the State, and to acquiescence in their existence by the economic community they affect and serve.

The privileges enjoyed by business in the foundational economy are great. What obligations should it observe as the price of enjoying those privileges?

The social licence: making the foundational economy part of the constitution

The heart of our proposal puts a social licence at the heart of the foundational economy. The notion of 'social licence' is most familiar in the mining industry, particularly in the developing world. It involves a formal or informal agreement between an investor seeking to extract natural resources, and the community affected by these activities. It may cover labour conditions, environmental standards, the sharing of economic benefits and other locally important concerns such as the protection of sacred sites (Socialicense, nd; miningfacts.org, nd). Our proposal is that something comparable to the more formal version of a mining social licence be applied to firms and sectors in the foundational economy. We work by analogy. The extractive industries seek immobile natural resources, but so too do private sector operators in the foundational economy which tap the household spend and taxes of an immobile population. In mining, as in the foundational economy, a limited number of operators are granted the right to extract. The fundamental rationale is thus the same. In the foundational economy, as in countries sitting on large mineral deposits, businesses need to earn the right to extract cash from a territory.

How might social licensing work in the foundational economy? Here are the two core proposals.

- Licensing would be an explicit arrangement that gave contracting enterprises or sectors privileges and rights to trade while placing them under reciprocal obligations to offer social returns. A formal licensing system would make the right to trade dependent on providing a service that meets negotiated criteria of community responsibility on issues such as sourcing, training and payment of living wages.
- The scale and scope of licensing agreements would vary. They might be with whole sectors, including all the firms above a certain size threshold. In other cases, where firm size and market position varied greatly within a sector, it might be more appropriate to have separate firm agreements. For example, the sourcing obligations on the big four supermarket chains would probably be different from those placed on smaller chains like Waitrose, or the regional chain of Booths. Note how modest and open ended is this suggestion. Firms in the foundational sector are not being made an offer they can't refuse. As important partners with the state they are invited to sit down to work out how they can deliver on their social obligations in return for their privileges.

The reasoning behind these proposals is straightforward, and is directly in the line of those observers like Berle who wanted to give the business enterprise a stable, legitimate foundation. Businesses in the foundational economy have a sheltered existence – and rightly so, because they deliver goods and services fundamental to civilised life, and they deserve shelter from the instabilities of the gale of competition that rages in so much of a modern economy. But the corollary is that the foundational cannot simply be about economic transactions, and the contracts under which it operates cannot simply be determined by bottom-line accounting. Reframing the foundational economy, as we have done here, makes plain that it is about reciprocal social relations within local, regional and national spaces. The provision of mundane goods and services in the foundational economy is intertwined with the multiple identities of people as consumers, workers and local residents.

The proposal is thus for an extension of government, but it is far from a return to the old world of command and control. It accepts that private corporate actors have a key role in the foundational economy – indeed so key that they are best considered governing institutions joined in relations of co-dependence with the state, because firms in the foundational economy already operate under the protection of government. As governing institutions they need to be recognised as part of the constitution – and in turn need to recognise their obligations, as would any other important constitutional actors. State protection may be explicit and contractual, as with rail franchising or social care, or regulatory, as in the relation between supermarkets and planning permission. Alternatively, the social licence may involve not disturbing de facto territorial monopolies as with bank branches, or may even include state inducements to invest as with rural broadband rollout.

The emphasis here is on a *constitutional settlement*. Like any constitutional settlement in a democratic state it needs to be freely negotiated. All important actors, corporate and non-corporate, need to have their voices heard and their interests defended. That will not be easy, but then democratic constitutional settlements are not meant to be easy, they are meant to be the way we govern in a civilised manner. The uniqueness of the foundational thus far is that it has provided privileges for corporate interests using state power, but has neglected to hammer out the constitutional terms of that state protection. Naturally, the particular terms of the settlement will vary in different parts of the foundational economy. But that is what democratic control of economic life is all about.

References

Berle, A. (1962) 'A new look at management responsibility', *Human Resource Management*, 1 (3): 1–5.

Bowman, A., Ertürk, I., Froud, J., Johal, S., Law, A., Leaver, A., Moran, M. and Williams, K. (2014) *The end of the experiment: From competition to the foundational economy*, Manchester: Manchester University Press.

Bowman, A., Ertürk, I., Folkman, P., Froud, J., Haslam, C., Johal, S., Leaver, A., Moran, M., Tsitsianis, N . and Williams, K. (2015) *What a waste: Outsourcing and how it goes wrong*, Manchester: Manchester University Press.

Braudel, F. (1981) *The structures of everyday life: Civilization and capitalism*, Vol 1 (trans Sian Reynolds), New York: Harper and Row.

Corbyn, J. (2015) *Investment, growth and tax justice: Corbyn outlines economic vision and fairer taxes for Britain 2020*, www.jeremyforlabour. com/investment_growth_and_tax_justice

Friends of the Earth (2005) 'How to oppose a supermarket planning application', www.foe.co.uk/sites/default/files/downloads/ campaigning_against_supermarkets.pdf

Johnson, B. (2013) The 2013 Margaret Thatcher lecture, Centre for Policy Studies, 27 November, www.cps.org.uk/events/q/ date/2013/11/27/the-2013-margaret-thatcher-lecture-boris-johnson/

Mazzucato, M. (2013) *The entrepreneurial state: Debunking public vs. private sector myths*, London: Anthem Press.

Miningfacts.org (n.d.) 'What is the social license to operate (SLO)?', www.miningfacts.org/Communities/What-is-the-social-licence-to-operate/

Mitchell, T. (2002) *Rule of experts: Egypt, techno-politics, modernity*, Berkeley: University of California Press.

Mitchell, T. (2008) 'Rethinking economy', *Geoforum*, 39: 1116–1121.

National Audit Office (2013) *The role of major contractors in the delivery of public services*, HC 810, London: The Stationery Office.

National Audit Office (2014) *Adult social care in England: overview*, HC 1102, London: National Audit Office.

Nussbaum, M. (2000) *Women and human development: The capabilities approach*, Cambridge: Cambridge University Press.

Sen, A. (1985) *Commodities and capabilities*, Oxford: Oxford University Press.

Socialicense (n.d.) 'The social license to operate', http://socialicense. com/

Part Three
Economic and political democracy: restoring the market-civil society balance

Editors' overview

In Part One our contributors have set out some broad themes that would break with neoliberal discourse and provide broad perspectives for movements and policies for change. To recap, these were: a platform of democratisation by O'Donnell; new or updated modes of collectivism by Gilbert; integration of lifeworld relations and environmental priorities by Coote and Benton; articulated, according to Coote in a new social settlement. Some of these perspectives were related to current fluctuations in structures of power and social context in the Part Two chapters by Farnsworth and Irving, and the Jones and O'Donnell chapter on the European Union. Thompson showed that there are some, though limited, shifts in the economic policy making within which progressive reforms may have to work. Both Jones and Johal, Moran and Williams identified specific changes that could make businesses and local economic institutions more accountable to civil society and local government criteria for socioeconomic amelioration. This final part of the book links the Part One perspectives to the Part Two institutional analyses by examining a number of fields of favourable political action.

Crouch begins these analyses by setting out the case for a revitalised form of social democracy in which the needs and interests of women are the 'motors' of change in a way that is analogous to that of trade unions and labour organisations in classical social democracy. Citing lifeworld aspects, such as the work–life balance and the gendered division of domestic labour, Crouch argues that a revamped and revitalised social democratic state could be the best mechanism for improving these popular concerns. The trends and projections which Crouch identifies, complement and 'materialise' the principles of 'natural' wellbeing for which Coote and Benton argued in Part One. Jones and Mike O'Donnell pursue this focus on social justice and change agents by identifying the analogous concerns in the evolution of social movements. They argue that, as well as often making explicit criticisms of neoliberalism, many of these campaigners and their organisations could play similar roles to those previously taken by labour movement organisations as advocates and facilitators of classical social democracy – a role for which their emphasis on more direct democracy in socioeconomic governance would render them especially relevant. An illustration of how such a new social democracy could be practised in more democratic and effective ways than both the statist social democracy and the neoliberal models is provided by Andrew Cumbers' chapter. He describes the principles on which 'the broadly conceived democratic approach to public ownership' might be based and offers a number of options for public ownership which emphasise social accountability and economic democracy – options which derive not from abstract formulae but popular ownership forms already practised in various other societies.

The Conclusion chapter brings together key points from the alternative macro-paradigms in Part One, the institutional parameters and reforms to these, discussed in Part Two, plus the political and economic restructuring advocated in Part Three. It argues that a new social democracy, needed to rebalance the market–state–civil society relationship which neoliberalism has distorted, should be based on democratisation and accountability in the social and economic spheres as well as in conventional politics – a paradigm and practice drawn from and substantially driven by a social base from recent social movements and more progressive NGOs. Applied in fields such as housing, finance and employment, its discourse would emphasise gender and practical environmental issues to ground a post-neoliberal politics in more relevant and popular concern than the stagnant and often obscure abstractions of economic discourse. It is argued that the related ideas and policies could, at the least, achieve a regime change within contemporary capitalism, comparable to the social democracy which successfully displaced the market hegemony of the 19th and early 20th century.

TEN

Neoliberalism and social democracy

Colin Crouch

Social democracy is in danger of the fate once suffered by British liberalism: to represent the core consensus of much of public life, but to be seen as somehow increasingly marginal to it. Neoliberalism enjoys an ideological hegemony, but no government can ever long pursue its true strategy of unregulated market forces. At the other extreme, of the political right, the new xenophobic forces frequently combine their nationalism with advocacy of strong social policy (restricted of course to natives). Social democracy, in contrast to both socialism and neoliberalism, stands for the search for creative compromises between markets and their regulation, rather than accepting grudging concessions with a preference at either pole. And it has a model of citizenship rights that can assert national identity without hostility to immigrants and people from other countries.

There is no need for social democrats to believe that their policy approaches have become outmoded. Indeed, a neoliberal economy, with increasing use of markets, requires moderation through social democratic interventions if it is not to produce a one-dimensional society of a kind that very few people find acceptable – the kind of outcomes which are described in the Introduction and Chapters One, Two and Three of this book. Social democracy's problem is not that its approach has become outmoded, but that its historical voting constituency has shrunk in size – though this is a problem that it shares with traditional conservatives. Even here, however, there are positive possibilities with the growth of a left-of-centre female electorate. Unfortunately historical electoral decline is blinding social democratic parties to both the dangers and the optimistic possibilities of the current situation and, particularly in the United Kingdom, they are instead sinking into internal recriminations between increasingly irrelevant positions of their own left and right.

The democratic deficit of neoliberalism

Neoliberalism became globally dominant because it captured the minds (and feeds the wallets) of political, economic and many other elites, not because it has become an irresistible democratic force. Political parties that have little to offer other than a neoliberal agenda are usually fairly small minority ones – like the Free Democrats in Germany, which has now lost its representation in parliament. Where neoliberal ideas achieve a stronger status it is because they form coalitions with movements able to build on deep roots in the electorate, usually conservative or Christian parties. Even in the USA, neoliberals have to make common cause with fundamentalist Christians and groups with implicit ethnic agendas within the Republican Party – political ideologies with which they have little in common. Sometimes, as with Clinton's New Democrats, Blair's New Labour or Schroeder's *Neue Mitte*, the partners are social democratic; but alliances with the traditional centre-right are more likely, as these are more likely to share neoliberals' rejection of redistribution and a strong welfare state.

Neoliberalism's central positive contention is not just that markets are always better guides to public welfare than anything that can be attempted through political action, but that values, interests, prejudices should only be expressed in ways that can be realised through the market. Those that cannot must either be transformed into market form or fall by the wayside. Very few people are willing to accept this restriction, except perhaps those rich enough to buy the practical realisation of any ideas or values that they hold. For example, culture and education have to be justified in terms of their economic contribution, unless they become the hobby of a wealthy philanthropist. While there are many such instances of such thinking in contemporary public policy, the core belief of neoliberalism that lies behind them is rarely expressed baldly in political debate. Neoliberals prefer to work behind the scenes. As this book's Introduction argues, they find democracy potentially very disturbing and try to limit its reach – as Wolfgang Streeck (2013) and Philip Mirowski (2013) have previously demonstrated in their separate, excellent analyses of the political ideas of Friedrich von Hayek.

Further, although the public rhetoric of neoliberals is couched in terms of markets, the freedom of choice and restrictions of government power that they bring, in practice, as Chapter Eight shows, they generally also imply 'and large corporations' whenever they say 'markets'. This is partly because it is impractical to have a pure market with masses of producers in many key sectors of the economy As I have tried to show elsewhere in a discussion of the decline of antitrust law, neoliberal economic ideas have adapted themselves to this reality by arguing that markets dominated by quasi-monopolies can serve consumer welfare better than those with large numbers of producers, because size equals efficiency (Crouch, 2011). Many economists have challenged that equation on efficient market grounds, but there are other problems. The crucial idea of 'freedom of consumer choice', one of neoliberalism's few popular slogans, becomes supplanted by the top-down notion of 'consumer welfare' as determined by corporate leaders and competition courts.

One of the ideals of a true market economy with no dominant firms is that no producers should wield a corrupting influence on politics. Once fortunes made in the economy can be deployed politically, the assumption of rough equality of political influence, fundamental to liberal democracy, falls. In private, neoliberals will argue that it will further advance economic efficiency if those who have made fortunes through economic activity can also control politics. But, as Mirowski (2013) has argued so well, the public and private discourses of neoliberalism are very different. The think tanks, movements and parties that most uncompromisingly promulgate neoliberal ideas depend heavily for their strength and influence on lavish funding from foundations which have their bases in large corporate and personal fortunes. This extends to ostensibly grassroots movements like the Tea Party, so aptly dubbed by Mirowski an 'astroturf' movement.

Markets and diversity

In these different ways, the claim to democratic plausibility of neoliberalism is highly vulnerable to attack, but this should not be read as a rejection of the idea of a market economy, or even of the idea of intensifying the role of the market where it can improve efficiency and true consumer choice. Social democrats do not need to be on the defensive when the advantages of a market economy are extolled over a state-controlled one, as they do not advocate state control, just state correction of the defects of the market.

What really matters here is the scope for diversity and innovative challenge within a political economy. Both its insistence on conformity in ideas of all kinds and its monolithic state ownership patterns were the fundamental flaws of state socialism that produced its perceived incompetent drabness. But today, as described in the Introduction, neoliberalism risks similar uniformity. A market economy will never become as bereft of innovative capacity as a state-controlled one, because there are always some free-floating resources, but a fully neoliberal *society* (that is, one where both economy and polity are dominated by neoliberal orthodoxy) would lose its capacity for change. Change comes through challenge and the confrontation of opposed or at least different backgrounds and perspectives. Once that ceases there is stasis, and in the case of total dominance by neoliberal orthodoxy, the deep ambivalence of Hayek and others about the rights of democracy can start to work a wider mischief.

In the strictly economic field, innovators are often outsiders of various kinds: immigrants, the religiously unorthodox, alternative people of various kinds. As they become successful and their corporations grow, these characteristics are often left behind, but they were crucial to the beginnings. Neoliberalism can sustain this kind of diversity-led innovation within the economy – provided its need to make alliances with other political tendencies does not lead it into coalitions with xenophobic and other intolerant right-wing tendencies within or between parties. But at the level of politics and society, what stimulating challenges await neoliberalism itself once it has disposed of all opposition to its project? While it extols the role of competition and freedom of choice in the economy, and while many of its leading protagonists believe in extending the reach of the market and analogues for it into virtually all walks of life, it does not extend this logic to ideologies and policy approaches. Here neoliberals seek a complete monopoly, guaranteed indeed by a state safely in their own hands and with many public institutions placed beyond the reach of democracy. This is where 20th and 21st century neoliberalism is such a narrow shadow of its 18th and 19th century predecessor, classic liberalism. This welcomed diversity and innovation in all areas of life. True, the clashes provoked by this openness produced some bloody conflicts from 1789 and 1948 onwards, but its long-term legacy was to liberate our lives and minds across a whole range, not just our ability to choose goods and services.

Once people gave up using violent struggle to resolve political conflicts, the abiding legacy of classic liberalism was to allow a continuing clash between rival world views. Sometimes these result in dull stalemates, but often in creative compromises. The part of the world where we see this most clearly is in the Nordic countries, where so many initiatives in economy, polity and society have originated. It is normal on the left to attribute Nordic successes to their past prolonged periods of social democratic political dominance, but it should be interpreted differently. These are also seriously market-oriented economies: small, open, dependent on world trade for many of the means of modern life and therefore needing to be able to export competitively. Powerful trade unions and social democratic parties were forced to develop forms of market regulation that were at least compatible with, and eventually came positively to advance, competitiveness. The economies remained primarily in private hands, in the Swedish case in particular an economy dominated by major firms that became global. Creative compromise between opposed political forces, neither social democratic nor neoliberal hegemony, were at the heart of the model. Today their economic performance continues to be among the best in the world, while their welfare states remain the world's most generous and the levels of inequality among the world's very lowest. Social democracy represented the culmination of liberalism's programme; the alternative project of total socialist dominance produced little more than stagnation, a police state and an inability to adapt that finally led to its total collapse.

This last point constitutes a case against unchallenged dominance by any one political force. The specific case against such dominance by neoliberalism is that made at the outset: people cannot be forced to accept that their only legitimate values are those sanctioned by the market. As Karl Polanyi ([1944] 1957) showed in his great study of the English enclosure movement, the introduction of markets tore into an existing social fabric, damaging forms of solidarity and social support developed over long periods. Modern social policy developed to provide new forms of protection, given the failure of the market to provide adequate solutions itself (see also Chapter Four, page 83). Similar processes have returned at various historical moments. We are living through another one now, as marketisation, especially in its globalising form, breaks down national economic arrangements, the 20th century welfare state, and even the mechanisms in the natural world that have protected our climate and physical environment. These varied incursions of the market into previously protected aspects of life require a diversified response, depending on one's particular values and associated interests. We might be pleased at the demise of national systems of economic protection, but when it comes to plunging the lives of relatively poor people into anxiety and insecurity over their livelihoods, or provoking natural disasters through climate change, many of us will take a different approach. Social democracy, reinterpreting itself as the structure of the economy and appropriate forms of regulation change, is the political tradition best equipped to address these issues.

However much we might disagree over an exact list of preferences and priorities in confronting the invasions of the market, very few people are really willing to delegate everything to the market in the way that true neoliberals do. For them, no other human institution, least of all that institution charged with surveillance of common interests, the state, has an accumulation of information, competence and efficiency to match that of the market – and, they have to add, the great corporations – though their theoretical basis for that argument is far less elegantly grounded than that of the pure market itself. For them, if a particular goal cannot be achieved through the market, then by definition its pursuit is either inefficient or not wanted by enough people. They have a major problem with market externalities, those issues that are affected by a market exchange but which do not enter into the cost calculations of the buyers and sellers involved; most cases of pollution and environmental damage fall into this category. Theoretical neoliberals deal with these problems in various ways, but neoliberals in government find themselves reacting differently, as concern for other values produces demands for protection of various kinds from the negative consequences of the market. For example, within its heavily neoliberal (but also partly xenophobic) manifesto for the 2015 general election, the British Conservative Party (2015) pledged itself to higher levels of public spending on rail, road and broadband infrastructure, research and development, and culture and sport. It promised regulation to protect the countryside and the marine environment. Whether or not these commitments were adequate or likely to be kept in practice is not at issue here. The key point is that a fully confident neoliberal party would have declared that all these things would be best left to the market. Despite the strong push towards neoliberalism that has taken place in this party's agenda over the past 30 years, it still stands on essentially social democratic territory, seeing a need to balance the market against other values.

The more we extend the role of markets, the more we damage interests, values and people that cannot protect themselves through the market itself – unless those values and interests can be fully redefined in market terms. Therefore, the more we have a marketisation project, the more we need a politics that can reflect on its consequences. Which aspects of this damage should simply be accepted, even welcomed? Which should be accepted, but with recognition that the victims should be compensated in some way? (For example, if marketisation is producing increased inequality, should there be increased taxation on high incomes? If labour markets are becoming more flexible, should there be improved income support for those temporarily thrown out of work?) In other cases again, damage may seem so severe that it should be reduced by attempts at regulating the market behaviour concerned. Examples here would be irresponsible banking behaviour, and environmental damage resulting from economic activity. There are no technical solutions to these questions; they are the appropriate business of political debate and conflict.

There are major issues here for European Union policy makers. The European project has always been primarily a market-making one, initially breaking down barriers to commerce across national boundaries and ensuring that member states traded with each other on reasonably level playing fields. But this has usually been accompanied by some, though limited, market-correcting measures, including social policy. Currently, however, the market-correcting aspects have been forgotten, and we have moved into a period of aggressive European marketisation without social policy rebalancing. A major instrument of this shift has been the extension of the single market to the services sectors, which is making it increasingly difficult to defend public services from privatisation. The crisis has intensified this problem, which is ironic given that it had been caused by a key part of the global neoliberal project: the rampaging of banks through the deregulated financial markets. Fears of economic stagnation lead politicians to conclude that only even more market deregulation can liberate economic dynamism. As part of this, Europe has given up its leading role in combating climate change. The policies that the EU, with others, has imposed on the problem economies of the Eurozone call overwhelmingly for the exposure of workers to radical insecurity. There is now a growing danger that marketisation will become a European force while compensation for it will be left to national policies. This will not help a fundamental challenge facing social policy: can it protect a purely national determination at a time when market making is a global project beyond nations' reach?

In the UK this problem takes a particularly subtle form, the issue of the respective roles of the EU and the nation state in marketisation and policies to contain it being seen the other way round. Romantic Conservatives and nationalists such as UKIP attack the EU by demanding that Britain should have unimpeded national sovereignty. But national sovereignty can achieve little in a globalised economy dominated by transnational corporations. Therefore, to confine political action on economic issues to the nation state is to condemn it to impotence. This is of course what neoliberals seek, but are reluctant to say too openly. However, in the UK they can advance their goal while appearing to be proposing the exact opposite by hiding behind nationalist flag-waving. As ever, neoliberalism hides behind other, often incompatible, political forces.

Finding a social base for opposition

Economic, political and social dynamism depends on permanent challenge and peaceful confrontation of opposed class interests. Without many of its members ever appreciating it, the organised industrial working class secured the creative compromises that in many countries characterised the second half of the 20th century. Today this class is in steep decline. True to what one should expect, in the absence of an alternative representative of major social interests outside the economically privileged, this decline is being accompanied by the rise to power of a new, uncompromising form of hegemony favouring the interests of the privileged. Neoliberalism is not however achieving an easy triumph; it is not overrunning abandoned trenches of the welfare state, but meeting resistance at many points.

The problem is that these forces of resistance are disparate and lack strategy. The great majority of people are not often politically active. Why should they be? Their chances of exercising any real influence remain close to zero, unless they make pursuit of a political career the overwhelming focus of their lives. Even then their chances of success remain small. Therefore their acquisition of a coherent political identity can never be taken for granted. Where such identities exist, they have been the result of particular historical processes, not some logical necessity. The achievement of universal democratic citizenship proceeded through a number of struggles over inclusion and exclusion. Some groups gained a political meaning to their identity by being excluded: on the basis of civil wars, religion, property ownership or type of work. Those included also acquired an identity, as the included, and usually concluded that they should support the leaders of their identity in maintaining the exclusion of the others; and vice versa for those excluded. This process came to a halt once universal political citizenship was achieved. Since that time, newly emerging identities, such as those occupational ones that have developed in the post-industrial economy, have not needed to struggle for inclusion; therefore they confer no sense of political identity. The dynamic process of identity formation through struggle has come to an abrupt end. The political landscape formed by our major parties comprises extinct volcanoes, survivors of an active past of religious and class struggles. By a curious irony the very process that finally ushered in mass democracy, universal citizenship, also undermined the basis of its continuing vitality.

There are two main exceptions: one dangerous, the other promising for social democrats. These are race and gender. Major struggles over the inclusion and exclusion of immigrants and ethnic minorities are becoming increasingly salient, spurred by the two different but connected issues of economic globalisation and Islamist terrorism. Almost everywhere in the democratic world, including and even in particular the former Nordic social democratic bastions, extreme xenophobic parties have grown in strength and either entered governments or pushed conservative and neoliberal governments into increasingly extreme actions. At present neoliberals, always in search of partners more popularly attractive than themselves and finding traditional conservatism to be losing its appeal, are increasingly likely to accept alliances with the extremists in order to keep social democrats out of office. Important current examples are Denmark and Norway; in the past it has also occurred in the Netherlands; it may yet happen in France. Indeed, a union of neoliberalism and xenophobia brings together the two most vigorous forces at work in contemporary politics. But such alliances are fraught with internal contradiction. Neoliberalism's agenda of globalisation, the end of economic protectionism and the free movement of labour contradicts all objectives of right-wing populism.

In a further problem for neoliberals, populist parties are increasingly adopting strong social policies. Do social democrats (who do not reject globalisation) then become the lesser of two evils as partners for neoliberals, producing new dilemmas of compromise for social democrats? Or do social democrats find themselves pressed closer to xenophobia and a general alliance of anti-neoliberal forces? Different answers will emerge to this major issue in different political systems. Neoliberals and social democrats will need to remember how much recent change in society has resulted from their tacit, even unconscious, cooperation against conservative and populist opposition: changes in family law and the position of women, the full acceptance of homosexuality, and (what will come increasingly under pressure) improvement in the rights of immigrants and ethnic minorities.

The second and more encouraging development in political identities is gender. Women possess four major characteristics that make them suitable candidates to be the carriers of a major, constructive challenge to neoliberal hegemony. First and most simply, they are not a minority. Second, although they long ago acquired political citizenship, many still suffer from a range of gender-based disadvantages in participating fully in life outside the home alongside men. Their identity therefore has a powerful political dimension. The fact that several of these disadvantages have been addressed in many countries in recent years does not weaken the force of this. History has frequently shown us that disadvantaged groups are most likely to press for change when they see some signs of improvement. Hopelessness does not create activism. Third, women constitute the majority of people working in middle and lower positions in the services sectors of the economy, the very social location to which one must look for any new challenge to dominance by elites (Oesch, 2006).

Finally, and more difficult to demonstrate than these three points, the lives of a large majority of women are, by both their long-term and the recent distinctive history, better equipped than the majority of men to resist the central thrust of the neoliberal project. Until now, there has not been much evidence of this outside some not very well known feminist literature. This is mainly for two reasons. First, as noted above, most successful policies for women's advance have been, against gradually shrinking conservative opposition, on a shared neoliberal and social democratic agenda for liberation from various constraints imposed by past law and custom. Except when it comes to demands for state support of childcare, neoliberals have no problems with this. If anything, social democracy might have been more threatened as its traditional male bastions in the work force were invaded; but the fact that, particularly in the more social democratic societies, women tended to work in occupations, especially in the care sector, where there were few men has rendered this unimportant in practice. A second factor has been that, in order to be successful in achieving leadership positions in most types of organisation, women have had to adapt themselves to stereotypically male approaches to work and life.

It is in relation to this second point that we should look for a stronger challenge to neoliberalism from women. Neoliberalism requires of members of society, if they are to avoid abject failure, a single-minded devotion to maximising interests that are defined according to a strict economic calculus. Areas of life that lie outside the scope of that approach are either to be ignored or forced to be redefined so that they can take their place within that calculus. Not many people of either gender can accept this over the long haul, but men are more likely to adapt to it. Men are more used to the single-minded pursuit of work goals at the expense of family life, friends and relationships. Neoliberalism, with its insistence on a single, non-social form of communication, the emission of market signals via numbers, is an ideology ill at ease with ordinary human relationships. The dual role that women usually play in contemporary society, balancing work and home, places them at the sharp end of these struggles (Walby, 2015). If gender relations become more balanced, then an increasing number of men will become like this too - a convergence on a hitherto predominately female life that is important to what I mean by a politics increasingly defined by women but benefiting many men too – a tendency explored in the Conclusion to this book.

Some aspects of this situation are readily understandable and turned into familiar political demands. For example, we need a politicisation of the problem of work/life balance, talked about by very many people but not by political parties (see also editor's Conclusion; for a good review of work–family conflict as it affects European societies during the crisis, see McGinnity and Russell, 2013). But there are deeper aspects that will become more pressing as the neoliberal strategy itself has more victories. For example, as Mirowski (2013, ch 3) has demonstrated, the marketisation of everything eventually requires a fragmentation of the self. In a highly flexible neoliberal economy where eventually all support for the unemployed will have been withdrawn, people need to be repeatedly representing and redefining themselves to be attractive to employers' constantly changing requirements. This is especially true in the personal services sectors, in which women predominate, where the self becomes part of the product. To present oneself effectively against a constantly shifting set of criteria requires constant attention to the signals one gives out by one's entire lifestyle – and therefore in one's life as a consumer, for in a fully marketed society there is little outside the realm of purchase and consumption.

Everyone is affected by this trend, and the great majority are likely to resent it. But if it is to be politicised and become part of a revulsion against neoliberalism, the move will come first from women, as they are hit by it most directly and fully. It will be a demand for the protection of whole areas of life and the self from the market, which in turn requires that the market ceases to become the main arbiter of value, right across the board of social life. There are further issues. Some observers have argued that an economy dominated by women would have a different character from the male one that we now experience (Heuser and Steinborn, 2013). How far one takes these arguments is not yet clear, but it opens exciting possibilities.

Conclusion

The large political movements that have dominated the democratic world have to redefine themselves from time to time. They need to reach out to new kinds of support while somehow keeping hold of old ones: managing to have multiple roots that enable them to be simultaneously weighty and adaptable. The British Conservative Party was able to change from being the protectionist defender of rural interests to the free trade spokesman of the financial sector. European Christian parties changed from orchestrators of intolerance to mild advocates of ecumenicalism. Social democratic parties throughout Europe have already made a transition from being mainly supported by male manual workers in manufacturing to securing more than 50% of their votes from women: especially those working in the care sector. US Democrats have had a similar experience. Almost everywhere in the advanced world, a majority of trade union members are now women.

The adaptation of social democracy to being a movement that primarily represents women's concerns in the new economy is already underway. It needs only to become more imaginative. Social democracy's existing repertoire of policies combines acceptance of the market, where it helps achieve people's goals, with checks on it by social policy, regulation and action by social partners and other non-state, non-market groups. It is from this stock that responses will be found to the emerging political imperative: to protect the human self from the insistent invasion of the market and the giant corporation, and to insist that the market cannot be the only institution through which we pursue human values.

Acknowledgements

An earlier version of this article appeared as 'Putting neoliberalism in its place' (2014), *The Political Quarterly*, 85 (2): 114-121.

References

Conservative Party (2015) *The Conservative Party manifesto 2015,* London: Conservative Party.

Crouch, C. (2011) *The strange non-death of neoliberalism,* Cambridge: Polity.

Heuser, U.J. and Steinborn, D. (2013) *Anders denken! Warum Ökonomie weiblicher wird* [Think differently! Why the economy is becoming more feminine], Munich: Hauser.

McGinnity, F. and Russell, H. (2013) 'Work-family conflict and economic change' in D. Gallie (ed) *Economic crisis, quality of work and social integration: The European experience,* Oxford: Oxford University Press.

Mirowski, P. (2013) *Never let a serious crisis go to waste,* London: Verso.

Oesch, D. (2006) *Redrawing the class map: Stratification and institutions in Britain, Germany, Sweden and Switzerland,* Basingstoke: Palgrave Macmillan.

Polanyi, K. ([1944] 1957) *The great transformation: The political and economic origins of our time,* Boston, MA: Beacon Press.

Streeck, W. (2013) *Gekaufte zeit*, Berlin: Suhrkamp. (English translation: *Buying time*, London: Verso, 2014.)
Walby, S. (2015) *Crisis*, Oxford: Wiley.

ELEVEN

Rethinking public ownership as economic democracy

Andrew Cumbers

Introduction

The 20th century was dominated by two opposing utopias. One was a vision of top-down state ownership that could overthrow capitalism and deliver the fruits of their labour to the masses; the other was Hayek's market-driven nirvana of the property owning democracy that could liberate the individual, creativity and enterprise. Ultimately, both visions ushered in centralising dystopias in the form of the totalitarian command economies of the Soviet Union and China on the one hand, and a corporate-driven, elite, Western project of globalisation, neoliberalism and privatisation on the other.

As the 21st century advances we seem to have the worst of all worlds. The messy confluence of these two dystopias has produced a global economy characterised by growing inequality, deepening uneven development and accelerating environmental destruction. A slightly revised and reheated form of neoliberalism has emerged from the ashes of the financial crisis in a regime of austerity and welfare retrenchment. Meanwhile, the state as a critical social actor is re-emerging – if indeed it ever went away – in different and often regressive guises to paper over the contradictions and 'market failures' of deregulated capitalism. The nationalisation of much of the banking sector in the wake of the financial crisis was enacted by the same political elites who had been telling us for years to learn to love globalisation, the market and private enterprise. At the same time sovereign wealth funds – whether they originate from Norwegian or Middle Eastern oil riches or East Asian developmental states – are increasingly important in shaping financial markets.

The contemporary political economy seems increasingly to be characterised by a state project around security and restriction of individual rights and freedoms on the one hand, alongside a more rapacious accumulation by dispossession, to use David Harvey's phrase (2003), of our remaining common resources and assets on behalf of financial and corporate elites. In this chapter, I want to engage critically with what progressives can do to challenge this situation. A key component of the solution is to rethink the concept of public ownership by taking economic democracy seriously (see Cumbers, 2012). In what follows, I argue that this is essential in tackling social and environmental justice and elite power in the years ahead.

Reluctant return of public ownership: its aftermath in the capitalist heartland

At the height of the 2008-9 financial crisis, the return of public ownership – in the form of massive bank nationalisations across the advanced capitalist economies –caused many on the left to think that perhaps the spell of neoliberalism had been broken. In the UK, hitherto independent bastions of finance capital such as the Royal Bank of Scotland and HBOS, as well as smaller former building societies such as the Bradford and Bingley and Northern Rock, were taken into public ownership. It wasn't just those on the left who thought that something seismic had happened. The country's main conservative broadsheet, the *Daily Telegraph*, proclaimed somewhat apocalyptically that 'October 13th 2008 will go down in history as the day the capitalist system in the UK finally admitted defeat'. Although the *Telegraph* was sadly proved wrong in the event, nevertheless only a massive injection of public money across the world's major economies prevented a complete collapse of the financial system and possibly the global economy.

At the height of the financial crisis, there were some grounds for hope that the political tide had turned after three decades in which governments across the world – of both right and left – had signed up to a form of free market fundamentalism. As the banking crisis began to ripple through to the rest of the economy, producing a collapse in the housing market, the freezing up of credit to business and a general downturn in consumer demand, it appeared that the political classes might be rediscovering the benefits of a more sophisticated form of economics. Hayek and Friedman might be about to give ground to Keynes, Polanyi and even Marx.

However, as the initial shock of the financial crisis wore off and state intervention appeared to have – at least temporarily – stabilised the banking system, it became clear that the grip of free market thinking or at least neoliberal ideas on the political mainstream was as strong as ever. Elite and mainstream policy discourse remained cloaked in the language of better regulation and management of market forms with a continued commitment to private ownership as the more efficient form of service delivery. In the USA and the UK the appointment of executives from the very banking sector that had caused the crisis to oversee stabilisation efforts and run the newly nationalised companies (Brummer, 2009) reinforced the point about the ability of financial and political elites to capture the mainstream economic discourse and ultimately the solutions to the crisis (Crouch, 2011; Blyth, 2013; Mirowski, 2013).

In effect, nationalisation changed very little. Not only was it used to save the financial classes from their own recklessness in 'blowing up' the economy (Harvey, 2010) but arguably it reinforced inequalities and deeply rooted power structures in the global economy (Panitch and Gindin, 2009). 'Socialism for the rich, capitalism for the poor' became a useful aphorism to encapsulate the way that in our contemporary economy profits have been privatised while losses and incidences of market failure are socialised. Nationalisation was used to allow the public sector to absorb bad debts from 20 years of financial market deregulation and subsequent hyper-speculative Ponzi-style capitalism. Seven years on from the financial crisis, a global elite has used the previously ridiculed policy of nationalisation to save the banking system from its own vices, while the ideology of 'the market' and the other two neoliberal tropes of 'private enterprise' and 'competition' seem to have emerged remarkably unscathed by events. Indeed, the austerity policies now being visiting upon much of Europe have re-embraced these failed nostrums while corporate and financial capital are restructuring and getting on with the job of accumulating profits and appropriating wealth.

For seasoned observers, there is no mystery to all this. As the veteran economic historian Douglas Dowd has pointed out, free market principles and neoclassical economics serve the distinct purpose of producing theories that can entrench the power of elites and vested interests (Dowd, 2000). If the left were to capitalise upon the brief 'nationalisation moment' of 2009 it would have needed to have built up, through a Gramscian war of position, a far more effective alternative economic vision and political mobilisation than is currently on offer. In the heartlands of capitalism – throughout Western Europe and North America – the very opposite had been happening. Dominant parties of the centre-left had spent the past decade and a half learning to love the market, particularly financial markets, and embrace neoliberal nostrums, notably privatisation (Cumbers, 2012, ch 3). The hegemony of corporate interests over the political classes was such that Labour

Chancellor of the Exchequer, Alistair (now Lord) Darling, showed little knowledge of history let alone socialism when he reassured business that nationalisation would be a temporary and necessary evil to get the neoliberal show back on the road:

> It is better for the Government to hold on to Northern Rock for a temporary period and as and when market conditions improve the value of Northern Rock will grow and therefore the taxpayer will gain. The long-term ownership of this bank must lie in the private sector. (Cumbers, 2012, p 97)

The grip of neoliberal tenets on ruling elites should come as no surprise but there is a surprising lack of alternative discourse on the economy among those identifying with a left-wing project. The dangers of this intellectual vacuum are clearly manifest as the free market right has successfully reasserted its grip on the mainstream of public debate (Mirowski, 2013; Blyth, 2013). In the UK, media discussion moved with frightening speed from the perceived immorality of the financial 'masters of the universe' to a renewed assault on the growing public sector deficit that had mushroomed following the financial sector bailouts (see Figure 11.1). In both the 2010 and 2015 UK general elections, all three UK mainstream parties signed up to the policy of cutting the deficit, the only difference being how far and how fast. However, the recent impressive left-wing mobilisation around the Scottish independence referendum, the rise of the Corbyn left-wing project within the Labour Party, further afield the rise of Syriza, Podemos and even the success of the US mobilisation around Bernie Sanders' presidential bid suggest a greater public appetite for a radical alternative.

Seeds of an alternative: emergent forms of democratic public ownership

Beyond the financial crisis and the tightening grip of the austerity agenda on policy agendas in the global north, there have been some interesting developments elsewhere. In Latin America a number of governments, municipal authorities and social movements have started down the path of attempting to reclaim their economies from multinational corporations and private profit to construct alternatives based around more collective ethics and values. Evoking the solidarity economy (see North and Scott Cato, 2016), public ownership has returned to the fore as part of these initiatives debates, with nationalisation agendas being pursued in Argentina, Bolivia, Ecuador, Venezuela and Uruguay – the latter becoming the first country in the world to legalise and nationalise marijuana. Bolivia and Ecuador have also instigated national constitutional frameworks for the recuperation of common lands and rights by indigenous groups across the region.

Figure 11.1 UK public debt as a proportion of GDP

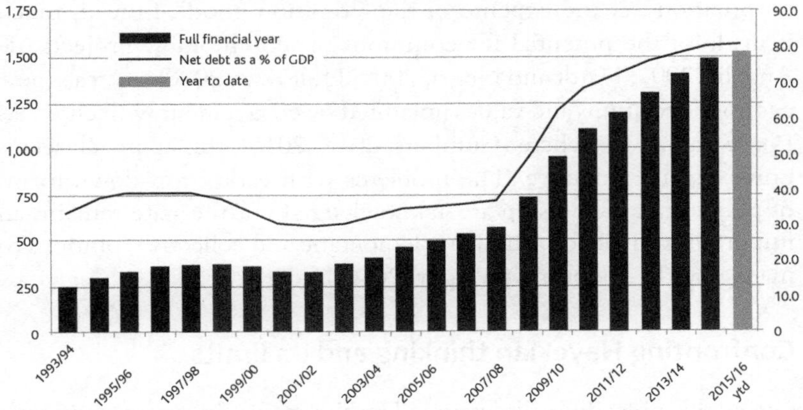

Source: ONS 2016.

Public ownership at the local level is also back on the policy agenda in the global North with significant remunicipalisation trends (Cumbers, 2016) – taking formerly privatised utility sectors back under local government control. Water services have come back under public control in France, Germany and even 58 cities in the US, not normally considered bastions of municipal socialism, such as Houston and Atlanta. Critically, such developments – often involving very diverse political identities – all recognise the importance of public and collective municipal ownership as policy tools and interventions. Local political actors are gradually acknowledging the importance of securing control of key resources and assets, taking these back from private rent-seeking interests to facilitate forms of more sustainable local development, in both the economic and environmental senses.

Despite such hopeful stirrings in the local, public policy arena, critical left-wing thinking on public ownership remains thin on the ground. Why is this? In part, this state of affairs can be traced to the influence of postmodern and anti-foundationalist thinking about the grand narrative and the distrust of socialist solutions that ended up being totalitarian rather than liberating. Partly it also reflects the failings of older, more centralised forms of public ownership. Much new thinking on the left has tended to dismiss the state as an avenue for progressive and radical reform, railing against both public ownership and private ownership (e.g. Hardt and Negri, 2009; Holloway, 2010) because both are viewed as forms through which resources and knowledge are appropriated on behalf of certain powerful interests, either state elites or private corporations, at the expense of the 'common good'. Instead, much is made of the potential for commons or 'commoning' projects (de Angelis, 2007; Hardt and Negri, 2009; Holloway, 2010) to create new economic relations and values untainted by engagement with elites. As I have argued elsewhere (Cumbers, 2012, 2015), this approach seems unnecessarily reductive. The problems with earlier top–down forms of public state ownership are acknowledged but the state remains an important vehicle for achieving democratic and collective solutions to managing the economy (Wright, 2010; Sader, 2011).

Confronting Hayekian thinking and its limits

Given the preceding discussion, Hayek's powerful critique of state planning and public ownership might not seem the most obvious place to start. However, in rethinking public ownership, it is important that we engage with this assessment as much of it occupies the same ground as these critiques on the autonomous left. We are now fairly familiar with the limits to Hayekian market utopias, which have been exposed through detailed examination of the effects of privatisation policies. In spite of the evident failings of policies of privatisation and marketisation, as we have seen, ruling elites have successfully resuscitated them. An important reason for this revival is that the left has critiqued neoliberalism but has not responded effectively to the powerful Hayekian critique of older forms of socialism, central planning and state ownership.

Whatever the problems of Hayek's free market vision in promoting individual liberty and democracy, his critique of planned economies under universal state ownership remains prescient, powerful and ultimately compelling. For an economic system to be democratic requires a level of devolved decision making, variety and choice which is simply not present under centrally imposed planning regimes. As Geoff Hodgson has put it in his excellent book on the subject:

No convincing scheme for durable economic decentralisation has been proposed, without the equivalent decentralisation of the powers to make contracts, set prices, and exchange products and property rights, through markets or other forms of property exchange. This does not mean that markets are regarded as optimal or ideal, nor that an entire economy is made subject to 'market forces'. It does mean, however, that markets and exchange are necessary to sustain genuine economic pluralism and diversity. (Hodgson, 1999, p 31)

One does not have to fully embrace Hodgson's endorsement of market solutions to recognise the salience of the wider point being made here about the importance of decentred forms of economic governance to tackle the central accretion of power that marked both market and planned utopias in the 20th century. Nor does it automatically become an argument for a radical green or anarchist, localist political economy. Instead, what is critical here is the importance of pluralism, diversity and tolerance of difference in creating more democratic forms of economy.

But the key point here echoes those of Johal, Moran and Williams in Chapter Nine and Jones (1995). In reimagining a publicly owned economy we should not be drawn into a totalising vision around a single dominant model or form – whether it is within or outside the state. Here, I take a deliberately broad definition of public ownership and prefer the term to that of commons or common ownership. The use of the term 'public' is advocated in opposition to 'private' in relation to economic ownership and the social relations that underpin the economy. For the pursuit of public ownership in its strongest sense implies an economy which is primarily owned collectively and, more important, subject to collective forms of decision making in opposition to private or, increasingly, corporate or financialised forms of ownership; which under capitalism involve the appropriation of both resources and labour for particular interests. Taking the three pillars of capitalism as the wage relationship, private property relations and the market, then all forms of collective ownership that seek to disturb and intervene in these spheres need analysis. Thus the concept of public ownership deployed is framed within a 'thin' version of socialism, which does not envisage one dominant all-encompassing model (see Cullenberg, 1992; Burczak, 2006; Cumbers and McMaster, 2010). By this, I mean that it involves certain principles – notably collective and democratic forms of ownership and the pursuit of more egalitarian social relations – but recognises that these can take diverse forms that respect local economic conditions and contexts.

Principles for constructing democratic public ownership

From these observations, five key principles for a broadly conceived democratic approach to public ownership arise. The first is the commitment to a 'fuzzy' but still egalitarian notion of the common good, which takes forward enlightenment ideals but does not seek to impose these universally in time and space. Critical here is the recognition of the conflict between the common good – in terms of using assets and resources for social needs – and vested interests that seek to appropriate resources for private gain and exchange value. The nature of this contest changes in time and space, but the ultimate underlying vision of upholding social and environmental justice through the common good does not. This notion of 'the common' employed here should be open both in its spatial imaginary – appealing to progressive rather than regressive localism – and its temporal vision of intergenerational and therefore sustainable management of resources.

A second principle relates to the importance of ownership. Collective ownership is not just important in the old Marxist sense of giving the workers or producers control over their labour but in the much wider sense of using resources for the benefit of the community as a whole. George DeMartino's work is very instructive here for the importance of 'appropriative justice' as class justice (DeMartino, 2003). Those who appropriate the surplus arising from the economy not only exploit the rest of us – arguably consumers as much as producers – but decide what is done with that surplus. In other words, they control investment decisions and the future shape of the economy. Taking this power back under public and collective control is arguably the most important set of economic issues facing society today – most evident in the battle to change direction over climate change.

Third, we need a commitment to dispersed decision making. Some of the most compelling critiques of nationalisation and public ownership in the 20th century, from writers as diverse as Hayek, Hodgson and Holloway, focused on the strong tendency to centralise and concentrate powers in party and state bureaucracies far removed from the everyday lives of workers and consumers. Both knowledge problems and alienation, a fusing of Marxist and Hayekian concerns, resulted. However, addressing this defect should not be interpreted automatically as a commitment to localism and decentralisation per se. There will remain the need for planning and ownership at higher geographical scales, but these in turn need not necessarily be overwhelmingly concentrated within particular places, organisations or social groups. What it does require is a commitment to the decentring of knowledge and decision-making power wherever possible both in geographical and functional terms. Within any territorial form of political governance, the key decision-making functions for different economic activities can and should be dispersed. Despite some recent devolution, we might contrast favourably here the decentralised and federalised polity of post-1945 Germany with the growing concentration of political and economic power in the UK around London and the south east of England.

A fourth principle concerns the importance of diversity, pluralism and tolerance in accepting different versions of collectivism and mutualism. One of the big failings of both the revolutionary and the reformist socialist traditions in the 20th century was their rejection of older forms of collectivism, particularly those from more conservative and religious underpinnings (for example, Macfarlane, 1996). Yet I would argue that there are strong possibilities for coalition and alliance building: bringing together statist commitment to public ownership with older localist collective and cooperative perspectives – as recognised by early left-wing thinkers like Klaus Kautsky and Otto Neurath, German socialists with otherwise opposing views (see Cumbers, 2012, pp 154–155).

A final critically important principle is developing ownership forms that allow public debate, discourse and collective learning processes. Many of today's problems are not just about the colonisation of economic decision making by an elite but its consequences for public participation and engagement in the economy. It is naïve to expect all of the public to take an interest in economics just because things become more collectively owned. However, we can at the same time develop institutional forms of public ownership that help spread participation and knowledge about the economy and its functioning. Many recognise economic decision making under neoliberal hegemony as increasingly characterised by post-political, technocratic discourse (Ranciere, 2001). Countering this removal of the economic sphere from democratic discourse (Crouch, 2004), means calling forth the kind of radical deliberative and participatory democracy envisaged by the great US radical pragmatist philosopher John Dewey (1927).

Dewey famously engaged with Water Lippman, for many the founder of modern political public relations. In the 1920s, in the wake of World War I, Lippman had cautioned against the limits of democracy, distrusting the masses to make informed and competent choices, arguing instead that democracy should be limited to electing more informed experts – an elite political class in effect. Dewey vehemently disagreed, arguing that:

> No government by experts in which the masses do not have the chance to inform the experts as to their needs can be anything but an oligarchy managed in the interests of the few ... The world has suffered more from leaders and authorities than from the masses. (Morris and Shapiro, 1993, p 187)

What this means for us here is that economic decision making should not stand outside of the greater public. It should be firmly embedded within ongoing and evolving processes of public deliberation, knowledge formation and collective learning: 'The essential need, in other words, is the improvement of the methods and conditions of debate, discussion and persuasion. That is the problem of the public' (Morris and Shapiro, 1993, p 187). By the late 1920s Dewey's political critique was aimed at liberalism rather than socialism. He attacked the way that an 18th century progressive doctrine, concerned with liberty and emancipation from the elite structures and interests of feudalism and clericalism could by the 20th century have become a conservative doctrine to bolster the interests of capitalist ruling classes (see Westbrook, 1991). Liberals had treated basic philosophical tenets as absolute whereas Dewey's radical pragmatism cautioned of the need for historical specificity and awareness of changing social and economic circumstances and an ongoing commitment to public debate and engagement. The same critique can also be levelled at the failings of socialism in the 20th century. If cast in stone and unable to confront technical and practical inadequacies in changed circumstances then rigid and outmoded models and practices both bolster elite interests and render progressive ideals redundant. Dealing with this danger requires a commitment to radical democratic processes of enquiry and knowledge exchange and a more flexible sense of what public ownership might constitute on the ground.

Constructing economic democracy: learning from actually existing alternatives

Implementing these principles in practice is of course another set of challenges. It amounts to the need for a long Gramscian war of position in opposition to existing neoliberal economic policy configurations. However, some useful examples from already existing alternatives illustrate the diversity of forms for a more democratic public ownership. Here, I briefly discuss three of these: the Norwegian experience of state-owned oil resources; the Danish renewable energy transition organised around localised forms of collective ownership; and Germany's recent experience of energy remunicipalisation.

Although Norwegian oil policy has partly been captured by elite interests in recent years, in the 1970s it developed as the most progressive and inclusive models of energy development ever seen (Ryggvik, 2010). Its experience is particularly interesting here because of the nature of state intervention, public ownership and democratic participation. The first North Sea oil discoveries in the 1960s adopted an approach having much in common with Third World countries in dealing with the power of the international oil cartel: setting up a nationalised entity for joint ventures with multinationals and, over time, indigenous expertise. This 'top-down' model of state ownership was led initially by elite groups within the central state apparatus. However, as the magnitude of oil resources became apparent, a much more wide-ranging debate over the impact of oil on Norwegian society and culture developed, going beyond narrow economic considerations. In the process, some interesting institutions and mechanisms embedded oil development within a more deliberative and democratic framework allowing more progressive agendas. (These issues are covered in much greater detail in Cumbers, 2012, ch 8; Rygvvik, 2010.) The main means for the exercise of an independent Norwegian oil policy was the creation of a state-owned entity Statoil in 1972. The new company was neither particularly democratic nor radical, but was a classic post-1945 state corporation run by executives at arm's length from government control. Nevertheless some important institutional configurations were developed around it that had the effect of embedding Statoil within wider public deliberation and discourse. The first was the creation of a Petroleum Directorate as a separate organisational actor to Statoil charged with administering, regulating and controlling oil and gas resources independently of the oil companies. From the early 1980s onwards this facilitated development of the safest offshore oil and gas regime in the world. But the Directorate also developed its own professional and technical expertise in all oil matters.

A second feature was what became known as the Paragraph 10 clause in the legislation that created Statoil. It stipulated the company presentation of an annual report to parliament on 'significant issues relating to principles and policy' (Ryggvik, 2010, p 100). Consequently the company and the broader impact of oil on Norway was opened up to scrutiny for broader civil society. A whole series of committees in the Storting (Norwegian Parliament) set up their own consultation exercises, including Social Affairs, Foreign Affairs and Local Government, to consider all aspects of oil development. This process drew upon a diverse range of knowledge and expertise from all sectors of civil society, including professional associations, fishing and farming interests, church groups and trade unions. Overall this impressive process of wide-ranging deliberation on questions of oil policy as well as collective learning meant that many parliamentarians also developed extensive knowledge of oil affairs. The outcome was a set of quite radical proposals, particularly when compared to the experience of oil development elsewhere. Proposals included government commitment to a 'socialised' model of oil, key elements of which were the priority that oil should create a 'qualitatively better society' and crucially a 'moderate rate of oil extraction' (Ryggvig, 2010, pp 34, 35) with a 90 million tonne ceiling that was not breached until the early 1990s. Additionally, emphasis was put on developing the resource in the most environmentally friendly manner, as well as using revenues to boost the country's spending on international development.

Denmark's emergence as a global leader in renewable energy (see Cumbers, 2012, ch 9) has taken a different form to the Norwegian experience. Though based upon public ownership and planned interventions it is neither a top-down state-driven process nor a grassroots achievement. Instead, it reflects a combination of national state interventions, grassroots social mobilisation and a diversified set of public ownership arrangements operating at different geographical scales.

The shift towards renewable energy reflected the country's attempt to escape foreign oil dependency in the 1970s (Cumbers, 2012). Much of the country's political and business establishment favoured nuclear power as an alternative to oil, but was opposed by a coalition of green, left-wing and rural communities around an alternative vision of a more localised, decentred model based on renewable energy. Important factors that probably helped to tip the balance away from nuclear were the continuing tradition of interest in wind power as an alternative, and engineering and scientific communities able to showcase the viability of non-nuclear technologies in a populist way: generating an alternative discourse around 'clean' and 'pure' energy.

By 1980 the Danish government had embarked upon a decisive strategy in support of renewables, emphasising decentred and localised forms of collective ownership based on three critical pillars of government policy.

- First, government funding for 30% of all investment in new wind turbines between 1980 and 1990, substantially boosted Danish windpower producers.
- Second, the 'Energipakken' requirement for electricity distribution companies to purchase annual quotas of energy supply from renewable producers was strengthened through a 1993 amendment to the Renewable Energy Act for a 'feed-in' fixed-price tariff for 'green energies' of 84% of a utility's production and distribution costs.
- Third, and most pertinent here, the encouragement of local and collective ownership of turbines, largely through laws known as 'residency criteria' or distance regulation laws, limiting ownership of wind turbines to residents of the municipality where the turbine is built.

Despite recent relaxation of these ownership laws, they gave critical political momentum to localised and collective forms of ownership which have had long-lasting effects. Wind turbine ownership remains dominated by either small-scale forms of private ownership, typically partnerships between local neighbours, or cooperative forms. The first Danish onshore 'wind farms', as larger scale activities that supplied more than a local neighbourhood, were all cooperatively owned. At its height in the late 1990s, it was estimated that 150,000 families or around 10% of the population were involved (Cumbers, 2012).

Together, the 'distance regulation' laws, state support for renewables and the localist and collectivist traditions of Danish society have been important in both dispersing economic power and creating the conditions for greater public participation, deliberation and economic democracy in energy. Particularly interesting is the emergence of a coalition that fuses older rural traditions of cooperative associations with more contemporary forms of local public ownership. An interesting hybrid form has been the ownership of the *Middelgrunden* wind farm off the coast of Copenhagen by a special-purpose public entity part owned by the city council with 50% owned by a residents' cooperative.

My final and more recent example comes from Germany's trend towards energy sector remunicipalisation with over 100 contracts for energy distribution networks or service delivery returned to the public sector since 2000 (Cumbers, 2016). As elsewhere, dissatisfaction with the consequences of privatisation has largely accounted for the return of local utility companies to public hands. The impressive scale of new enterprises, 72 new public energy companies since 2005, is matched by the diversity and innovation in forms of collective ownership. These range from new local state-run entities, such as Hamburg Energie, set up in 2009 by the Green Party in its then coalition with the CDU in the city government, to smaller scale rural cooperatives – *Genossenschaft* – found throughout the former West Germany.

There is nothing necessarily radical or even democratic about these developments. Many were undertaken by the same class of mainstream, Christian Democratic Union (CDU) and Social Democratic Party (SDP), politicians that privatised originally. For many city and local governments, remunicipalisation is primarily aimed at regaining control of revenue-producing assets during a period of heightened fiscal austerity and welfare retrenchment. There is also the local commitment to tackling climate change (Cumbers, 2016). However, something interesting is happening here that has broader lessons for how we begin to reverse neoliberalism and develop more democratic and collective forms of economy. The growth in local collective ownership, both through new *stadtwerke* but also smaller cooperatives, has facilitated public engagement and participation in the process of low carbon transition. Underpinned by considerable political mobilisation, citizen initiatives are beginning to contest neoliberalism and articulate alternatives in the largest German cities like Berlin and Hamburg (see for example Becker et al, 2015). The growth of massive campaigns and movements attest the degree to which individual and collective ownership draw citizens into the movement for low carbon transition and the battle against climate change. Both personal commitment and important socialised and collective learning processes are forged around important goals that develop a public policy agenda for the common good.

Conclusion

In a harsh global political and economic environment the prospects for progressive democratic alternatives seem remote. Yet it is important to emphasise that forms of public ownership are alive and well. With the right political will and social mobilisation, these can be used to counteract the worst excesses of neoliberalism and austerity. The resuscitation of nationalisation to save the world's financial sector from its own excesses, in the midst of its own self-induced crisis, shows the potential but also the problems inherent in bringing in public ownership to correct the inevitable contradictions and market failures of mainstream economic doctrine. A critical aspect of my argument is the need to rethink our basic understanding of public ownership in terms of radical democracy and social empowerment to deal with the left's current predicament.

In particular, we need to rethink the basic structures, institutions and ownership forms required for a more collectively owned democratic economy. Perhaps controversially, I argue here and elsewhere (e.g. Cumbers, 2012, 2014) that this needs a response to Hayek's devastating critique of older forms of state ownership and planning to challenge neoliberals' linkage of liberty, markets and private property. The response should be a radical democratic project of public ownership with greater pluralism and diversity in developing coalitions around the common good, even working with older and more conservative traditions of mutualism and cooperative practice.

Despite contemporary alienation and disengagement from the economy, this project also requires the development of greater public engagement, collective learning and knowledge formation in the economy. The global economy is largely owned by elites, but even where we have forms of state ownership, they lack the public deliberation and democratic scrutiny that might afford more progressive forms of decision making. Current examples illustrated here from Norway, Denmark and Germany all show the potential of more participatory and democratic forms of public ownership for forging new economic relations. They also illustrate that not one model but a diversity of forms of collective ownership are required in time and space to encourage open and collective learning economies

Finally, however modest we are about accepting the limits to utopias and grand narratives, the progressive project must find ways of reinventing some notion of the common good. In other words, a radical and egalitarian environmental and social justice project that challenges appropriation of the economy, its assets and resources, by elite and vested interests. Those interests and antagonisms vary in time and space, but they remain the basic tension underpinning the global capitalist economy – in Marx's terms the conflict between private appropriation and the collective public sphere.

References

Becker, S., Beveridge, R. and Naumann, M. (2015) 'Remunicipalization in German cities: Contesting neoliberalism and reimagining urban governance?', *Space and Polity* 19:76-90.

Blyth, M. (2013) *Austerity: The history of a dangerous idea*, New York: Routledge.

Brummer, A. (2009) 'Mr Brown's Bankers', *New Statesman*, 22 January, http://www.newstatesman.com/economy/2009/01/government-banks-bankers

Burczak, T. (2006) *Socialism after Hayek*, Ann Arbor: University of Michigan Press.

Crouch, C. (2004) *Post-democracy*, Cambridge: Polity Press.

Crouch, C. (2011) *The strange non-death of neoliberalism*, Cambridge: Polity.

Cullenburg, S. (1992) 'Socialism's burden: Toward a "thin" definition of socialism', *Rethinking Marxism*, 5: 64–83.

Cumbers, A. (2012) *Reclaiming public ownership: Making space for economic democracy*, London: Zed.

Cumbers, A. (2014) 'Responding to Hayek from the left: Beyond market socialism on the path to a radical economic democracy' in G. Nell (ed) *Austrian theory and economic organization: Pushing beyond free market boundaries*, New York: Palgrave Macmillan.

Cumbers, A. (2015) 'Constructing a global commons in, against and beyond the state', *Space and Polity*, 19: 62–75.

Cumbers, A. (2016) 'Remunicipalisation, low carbon transition and energy democracy' in Worldwatch Institute, *State of the world report 2016*, Washington, DC: Worldwatch Institute.

Cumbers, A. and McMaster, R. (2010) 'Socialism, knowledge, the instrumental valuation principle and the enhancement of individual dignity', *Economy and Society*, 39 (2): 247–270.

DeMartino, G. (2003) 'Realizing class justice', *Rethinking Marxism*, 15: 1–31.

Dewey, J. (1927) *The problem of the public*, New York: Holt.

De Angelis, M. (2007) *The beginning of history: Value struggles and global capital*, London: Pluto.

Dowd, D. (2000) *Capitalism and its economics*, London: Pluto.

Graeber, D. (2013) *The democracy project, a history, a crisis, a movement*, London: Allen Lane.

Hardt, M. and Negri, A. (2009) *Commonwealth*, Cambridge, MA: Harvard University Press.

Harvey, D. (2003) *Accumulation by dispossession*, Oxford: Oxford University Press.

Harvey, D. (2010) *The enigma of capital and the crises of capitalism*, London: Profile.

Hayek, F. (1944) *The Road to Serfdom*, Chicago, IL: University of Chicago Press

Hayek, F. A. (1979) 'The political order of a free people', *Law, legislation and liberty* (Vol 3), Chicago: University of Chicago Press.

Hodgson, G. (1999) *Economics and Utopia*, London: Routledge.

Holloway, J. (2002) *Changing the world without taking power: The meaning of revolution today*, London: Pluto.

Holloway, J. (2010) *Crack capitalism*, London: Pluto.

Jones, B. (1995) 'Common ownership: Asset or relic?', *Renewal*, 1: 55-61.

Macfarlane, L. (1996) 'Socialism and common ownership: An historical perspective' in P. King (ed) *Socialism and the common good*, London: Frank Cass.

Mason, P. (2012) *Why it's kicking off everywhere: The new global revolutions*, London: Verso.

Mirowski, P. (2013) *Never let a serious crisis go to waste: How neoliberalism survived the financial meltdown*, London: Verso.

Morris, D. and Shapiro, I. (eds) (1993) *John Dewey: The political writings*, Minneapolis: Hackett.

North, P. and Scott Cato, M. (eds) (2016) *Towards just and sustainable economies: The social and solidarity economy North and South*, Bristol: Policy Press.

ONS database, https://www.ons.gov.uk/economy/ governmentpublicsectorandtaxes/publicsectorfinance/timeseries/ hf6x/pusf

Panitch, L. and Gindin, S. (2009) 'From global finance to the nationalization of the banks: Eight theses on the economic crisis', *The Bullet: Socialist Project*: http://www.socialistproject.ca/bullet/ bullet189.html

Rancière, J. (2001) 'Ten theses on politics', *Theory and Event*, 5 (3).

Ryggvik, H. (2010) *The Norwegian oil experience: A toolbox for managing resources?*, Oslo: Centre for Technology, Innovation and Culture.

Sader, E. (2011) *The new mole: Paths of the Latin American left*, London: Verso.

Westbrook, R.B. (1991) *John Dewey and American democracy*, Ithaca, NY: Cornell University Press.

Wright, E.O. (2010) *Envisioning real utopias*, London: Verso.

TWELVE

Turning the tide: a role for social movements

Bryn Jones and Mike O'Donnell

The Introduction to this book emphasised that the adoption of a few disparate policy alternatives will not shift the dominant neoliberal paradigm. Nor can displacement be achieved by a Damascene conversion of a handful of senior politicians and policy makers. Nor, we must concede, solely by illuminating ideas and prescriptions from academics and commentators. Historically, shifts of the sociopolitical consensus 'at the top' have involved the intermeshing of all of these actors with the aims and beliefs of broader social movements. Social movement can be defined as groups of people pursuing a shared cause or grievance requiring some social change and/or material or other gain. Activists may be closely or loosely organised – typically these days via the Web.

The rise of classical liberalism in the 19th century was propelled by the ideas and manifestos of campaigns by movements such as Chartism, Free Trade and anti-slavery. More recently, principles of the Keynesian-social democratic paradigm, which defined the policies and institutions making up the welfare state, were seeded, debated and promoted through the labour movement. Even the political acceptability of some of today's progressive causes, such as environmental responsibility, women's rights and anti-discriminatory practice can be tracked back to the so-called 'new social movements' stemming from the cultural ferment of the 1960s.

So what, if anything can the social movements of the early 21st century contribute towards alternative politics and economics to replace neoliberalism? To answer this question we briefly survey the tenor and aims of the most potent or influential, contemporary social movements. This account, in turn, presupposes a short history of their development. After these assessments we evaluate the transformative potential of relevant social movements with particular reference to their interactions with the political sphere. Some social movements have, for decades, been combining a critique of neoliberalism's globalisation dimension, with concrete proposals and attempts to develop alternatives. After 2008, and with the partial collapse of the globalisation hubris, some of these ideas and the activists promoting them have been devolving towards national issues and problems.

Distinctiveness and origins

The Occupy and Indignados activities of 2011 in the Western world were not simply expressions of protest. They also rechannelled ideas and practices from earlier anti and 'alter' globalisation campaigns back to formerly affluent metropolitan economies. These reoriented movements have in turn inspired and helped propel both local and national campaigns for sociopolitical change. The conjunction of the Greek *aganaktismeni* protesters with the Syriza political alliance is perhaps the most prominent example of a national catalyst. But many more subnational campaigns, targeting the poverty, homelessness and indebtedness of specific communities have also appeared and grown. The question is whether most of these national and local movements embody mainly negative opposition and rejectionist ideologies, such as nihilistic anarchism. Or, alternatively, have they developed at least the seeds of a paradigm capable of superseding national centres of neoliberalism?

From the early 1990s to the present the upsurge of newer social movements has been wide-ranging: student, housing, tax justice, anti-fracking, migrant rights, anti-austerity, corporate accountability and anti-sexist women's rights being the most prominent. Their beliefs and explicit aims cross most of the ideological and political spectrum. The most common feature is that they operate significantly outside of the conventional party and parliamentary system, although they often demand action from it. In Spain and Greece anti-austerity and avowedly anti-neoliberal movements have been important drivers of the formation of political parties, such as Spain's Podemos party. In other countries, such as Britain, the movements have not gained a distinct presence within the party system. However, the still unfolding relationship between the British Labour Party and social movements, fired by the unexpected leadership candidacy of veteran left-wing MP Jeremy Corbyn, involved tens of thousands of apparent activists in the Labour Party and helped secure his victory.

The historical antecedent of this recent upsurge can be traced back the 1960s and 1970s campaigns for minority rights, including those of women, gay people and ethnic minorities, the pursuit of peace and a politicisation of environmental causes. Indeed, for one commentator on the new Greek movements, the recent upsurges 're-start the 1968 cycle' (Douzinas, 2015). Major aims of this current phase are the deepening and extension of demands for both equality and democratic participation. The (re)emergence of direct action groups, such as UK Uncut, or online campaigners, such as 38 Degrees, illustrate the wave of interest and experiment in more direct forms of democratic engagement – as do some developments in mainstream politics such as the interaction between Jeremy Corbyn and grassroots activists. The multidimensional approach to equality encompasses ethnicity, gender, age, disabilities and – increasingly with the recession and austerity – the reversal of economic inequalities. Analysts conventionally differentiated the post-1960s 'new' social movements from the 'old' social movements, because the former prioritise cultural and identity equalities over the redistribution of resources and improvements in welfare, wages and working conditions championed by the 'old' labour and union movements. Over time, equality in the form of equal human rights, including equal protection under the law, became a mainstream political issue; whereas the democratisation aim stalled.

Between roughly 1990 and 2009, the focus of many campaigns and activists was on international inequalities and injustices. Many believed this approach was necessitated by an apparent transfer of power from the national to the global. As Saskia Sassen (2006, p 1) put it:

> globalization is taking place inside the national to a far larger extent than is usually recognised … an enormous variety of micro-processes … begin to denationalise what had been constructed as national – whether policies, capital, political subjectivities urban spaces, temporal frames, or any other variety of dynamics and domains.

The recent social protest waves in Britain need to be seen in relation to the ideas and strategies of these anti-globalisation campaigns. The internationalised movements opposing neoliberal globalisation have had no single formally organised coordinating body. But they have shared the idea of *alter*-globalisation: that 'a different world is possible' as a unifying aspiration and rallying call. Geoffrey Pleyers (2010, p 10) writes that the alter-globalisation movement established itself as 'a single integrated movement' from the early 1990s, albeit losing some impetus towards the end of the first decade of the new millennium.

Pleyers' influential analysis identifies three stages of this alter-globalisation movement: (1) an initial surge of opposition to neoliberalism among intellectuals and activists during the 1990s, with a climactic 1999 protest against the Seattle conference of the World Trade Organization; (2) a rapid growth in the size and organisation of the movement from 2000 to 2005, with more proactive stances such as a 'World Social Forum' from 2001 as a popular alternative to global elite convocations such as the Davos Forum, and huge demonstrations in Genoa (2001), Barcelona (2002) and worldwide against the war in Iraq (2003), widely perceived as a war to facilitate Western business investment in an oil-rich region; (3) a third, slowdown, phase of alter-globalisation from roughly 2005 to the end of the decade when the 'movement experienced several less than successful events and entered an irresolute phase' (Pleyers, 2010, p 9). Since this analysis, however, the alter-globalisation narrative after the 2007–8 crash took another twist in the surge of popular protest movements against inequality and poverty in Europe and the United States as well as opposition to authoritarianism in 'the Arab Spring' states and elsewhere. This apparent, post-crisis, fourth phase is refocusing on in/equality, anti-austerity and democracy in response to elite mismanagement and corruption on an even larger scale than previously in the West.

Some nongovernmental organisations (NGOs) and international nongovernmental organisations (INGOs) overlap with the wider, more informal social movements in their radical and humanitarian activism and goals. Some NGOs are effectively social movement organisations (SMOs). INGOs such as Greenpeace and Amnesty International have been as engaged and arguably as effective as less formally organised activist groups. Although in some cases NGOs' sources of funding and their own investment of self-interest in charitable work has provoked criticism (see Mowles, 2007). With the post-2008 regression of the affluent 'northern' economies to similar problems encountered in less developed societies, some SMOs have been reapplying their perspectives to countries such as the UK. Their social democratic content is clearly stronger than much present mainstream politics. They are also more ambitious in targeting the neoliberal stronghold in financial institutions. Behemoths against which the mainstream left, even the more radical new Labour leadership, has been more circumspect.

As well as the above periodisation, Pleyers offers a useful distinction within social movement activities – one following what he terms 'the way of subjectivity' and the other 'the way of reason'. Those tending to the former 'construct themselves ... through performances and lived experiences'. They 'assert their creativity and their subjectivity understood as the affects, emotions and thoughts raised by the will to think and to act by oneself'. By contrast, the way of reason 'passes through objective, quantifiable and technical content ... acquired through training' (Pleyers, 2010, pp 35-36, 112). Rational movements seek alternatives to the dominant neoliberal system through intellectual and policy methods and perspectives: proposing more effective alternatives and probing for change through formal pressures on the established political system.

By contrast, the more subjective approach acts through a grassroots, bottom-up strategy of change which is wary of collaboration with sympathetic politicians and of compromising its fundamental values. Pleyers contends that both 'ways' can operate in the same movement, group or even individual with greater effectiveness when the two 'ways' combine (Pleyers, 2010, pp 260-263). International campaigning for women's rights is a particularly prominent and significant force within the global justice movement; and one which has, effectively, integrated the subjective with the rational. This movement has had some success in getting gender perspectives on the agendas of international governmental organisations. In so doing it identifies as 'feminist' principles of leadership 'based on non-hierarchical, democratic, inclusive and accountable practices' (BRIDGE, 2013, p 3), ideas which are fully congruent with the distinctive democratic ethos of the wider alter-globalisation movement.

More generally, the rationalist approach has, so far, been pursued through cooperation with, and even integration with, an established party of the left, and only occasionally through the founding of a new radical party. Pleyers advocates a more conscious and strategic approach to change combining the strengths of both 'ways'. Some vindication of this synthesis appeared in the initial successes of the Greek political coalition known as Syriza, whose main component organisation, SYN, explicitly aimed 'not to guide but participate in movements and try to influence them while learning from them' (Tsakatika and Eleftheriou, 2013, p 11). This relationship between formal politics and anti-neoliberal movements and organisations in the UK context is analysed in the final section of the chapter.

Radical social movements' aims after 2008

The growing appreciation of the stark facts of global inequality is not confined to politically aware social movement activists (See *New York Times*, April 20, April 27, May 3, May 10, May 18, May 31, June 7, June 14, June 21 2014, http://opinionator.blogs.nytimes.com/category/the-great-divide/). The long challenge for contemporary activists is to find ways to catalyse discontent into an effective strategy for major change. The iconic Occupy slogan 'the 1% and the rest' came out of Occupy Wall Street. Social scientists, including Thomas Picketty (2014) have since provided more substantial analysis and evidence supporting activists' gut sentiments. As in the United States, in Britain and elsewhere in Europe, notably Spain, Portugal and Greece, post-crisis public austerity programmes shifted some social movement focus from the plight of the global South to include the threat to economic and welfare rights in advanced economies, as well as to the flaws and limitations of Western democratic institutions.

Oxfam GB's work in Britain is an example of the potential range of action and influence of a large nongovernmental organisation, translating its 'third world' case for a rights-based approach to poverty and inequality to this country. Oxfam GB has campaigned to combat gender inequality by increasing rights and services for the many women in informal employment, such as home-working jobs. By the same token, it claims, asylum seekers and migrant workers should be given proper employment rights, with specialised education and information services and controls over abusive employers. More generally, Oxfam's campaigns make a critical connection between poverty and inequalities of power. 'People facing poverty', Oxfam argues, should have structured input into policy and decision-making . . . at UK, devolved and regional levels' (Oxfam 2005, p 1); echoing the Poverty Alliance demand that they should not be regarded as passive objects for discriminatory policymaking' (Poverty Alliance, 2014, p 3). Similar sentiments emerge in many social movement campaigns, such as those for corporate accountability (see Jones, in Chapter Eight).

The worldwide Occupy and Arab Spring protests gave almost unprecedented publicity to the themes of popular democracy and equality that had been developing in the alter-globalisation movement over a quarter of a century. Despite a capacity for populist slogans and sentiments ('the 99% against the 1%') these campaigns also imported, explicitly, the intellectual concept of neoliberal capitalism from the anti-globalisation movement into popular domestic politics (for example, http://occupywallstreet.net/tags/neoliberalism). The broadly anarchist form and strategy of Occupy (Gittlin, 2012, p 80) has remained highly influential. However, it is not now the dominant political-ideological and strategic approach of the anti-neoliberal movement in Britain and Europe more generally. The emphasis on radical participatory and egalitarian values and policies, embodied in the forums and decision making in the Occupy sites, has subsequently fed into mainstream political and social life – at least in cases such as the new parties of Podemos and Syriza and, less dramatically, in debates surrounding the British Labour Party leadership elections. Themes of participatory democracy, which social movement activists had found lacking in the main parliamentary parties, became more visible. Here is a young activist addressing a group of Labour Party members.

> The experience of organising along participatory lines, I suggested, had been an empowering one for many young people who know they are unlikely to experience the same thing within the stifling routines of party bureaucracies. Clearly this resonated with members of an organisation that has been gutted of democracy at the local and national level. (Aitchison, 2011)

The kind of direct action and mass participation campaigns of, respectively, UK Uncut and 38 Degrees is underpinned by broadly participatory democratic values. Although its own internal democracy is a work in progress, most supporters of the latter rally behind central initiatives while an embryonic network of local groups is still defining its relationship to the professional leadership.

While 38 Degrees and similar internet-based organisations illustrate the 'path of rationality', UK Uncut exemplifies Pleyers' 'path of subjectivity'. UK Uncut was actually a spiritual precursor to Occupy. Formed to oppose the public spending cuts of the Coalition government of 2010–15, it has brought public attention to the broader field of corporate neoliberalism. Focusing on the tax avoidance of large, high-profile retail companies such as the Arcadia group that includes Burton, Dorothy Perkins and Topshop, in December 2010 it occupied various Arcadia businesses forcing the temporary closure of over 50 stores. Loose organisation without official leaders enabled participants, using the internet to coordinate local actions, thereby giving indirect support to more 'rational' campaigns, such as Tax Justice.

In contrast, 38 Degrees is more oriented to conventional political reforming tactics; closer to being a non-profit NGO than a social movement network, it has salaried managers and full-time organisers. Nevertheless, there is a distinctively radical democratic ethos to its campaigning on causes such as opposition to neoliberal trade pacts like the Transatlantic Trade and Investment Partnership. It has coordinated campaigns ranging from a demand for a recall law enabling voters to remove MPs between elections to the registration of new voters. Claiming 2.5 million supporters, its main methods involve internet activity to gather petition signatures and, more recently, via semi-independent, offline groups, to promote local activism. It is unclear, however, whether such SMOs can, or even wish to connect this issue-oriented campaigning to the politics of systemic change for more democracy.

Since the 1999 Seattle protests, the power of 'the Web' has augmented and cemented the 'horizontalist', anti-hierarchical and participatory sentiments of subjectivist social movement activism. Although internet activism does not prevent the exercise of neoliberal power, Hilary Wainwright associates it with a 'growing scepticism of supposedly authoritative or official versions of events of recent decades' encouraging an increasing production of alternative versions and interpretations (Wainwright, 2010). The logic of these 'subjectivist' movements may have lessons for pathways between the centralised social democratic state and the market authoritarianism of corporate neoliberalism. Partly with the media in mind, the protests and campaigns emphasised the values to which grassroots activists and possibly like-minded citizens aspire on an everyday basis. In Habermas' lexicon they resonate with the lifeworld of communities, friendships and families which contrasts with the colder rationality of markets and bureaucracies.

A community-based network that has successfully blunted excesses of neoliberal economics is Citizens UK, which straddles the charity sector and grassroots campaigning. Inspired by the 1960s US activist Saul Alinksy, Citizens UK began as Citizens London, an alliance of local community groups, trade unions, mosques and churches. Citizens London campaigned for a London Living Wage in some of the most exploited jobs, such as cleaning; and also for affordable local housing. It was prominent in campaigns against the loss of social housing. Its 2015 Election Manifesto, to which all the main parties responded in a special hustings, featured distinctive anti-market policies on housing, employment and incomes. Expanding to become nationwide organisation as Citizens UK, it has been credited with shaming several big employers to cede higher than Minimum Wage awards.

> After several public actions over a period of three years, which threatened the reputation of the bank and its chairman, Sir John agreed to a meeting with TELCO leaders and HSBC implemented the Living Wage in May 2004. (Baskerville and Stears, 2010, p 68)

In 2015 then Chancellor of the Exchequer George Osborne surprised critics and pundits by embracing the Living Wage as government policy. The exact impact of this policy is, of course, debatable. However, Citizens UK's success in pushing back one of the worst excesses of neoliberal economics by community-based activism shows that social movement campaigning can be a promising platform for alternative policies and values. It is also significant that another of Citizens UK's manifesto demands was for an increase in participatory democracy. 'Community organising is democracy in action' (Citizens UK, 2015). Before the 2000, 2004 and 2008 London mayoral elections, Citizens London organised Accountability Assemblies with the main mayoral candidates. As Citizens UK, the network's growing support was reflected in an assembly before the 2010 General Election, which rallied an estimated 2500 (Parry et al, 2010).

London Citizens and Citizens UK have some of the same values, and possibly activists, as the global justice and sustainability campaigns, but in local rather than global campaigning. More generally there has been movement from the ephemeral focus to the continuous, with 'regular organisational practices ... citizens' organisations [that] are robust, rooted, and have continuity across time – so ... both the state and the market can be rendered more accountable and more susceptible to influence' (Baskerville and Stears, 2010).

Moving on from Occupy: social bases for political action

As suggested by Gilbert and Crouch (Chapters One and Ten), if they are to have a comparable impact to that of the 'old' labour movements on social democracy, today's social movements require a sociodemographic base. In other respects, there are obvious echoes of the 1960s in the cross between a sit-in and a commune of the 2011 protests. Occupy Wall Street, for example, attempted, not always successfully, to integrate values, ideas and practice holistically, thus modelling what a different society might look like (Gitlin, 2012; see also O'Donnell, 2008). As one participant claimed, many occupants were 'prefiguring the kind of society they want to live in' (Gitlin, 2012, p 73). Todd Gitlin, a former 1960s activist and President of the American Students for a Democratic Society (SDS), adopts the term 'anarchism' to describe his own half-century experience of American social movement radicalism. Anarchist and anarchist-influenced thinking also features prominently in Pleyers' 'subjective way' in some anti- and alter-globalisation movements. Occupy's distinctive aspect of 'mass' engagement has prompted the hybrid term 'anarcho-populist' (Gerbaudo, 2013), which captures both the democratic decentralism and search for mass appeal of Occupy. The prevalence of such themes as in Occupy Wall Street activist and academic David Graeber's *The Democracy Project* (2013) and Serbian activist Srdja Popovic's (non-violent) *Blueprint for Revolution* (2015) suggest that alternatives to neoliberalism's centralised state–corporate markets model could have considerable appeal if based on more expansive forms of democratic decision making.

Yet despite its occasional effectiveness mass protest has proved to be neither easily sustainable nor a reliable path to power for social movements in Europe or the Arab Spring countries. The question is whether these protest campaigns represent an atypical, radicalised minority or whether they are the vanguard of a broader social base. The new protests have been premised on the idea of an elite-mass division, which diverges from traditional Marxist class analysis by adopting the 1% versus 99% slogan. At a more theoretical level it opposes the 'mass' to 'globalising elites' (Gill, 2008), expressed in Di Muzio's (2015) thesis that government personnel blending with controllers of capital form part of a wider interlocking of business and financial, political, military and professional elites exercising global and/or national power (see also Williams, 2006; Stiglitz, 2015).

Di Muzio's more precise mapping distinguishes between the comfortable but relatively powerless 'millionaire next door', who just scrapes into the top global 1% from the world's most wealthy 10 billionaires (0.0000002%) and the total number of 1426 billionaires (0.00003%). These enjoy serious decision-making power and lifestyles increasingly detached from 'the rest', pitching their 'conspicuous consumption' into forms of media entertainment (Di Muzio, 2015, p 34).

As for the rhetorical 'mass', or the 99%, the vast majority of the world's population are obviously stratified in more complex ways than mere differences from the global elite. Guy Standing (2014, p vii) controversially merges Marxist and elite terminology by referring to an emerging 'mass class' which he terms 'the precariat'. Characterised by insecurity in relation to work and income/support, the precariat lacks a stable work status and effective political representation. On this basis the precariat would extend from the migrant workers in casual agricultural work to many sections of the middle class. As Gilbert's chapter explains, some of the latter may feel their life situation is precarious; and he may be objectively right as corporate employment and pay practices plus technological change threaten the security of middle-level technical, managerial and professional jobs. However, the social connections and 'social capital' of these groups may render them less vulnerable than more conventionally 'proletarian' types of worker.

Moreover, social justice campaigns have recognised that many of the world's poor and less affluent seldom or never work in standard wage-labour roles. Even if they have such work, they do not represent an organised working class: the historic Marxist agency of change.

Occupy and spin-off movements now focus on the development of similar insecurities in Europe and the United States. Unemployment among the 16-24 age group has consistently been about twice the rate of the national average since the 2007-8 crash and the situation is more acute in Greece, Spain and Portugal. According to a European Social Survey, already in Britain well over half of graduates do not get graduate calibre jobs (CIPD, 2015).

Youth may constitute a new dimension of inequality (Savage, 2015) but it is one that is multifaceted and variable. Moreover, despite the activism of a minority, as an entire age group, young people are as unlikely a main agency of change as the precariat, at least in Britain. The 1960s thesis that youth itself, particularly students, may be the main agent of change (Roszac, 1971) is even more implausible today. Young people are as socially divided as the rest of the population and are not exceptionally politically minded. Compared to the over-65s, political participation among the majority of the 18-24 age group is low, with less than half voting in the last general election. However, redistribution from the wealthy rather than older people as an age group, some of whom are among the poorest, is clearly a fairer and more tractable political project, if young people are among the substantial beneficiaries of appropriately targeted redistribution.

Despite differentiating internal conditions, widespread 'precarity' across sociodemographic groups at least among activists from such circumstances or protesting against them, may create overlapping circles of people. In line with the classical sociology of Simmel, common concerns and frequent association may, especially now with the assistance of the internet, gradually create a shared community of interest and identity (Diani, 2000). Could such groups act as a social vehicle to support or disseminate alternatives to neoliberalism? In a long-standing model of collective action and identity, the sociologist Michael Mann distinguished four key subjective dimensions for institution-changing action.

These dimensions were: a shared and distinctive identity, a recognition of opposed interests to those in positions of power, an understanding that these differences constituted a totality rather than unconnected institutions and, finally, some kind of vision of an alternative system of social or economic relationships. Although this IOTA model was conceptualised as a means of assessing organised working class movements, it can be relevant to contemporary social movement challenges to neoliberalism. In our judgement these movements score relatively highly in recognising opposed interests (the 99% versus the 1%) and the totality of neoliberal capitalism. However, the existence of a shared identity seems more problematic. Participants in social movements have multiple identities and a shifting web of ties which rarely fully overlap. Evidence of a coherent vision of an alternative system is also limited. On the other hand, such a vision also depends partly on models and proposals elaborated by intellectuals, politicians and movement leaders. The rise and ascendancy of socialist and social democratic paradigms, for example, came from the interaction of economic theories, ideological principles and experiments with collective institutions, such as cooperatives, community healthcare and public corporations.

The institutions most recently affected by neoliberal austerity are of major concern to most women, leading to distinctive feminist attempts to displace neoliberalism. Some feminists see neoliberal anti-state projects as resurgent patriarchy replacing social democratic entitlements: 'In its place we have a new articulation of neoliberalism and patriarchy. Neoliberalism has constructed itself in such a way that it depends on forms of male domination' (Massey and Rustin, 2012). From the same worldview, feminist writer Beatrix Campbell sees 'neoliberal neo-patriarchy' as immovable without 'a gender revolution' (Campbell, 2014). However, Walby (2015), along with other feminists, suggests that the resurgence of neoliberalism since the financial crash is reversing previous trends of a social democratic transition from a family-based gender regime, where women were confined mainly to childcare and domestic roles, to one where public programmes and rights supplemented or freed women from these roles. In this view, neoliberal austerity regimes are cutting or withdrawing such public support while women are still supposed to participate in increasingly exploitative labour markets.

As Walby (2015, pp 157-160, 177-178) explains, the insecurities, pressures and stresses on families, and women in particular, in this long hours/low pay situation should engender considerable support for a new, gender-focused social democratic programme. A slate of state-led support and rights for childcare, decent employment and more equal domestic roles have been proposed by the Women's Budget Group (see Box 12.1).

Box 12.1 Women's Budget Group
Plan F, a feminist strategy for economic recovery

*Gender budgeting into overall economic strategy for financial autonomy, inclusion, rather than fiscally determined exclusion in paid employment, prioritisation of care

*Fairer contribution from the wealthy, companies or taxation of financial transactions to reverse the most damaging spending cuts

*Adequate incomes for all women by reversing the cuts, freezes and caps to social security and tax credits upon which women rely for themselves and as carers

* Adequate incomes from paid employment to lift people out of poverty, lifting the minimum wage to a living wage and action to close the private sector gender pay gap, especially for part-time workers

* A fundamental reconceptualisation of social care services as social infrastructure

* Encourage social infrastructure investment as capital investment rather than current spending

* Equal benefits from the employment opportunities presented by investment in physical infrastructure (jobs and apprenticeships in construction, science and technology)

* Make these jobs more family friendly, and overcome gender stereotyping

* More women involved in economic decision making in the Cabinet, the Treasury, across spending departments plus voices of women from outside Westminster

Source: Annesley (2014).

Of course, influential neoliberal versions of feminism work against such movements. Aimed mainly at the middle and professional classes, these perspectives see women's opportunities as enhanced through successful competition in meritocratic labour markets. Here, women may even be expected to exploit their intrinsically feminine human capital to achieve individual goals (see Hakim, 2011). However, the US sociologist Nancy Fraser (2009, p 115) rebuts such discourses, arguing for campaigns and programmes and feminist cultures which

1. Bring back together the dimensions of redistribution, recognition and representation 'that splintered in the previous era';
2. break spurious neoliberal links between the family wage with the requirements of flexible capitalism, to press for a 'form of life that decentres waged work and valorizes uncommodified activities, including carework';
3. develop participatory democracy to rehabilitate the state and subordinate 'bureaucratic managerialism to citizen empowerment and so tame markets' .

These possibilities are examined in the UK context in the chapter by Crouch and in the Conclusion to this book. More generally, the rootedness of gender issues in the materialities of the lifeworld parallels and partly overlaps some of the environmental or 'green' challenges dissected by Benton in Chapter Three. Such proposals also mesh coherently with emphases both on an updating of social democratic principles and the new social movement expansion of equalities. The vehicles for propagating such values and demands are however less apparent. The scale of successive waves of feminism has entailed diverse initiatives so that there is not a single or inter-linked set of feminist social movement organisations. Denise Osted's Global List of Women's Organisations lists over 100 women's centres and organisations operating in the UK. The f-word website cites around 40 campaigning organisations (www.thefword.org.uk/2011/05/websites_organisations_and_charities_uk-based/).

The paradox of this diversity and the continuing power and relevance of traditional bodies means that campaigners for women's causes have to participate in these originally male institutions. Veteran feminist Beatrice Campbell summarises feminism as having:

> an institutional presence which is precarious, it is both there and not there, its impact depends on champions and consensus, its priorities always risk being lost in translation … mediated through other political parties, professional and workers' organisations constructed in the image and interests of men.

Suspending judgement on the more single focus Women's Equality Party, the feminist dynamic seems, therefore, to involve interdependent alliances in and with other social movements. Or, as Rahil Gupta (2012) argued in a critique of neoliberalised feminism: 'We need to get involved in the major movements of our time, to redraw the links, participate in Occupy London, fight religious fundamentalism as well as sexual violence, wage inequality and poverty. These may be old goals for a new culture.'

Social movements, political parties and the state

Social democratic and liberal parties in Britain have tended to see democracy in terms of conformity to established practices of parliamentary representation and accountability, replicated in local government. As Jones shows in Chapter Eight, social democratic institutions such as nationalised industries were designed with only token worker and consumer participation. Reforms have concentrated, at best, on replacement of Britain's undemocratic, semi-feudal institutions of patronage, such as the House of Lords. To put it mildly, representation of social movements within or in alliance with a party such as Labour has had a chequered history. It could also be argued that the Third Way neoliberalism of Tony Blair and his supporters was in lock-step with the suppression of the various gender, ethnic and other equality campaigns which had found niches in the party during the 1970s and 1980s. Although committed to a positive discourse of gender and ethnic inequalities, New Labour promoted relevant policies in a top-down fashion. Under Blair and his faction, internal Labour democracy, and therefore rank-and-file participation by women's groups and ethnic minorities, was discouraged.

Yet if Labour is to regain any roots, loyalties and energies within the wider society, and also to transcend its Blairite consumerist orientation to swing voters in marginal constituencies, then such an opening out is essential. Anne Perkins wryly commented that at the outset of his campaign Corbyn surely 'didn't anticipate launching what can look like the political wing of Occupy' (*Guardian*, 24 July 2015, p 4). Perhaps; but such a wing may now be emerging. For activists willing to engage with the state to achieve their goals of collective action, Jeremy Corbin's 'Momentum' initiative is a potentially useful, if uncertain step towards a re-engagement with civil society.

Such moves would involve debate, discussion and probably divisions between those who, as Hilary Wainwright (2009, p 222) pithily puts it, want to 'reclaim the streets' and those who want to 'reclaim the state' – a cleavage roughly equivalent to Pleyers' (2010) 'subjective and rational ways'. New UK parties of the left struggle to establish a base and significant votes – even when, as with Left Unity, they get trade union financial backing. This does not augur well for the alternative of establishing new parties. Although successful with particular electorates, even the Greens and, in a different way, the Scottish National Party (SNP) have struggled to get wider acceptance in the UK's political system. All of which suggests that the UK, or even the non-Scottish British mainland, has insufficient space there for the kinds of innovations and re-formations that countries like Greece and Spain have experienced. Conditional strategic cooperation or extra-parliamentary 'coalitions' by movements with a political party or parties is another option. Although such alliances have been made more difficult by the restrictions on campaign financing introduced by the so-called 'Gagging Act' (Transparency of Lobbying, Non-Party Campaigning and Trade Union Administration Act) passed in 2014.

In sum

Social movement leaders and activists on the one hand and left-wing parties on the other face crucial choices in the next few years. For parties such as Labour, will they risk turning away from the voter-consumer model and its invisible links to a range of pro-market policies? Such a turn would entail conceding deeper weaknesses and allying with both social movements and smaller parties. Will social movements give Labour one last try? Or will they cast their lot more decisively for parties such as the Greens, which are more receptive but lacking in electoral resources? There does not seem to be a single and separate sociodemographic base – youth, precariat or women – on which an alternative politics could be based, but the social movements engaged with these groups could form the catalyst. Thus the question which we pursue in the Conclusion chapter: can the social movements, which have picked up the baton once carried by 1960s liberation and anti-globalisation movements, forge firmer links with both the new social movement (NSM)-inclined precariat and the now alienated working classes. Should they do so, they could take on a role similar to that once played by the 'old movement' organisational stalwarts of social democracy.

References

Aicheson, G. (2011) 'Labour and the anti-cuts movement', www. opendemocracy.Web/ourkingdom/guy-aitchison/labour-and-anti-cuts-movement

Annesley, C. (2014) *UK austerity policy – A feminist perspective*, Berlin: Friedrich-Ebert-Stiftung.

Baskerville, S. and Stears, M. (2010) 'London citizens and the Labour tradition', *Renewal*, 3-4: 18.

BRIDGE (2013) *Gender and social movements. Cutting edge programme: Focus, audience and purpose*, Sussex: Institute of Development Studies.

Campbell, B. (2009) *Supping with the devil? Second wave feminism and neo-liberalism*, www.beatrixcampbell.co.uk/media/published-articles/supping-with-the-devil-second-wave-feminism-and-neo-liberalism/

Campbell, B. (2014) 'Neoliberal neopatriarchy: The case for gender revolution', *Opendemocracy*, 6 January, https://www.opendemocracy.net/5050/beatrix-campbell/neoliberal-neopatriarchy-case-for-gender-revolution

CIPD (2015) *Over-qualification and skills mismatch in the graduate labour market*, CIPD Policy Report, www.cipd.co.uk/binaries/over-qualification-and-skills-mismatch-graduate-labour-market.pdf

Citizens UK (2015) *Citizens UK manifesto 2015*, www.citizensuk.org/citizens_uk_manifesto_2015

Diani, M. (2000) 'Simmel to Rokkan and beyond: Towards a network theory of new social movements', *European Journal of Social Theory*, 3 (4): 387–406.

Di Muzio, D. (2015), *The 1% and the rest of us: A political economy of dominant ownership*, London: Zed Books.

Douzinas, C. (2015) 'Syriza: the Greek spring', openDemocracy, 5 February, www.opendemocracy.net/can-europe-make-it/costas-douzinas/syriza-greek-spring

Fraser, N. (2009), 'Feminism, capitalism and the cunning of history', *New Left Review*, 56: 98–117.

Gerbaudo, P. (2013) 'When anarchism goes pop', www.opendemocracy.net/paolo-gerbaudo/when-anarchism-goes-pop

Gill, S. (2008) *Power and resistance in the new world order*, Basingstoke: Palgrave Macmillan.

Gitlin, T. (2012) *Occupy nation: The roots, the spirit and the promise of Occupy Wall Street*, New York: HarperCollins.

Graeber, D. (2013) *The democracy project: A history, a crisis, a movement*, London: Penguin Books.

Gupta, R. (2012) 'Has neoliberalism knocked feminism sideways?', *openDemocracy*, 4 January, www.opendemocracy.net/5050/rahila-gupta/has-neoliberalism-knocked-feminism-sideways

Hakim, C. (2011) *Honey money: The power of erotic capital*, London: Allen Lane.

Howker, E. and Malik, S. (2013) *Jilted generation: How Britain has bankrupted its youth*, 2nd ed, London: Icon Books.

Mann, M. (1973) *Consciousness and action among the western working class*, London: Macmillan.

Massey D. and Rustin, M. (2015) 'Displacing neoliberalism' in S. Hall, D. Massey, and M. Rustin, *After neoliberalism? The Kilburn Manifesto*, London: Lawrence and Wishart.

Mowles, C. (2007) 'Promises of transformation: Just how different are international development NGOS?', *Journal of International Development*, 19: 248–269.

O'Donnell, M. (2008) 'Nineteen sixties radicalism and its critics: Utopian radicals, Liberal realists and postmodern sceptics', *Psychoanalysis, Culture and Society*, 13 (3): 240–260.

Osted, D. (n.d.) *Global list of women's organisations (UK)*, www.distel.ca/womlist/countries/unitedkingdom.html

Oxfam (2005) *UK Policy agenda: Oxfam's UK policy programme*, http://policy-practice.oxfam.org.uk/publications/uk-policy-agenda-oxfams-poverty-programme-112334

Perkins, A. (2015) 'Milifandom lives, and it's running Corbyn's campaign phone banks', *The Guardian*, 24 July, p 4.

Picketty, T. (2014) *Capital in the twenty-first century*, Cambridge, MA: Harvard University Press.

Pleyers, G. (2010) *Alter-globalization: Becoming actors in a global age*, Cambridge: Polity.

Popovic, S. (2015) *Blueprint for revolution*, London: Scribe.

Poverty Alliance (2014) Poverty Alliance Briefing 20, *Human rights and poverty*, http://www.povertyalliance.org/userfiles/files/briefings/PA_Briefing20_HumanRights%26Poverty_FINAL.pdf

Roszac, T. (1971) *The making of the counterculture: Reflections on the technocratic society and its youthful opposition*, London: Faber.

Savage, M. (2015) *Social Class in the 21st Century*, London: Pelican.

Standing, G. (2011) *The precariat: The new dangerous class*, London: Bloomsbury Academic.

Stiglitz, J. (2015) *The great divide: Unequal societies and what we can do about them*, London: W.W. Norton.

Tsakatika, M. and Eleftheriou, C. (2013) 'The radical left's turn towards civil society in Greece: One strategy, two paths', *South European Society and Politics*, 18 (1): 81–99.

Wainwright, H. (2009) *Reclaim the state: Experiments in popular democracy*, Salt Lake City, UT: Seagull Books.

Wainwright, H. (2010) 'Rethinking political organisation' in J. Pugh (ed) *What is radical politics today?*, Basingstoke: Palgrave.

Walby, S. (2015) *Crisis*, Cambridge: Polity Press.

Williams, H. (2006) *Britain's power elite: The rebirth of a ruling class*, London: Constable.

A Brexit from neoliberalism?

Bryn Jones and Michael O'Donnell

Introduction

> [W]hen neoliberalism fell apart in 2008 there was ...
> nothing. This is why the zombie walks. The left and centre
> have produced no new general framework of economic
> thought for 80 years. (*The Guardian*, 2016)

Despite 40 years of neoliberal application, the UK economy is failing
to meet basic human needs in economic security, health, shelter and
sustenance for many citizens. The UK economy has massive inequalities
in wealth and income, public and private debt, and international trade is
based on unaccountable, and undertaxed corporations, many benefiting
from exploited labour. As a society, it is riddled with multiple social
problems in family and personal relationships and caring responsibilities
– problems compounded by a dysfunctional political system and more
incrementally, but toxically, by a deteriorating natural environment. A
departure from the EU may intensify global competition, deregulation
and corporate powers, reduce social safeguards and cosmeticise
neoliberal policies behind a mask of xenophobic patriotism. Like the
Brexit project, the impending Trump presidency in the USA offers a
right wing, nationalist variation on neoliberal economics but, in terms
of overall governance, it seems like 'business as usual'. The tax-cutting,
corporate friendly and public-service slashing policies promised will
only intensify the neoliberal hegemony – despite multi-billionaire
Trump's populist protestations to the contrary. Monbiot rightly says that
history shows that 'it's not enough to oppose a broken system', and that
a 'coherent alternative', 'a conscious attempt to design a new system,
has to be proposed'. However, the thrust of the alternatives discussed
here goes beyond simply another 'economic ... programme' (Monbiot,
2016). The scale and depth of neoliberalism requires a *social* and *political*,
as well as an economic project to challenge and supersede it.

Neoliberalism has dangerously unbalanced the relationships between state, market and civil society, which we describe as a *trilateral interdependence*. State functions have been marketised and subverted, with economic relationships – based on commodity exchange and maximisation of financial returns – expanded throughout the economy, the public realm and civil society. As Crouch explains, in Chapter Ten, the result is restricted or atrophied democratic and public sector institutions which fail to curb neoliberalism and only accentuate the social stresses inherent in capitalist societies. Previously, traditional social democracy empowered the state at the expense of the market and, in some respects, to the detriment of civil society. Neoliberalism has aggrandised markets and business at the expense of democracy and civil society. The only remaining path now available is to rebalance by empowering civil society. The preceding analyses strongly indicate that this empowerment needs to take the form of greater participatory democracy; rather than merely to reconfigure representative democracy – valuable though this might be in other respects.

Opposition to neoliberal policies is now well established, with qualified criticism even in former bastions like the International Monetary Fund (Ostry et al, 2016). Yet neoliberalism's continued, if faltering, hegemony remains a formidable obstacle. Following Johal et al (Chapter Nine) we would not advocate a wholesale return to the Keynesian economic approach. From the various political, economic and discursive alternatives to the neoliberal regime, outlined in previous chapters, some clear and overlapping themes and proposals stand out. In this Conclusion we identify and elaborate the most distinctive and promising ideas: wider democratisation and accountability, a social base in recent social movements, expressed in a 'lifeworld' discourse which emphasises gender and practical environmental issues. We adapt Habermas' concept of the 'lifeworld' to develop the recurrent theme of local and communal engagement. From his seminal definition of this sphere of society, we see the lifeworld as sets of social relationships based on open and non-hierarchical interactions – typical of most families, friendship groups and un-formalised community groups and organisations: the heart of civil society.

Some contributors' alternatives, such as Benton's in Chapter Three, involve transformations of dominant institutions. Others, such as Jones's in Chapter Eight, focus on narrower institutional reforms that might nevertheless be triggers for broader transformative change. In the present ideological confusion, however, a measure of utopianism may be needed as a guide for even modest changes. An alternative, well-grounded vision could successfully rival neoliberalism's own fractured utopian ideal. As Benton argues, the scale of unfolding socioecological problems could mean that only *system change* will achieve an equitably and environmentally stable society. However, achieving a post-capitalism system would be both a lengthy process and depend on agents of change that have not yet clearly emerged. The alternative is 'regime change': replacement of neoliberal policies and practices with a more democratic or accountable form of capitalism. But 'reform' and 'revolution' are not necessarily binary opposites. Small, incremental, but key reforms could eventually lead to societal transformation. Indeed, this has been the logic of the neoliberal success.

The kinds of social/societal change cited throughout this book, whether on a regime or system scale, are synthesised in the first section below. These would shift the trilateral relationship referred to above, rebalancing it through greater democratic participation. The second section tackles the values and discourse needed to communicate these ideas, particularly by a pursuit of equality and democracy through an integration of human and environmental welfare as lifeworld issues. Section three evaluates how these values could be applied to three currently overcommodified spheres: 'fictitious commodities', of land use, labour and money. These could be restored in some measure as Polanyi's historic 'commons' – collectively shared resources (Polanyi, [1944] 2001, ch 6). The fourth section assesses some of the institutional and political conditions for, and obstacles to the above objectives. In other words, these analyses address the following questions.

1. Where and how should the boundaries between state, market and civil society be reset?
2. How can 'lifeworld' values and discourse integrate welfare, environment and democracy for a rebalanced society?
3. What policies for overcommodified spheres – 'land, labour, and money' – might such values generate?
4. Which political and institutional conditions impede or facilitate such alternatives?

Resetting the boundaries between state, market and civil society: a trilateral rebalancing

As Karl Polanyi ([1944] 2001, p 257) said: 'The true criticism of market society ... is that its economy is based on self-interest'. The case for a more democratic society is that it is more likely to act in the public rather than elite interest. However, classic social democrat formulae may not now be realisable. As described in the Introductory chapter, instead of neoliberals' recipe for more competition to improve accountability and need satisfaction, social democrats demand more or better regulation in the public interest and economic redistribution. In finance, for example, closer central controls of the banking sector are clearly desirable. However, 'regulatory capture' by business has meant that much existing business regulation favours investors, rather than workers or consumers (Jones, 2015).

Financial redistribution is still widely and understandably regarded as the fundamental mechanism to diminish economic inequality (Krugman, 2013; Stiglitz, 2015; Piketty, 2014). More effective taxation is, of course, essential, not only for income redistribution and to fund basic public protection and care services like the NHS, but also the citizens/basic income scheme outlined in the Introduction. More could be done, and is being attempted, to collect the estimated £12 billion of corporate tax legally avoided by corporations (TUC, 2010; Murphy, 2015). However with an economy locked into global structures, which now promise little or no conventional growth (OECD, 2016), expanded revenues sufficient for additional redistribution seem unlikely.

We explained in the Introduction the case against state-centred rebalancing through more traditional socialist measures: nationalisation, or at least state control, of major businesses. The necessary political power and popular support for wholesale nationalisation is unlikely to be forthcoming; nor is this route required to achieve greater economic equality. For some national utilities, such as railways, state/public ownership might be both low cost and popular. However, state-controlled capitalism does not necessarily advance equality. It assigns control to state and public sector elites precluding democratic participation and thus the advance of political equality. More socially balanced capitalist societies, like those more social democratic ones discussed in Andy Cumbers' chapter, have had some success without full-blown nationalisations. With appropriate safeguards against a return to neoliberal ultracapitalism, reformed capitalist institutions could be reduced to a more restrained and useful core role: more compatible with the authentic needs of civil society and democratic control.

Building on the analyses in Chapters Four and Eight to Eleven, we propose that *economic* equality, the goal of traditional social democracy, presupposes greater *political* equality. Both neoliberalism and social democracy usually ignore or play down democratic controls. Classical Marxism postpones democratisation until the completion of economic emancipation. In the light of these paradigms' failings we advocate equality of *participation* in the institutions that shape the use of social and economic resources, whether public or private. This basis for an evolving alternative to neoliberal capitalism would retain some economic equalisation based on redistribution, but it would not have to bear all the bureaucratic and financial burdens associated with conventional welfare states.

The value of equalising strategies which avoid the present cul-de-sac of limited economic growth – and the associated neoliberal attacks on redistribution as 'tax and spend' – have already been recognised. Former advisers to ex-Labour leader Ed Miliband advocated policies of 'pre-distribution', involving more protection for workers to stabilise and increase wages with rights to access earnings information and family-friendly leave and working times. Related policies would authorise civil society agencies to police executive pay and help specific disadvantaged groups including the young 'precariat' with education, skills and microbusiness development (Hacker et al, 2013). The ideas of democratic equality and participatory democracy, outlined in Chapters Four and Twelve, could be broadened into countervailing powers against market inequality.

But participation either in civic or political activity requires time and some relief from the pressure to earn. Here the right to participate needs material support, as with Atkinson's proposal for a conditional citizens' income, described in the Introduction. The standard entitlement of other citizens' income proposals would be conditional, for those of working age, on contributions to family, community or nonprofit activities. Caring for a relative or children, or engagement with charities, or social movement or voluntary organisations, would be properly rewarded. Women especially could gain more opportunities for civic participation through more self-directed time and the reduction of dependency on a male 'breadwinner'.

One strategy for rebalancing the trilateral relationship might be a more comprehensive 'social settlement' (see Chapters Two and Nine) rather than simply the accumulation of discrete reforms. Inspired by the political and social compact of '1945' and the inception of the UK's social democratic welfare state, both Coote and Johal, Moran and Williams argue for settlements which prioritise the 'core' or 'foundational' economy of local provisioning of essential goods and care services. Coote also argues for employment practices which promote more gender equality and a refocusing on family and community priorities: a transformation of economic priorities and power balances in employment relationships. For Johal, Moran and Williams, a new social settlement should be pursued through the local dimension of the foundational economy – for example by local government licensing of corporate supermarkets according to employment or environmental conditions. This more selective 'settlement' could still have potentially significant impacts on local and community economies.

The 1945 social settlement followed the economic, political and military catastrophes of the early 20th century which, as Polanyi impressively argued, stemmed from (neo)liberalism's atavistic political economy. In his depiction of that period this paradigm inflicted unemployment, privation and economic repression on civil society, leading to grievances which contributed eventually to the socialist and social democratic responses. For Polanyi, this 'double movement' of market dictatorship followed by social reclamation is almost inevitable when essential human social relationships are distorted and degraded by excessive and relentless extension of commodity markets – particularly the 'fictitious commodities' of land, labour and money (see Benton, Chapter Three, and Coote, Chapter Two), policies for which are therefore outlined below.

'Lifeworld' values to integrate welfare, environment and democracy

We see the lifeworld as the heart of civil society: as sets of social relationships based on open and non-hierarchical interactions. These are typical of most families, friendship groups and un-formalised community groups and organisations. They should be the central concern of progressive alternatives to neoliberalism. Following Monbiot (2016) and Crouch (Chapter Ten) renewal or reinvention of social democracy's values of liberty and equality, underpinned by social solidarity, necessitates acknowledgement of the negative aspects of their previous applications and identification of new versions.

Arising from these sectors of civil society, the new social movements have provided much of the resistance to neoliberalism as globalisation and also generated alternative ideas. For that reason – and reflecting their popularity with younger generations (Pleyers, 2010, pp 86–88) – their attempts to go beyond the three social democratic values above deserve serious consideration. The fusion and overlap of anarchistic, green, feminist, human rights and social justice values in the 'movement of movements', identified by Benton in Chapter Three and analysed in Chapter Twelve, rival but also supplement and, arguably, further social democratic values by emphasising deeper democratisation and environmental sustainability.

Several contributions in this book, reflecting wider debates, propose a broadening of British democracy and a deepening of popular participation in key institutions. A marriage between social movements' commitment to more fundamental democracy and social democratic and socialist credos of equality could transcend the imbalances involved in both state-bureaucratic and corporate market power. This alternative paradigm stresses democratic, as well as economic equality. The principle of a 'right to participate' could open up this possibility in practical ways.

Reworking traditional social democratic concepts of equality also requires a distinct and much more substantial place for gender equality. Amongst the many relevant feminist approaches, the most favourable for a new, post-neoliberal paradigm could be the kind elaborated by Walby (2015) and Coote (Chapter Two) which emphasises breaking barriers between the polity, the formal economy and what we have here called the 'lifeworld'. Centring the nexus of family, community and personal relationships, in which most unpaid female labour occurs, within a new sociopolitical paradigm could simultaneously enhance gender equality and democratic participation. A political discourse centred on the prioritisation of health, family and personal relationships, security and caring could also have more popular appeal than such neoliberalistic totems of competitiveness, productivity, GDP and public debt.

Relentless application of market mechanisms to maximise profit has inflicted damaging and intrusive effects on family and personal life and privacy – outcomes not relieved by the costly commercialisation of caring responsibilities. Intensification of work and degraded employment conditions have fractured the work-life balance through shift-working and the necessity of maintaining dual-earner households because of downward pressures on wage levels and longer and antisocial hours. Precarious employment contracts have meant greater material and psychological insecurity for many, especially women.

As the contributions by Benton, Coote and Cumbers show, the welfare of people is becoming inextricably linked with that of the planet. As Coote, the New Economics Foundation (NEF) and others have argued, welfare and wellbeing provision increasingly needs to be reinterpreted to address those needs which commoditisation, market colonisation and their environmental consequences subvert or deny. Potential reinterpretations can be gleaned from from the five concerns of the Institute for Policy Research (IPPR) in its *The Condition of Britain: Strategies for Social Renewal* (2014). These are Beveridge's five 'giant evils' – want, disease, ignorance, squalor and idleness – described, in current terms, as inequality, chronic disease, isolation, squalor and digital exclusion (Brindle et al, 2014).

Historically high levels of inequality and poverty have become entrenched since the crisis of 2008; particularly in the areas of low pay and housing – analysed below. The relative incidence of ill-health is also substantially linked to social inequality and natural environmental conditions. Marketised lifestyles and addictive consumption induced by corporate sales targets, for example for high fat and sugary products, need similar controls to tobacco. The social licensing of supermarkets, proposed by Johal, Moran and Williams, could help promote such measures.

The emotional and mental distress accompanying isolation needs better resourced welfare provision. But it could also be alleviated by mobilisation of community and family resources, as suggested elsewhere in this book. Similar combinations of public and community support could help the estimated 6.4 million people excluded by lack of digital skills. Medical treatment in the contemporary form of cost-driven, bureaucratic – and often privatised – delivery fails to treat people as individual persons (Zigmond, 2015). In health, social work and education, increasingly impersonal and overstretched systems could be humanised by supplementing them with the collective capacities of families, friendships and communities, albeit on different social principles to the subcontracting ethos of the Conservatives' Big Society initiative.

Revitalisation of this 'lifeworld' will involve adjustments in lifestyle and politically and socially directed action from within civil society – supported by 'participation income' and equitable funding. Kinship and community groups are also the location of what Coote (2015) called the 'core economy of unpaid work, everyday wisdom and social connections on which all our lives depend'. As Johal, Moran and Williams point out, this nexus also overlaps with their 'foundational economy'. Market capitalism imposes obvious economic handicaps and limitations on the lifeworld. Its viability is also inhibited by the critical frictions between ethnicity, religion and gender differences. Chapter Four described associational democracy's role in collaborative networks in between diverse groups to achieve mutually desired outcomes. Such cooperation, between different ethnic groups, to address shared problems, such as housing, could have the latent effect of defusing interethnic hostility. However, gender roles cut across each of the other lines of differentiation, rendering them the crucial focus of cross-communal support.

As we saw in the Introduction, far from liberating women, neoliberalism promotes more stressful roles: competitive participation in the labour markets combined with the need either to purchase care and domestic services, or to play an intensified housewife role. Neoliberalism didn't create these conditions but it has added pressures and 'choices' which have actually worsened many gender inequalities and further complicated family life. It is here that gender equality and participatory democracy could come together. Reforms to the tyranny of contemporary working practices could provide equal opportunities for men and women to share childrearing and domestic roles and enhance women's capacity for democratic participation and/or careers.

The lifeworld is also the crucible for environmental change. Many of the influential NGOs shaping today's debates began, like Greenpeace or Friends of the Earth UK, as small civil society initiatives and networks. Much environmental degradation – energy-inefficient homes, traffic-blighted neighbourhoods, toxic emissions – afflicts lifeworld locales, so they should also be priority sites for improvements to the quality of life. Wellbeing, health and sustainable local environments could go hand in hand under the kind of policies advocated by Coote and the NEF's 'new social settlement' (see Chapter Two).

There is also a potential synergy between socially organic forms of civil society engagement and collaboration and the participatory democratic reforms suggested in Chapters Four, Nine, Eleven and Twelve, involving more formal institutions. Thus the opening up of shareholder democracy, already partly realised in Sweden and described by Jones in Chapter Eight, could enhance the opportunity for transmission of lifeworld values through stakeholder and civil society activists' participation into business decision making, from which they have so far been excluded.

Policy priorities: 'land, labour and money'. Restoring the commons

The policy priorities for developing greater participation and accountability are in spheres where neoliberal capitalism has particularly disturbed the trilateral balance. For Polanyi, three 'fictitious commodities' of land, labour and money are, in principle, 'commons': that is, fundamental aspects of nature and social life best organised for 'the common good' rather than for private profit. This is already widely recognised in the case of ecological-environmental degradation (see Benton, Chapter Three); less so for labour and money. But, as in Polanyi's period, market liberalism has brought, inter alia, a dearth of affordable housing, exploitative/insecure employment with widespread in-work poverty, reckless and unproductive banking practices, massive and probably unsustainable personal debt; accompanied by predatory practices like payday lending. These sectors can be decommodified and re-embedded in some kind of social accountability for the public good. This would represent a major part of the trilateral rebalancing, which we advocate alongside greater democracy and increased civil participation.

Land and housing

The primary human needs and purposes of land are for production (for example agriculture) and for habitation. Under capitalism housing has long been a marketed resource. However, at least in the UK, the post-World War II social settlement did semi-socialise housing provision. It comprised three sectors: a relatively small private rented sector, a larger bloc of publicly owned 'council housing' controlled by local municipalities and privately owned dwellings financed by mortgages – largely provided by mutual building societies. Mergers between mutuals and financial deregulation attracted more commercial institutions, such as banks, into the mortgage market. Related forces commercialised the remaining building societies with many offering banking-type service. Larger societies abandoned their mutual status leading to their takeover by commercial banks (Pollock, 2008; Tayler, 2003). The commoditisation of mortgages, accelerated by Thatcherite privatisation of thousands of council houses, fed a mushrooming of owner occupation from less than 10% of all homes in the early 20th century to 70% by the early 2000s.

Financial crisis has partly reversed this trend but mainly to the benefit of large and small capital owners who invested in 'buy-to-rent' properties - trends which have simultaneously made renting a more costly option while restricting personal mortgages to the relatively affluent. Average house prices in 2014 were around six times median earnings; requiring mortgages too high for most workers and families (GMB, 2014). All of this has meant that, except for the vestiges of council housing and the 10% of homes rented from not-for-profit housing associations, the market has dispossessed huge numbers of non-house owners from a basic human need (AMA Research, 2015). By 2013 nearly 10% of the population in England had experienced homelessness, and by 2015 around 200,000 faced or were 'at serious risk of homelessness'. An estimated 1.8 million families in England and Scotland were seeking unavailable council housing (Fitzpatrick et al, 2013).

The solution of neoliberals and their fellow travellers is for developers to build more houses for the market. However, house building presupposes land which is a natural, fixed resource, limited not only by environmental considerations ('green belt' restrictions and planning controls) but, as the 2015 floods illustrated, natural hazards. The restricted availability of mortgage finance also checks supply and here the damaging fictitious commodity status of money, described below, comes into play. A social democratic solution would be to loosen local authority financing for more council housing; which assumes lifting of neoliberal and austerity limits on public spending and borrowing. But, as Gilbert argues (Chapter One), more imaginative and participative solutions are conceivable. The civil society solution could be Coote's 'coproduction' principle with combinations of local voluntary groups with cooperatives or consortia of local builders in 'self-build' schemes.

Such initiatives would presuppose reduced land prices, perhaps by restrictions on the financial power of wealthier buyers and investors in congested cities, such as London. Empowerment of the growing number of housing protest groups could help campaigns against rent maximising investors, buy-to-let purchasers and speculative overseas buyers (Garland, 2016). More radically, most housing should be detached from the commercial financial system, because profit targets for investor returns incentivise higher house prices and rent levels. Instead, why not stronger, more democratic housing associations, with state-guaranteed borrowing and lending powers from a restored sector of old-style building societies or similar mutuals?

Money and the financial system

Polanyi called money a fictitious commodity because its supply cannot be expanded to meet demand - without eventual catastrophic economic consequences. The neoliberal deregulation of the commercial financial system allowed banks' credit expansion into unsound financial investments, leading to debtor defaults and the near collapse of the international financial system in 2008. In the UK, banking finance and house ownership resemble conjoined twins: namely the destabilising defaults on loans to the other fictitious commodity of land-restricted residential property. Banks and their investments (expanded credit) became 'too big to fail' without crashing the economy (Haldane, 2012). State-funded bank rescues unfortunately increased government debt, which neoliberal hawks in the UK and the EU used as a weapon to advocate austerity to avoid unsustainable public sector debt and possible state bankruptcy. (Later governments further boosted banks' 'money supply' by buying their bonds from banks – the 'quantitative easing' described in Thompson's chapter.) Banks have, mainly, failed to invest these extra funds into productive businesses in the 'real economy'. Instead they facilitate immoral, routinely hidden and, in an unknown number of cases, illegal diversion of funds to offshore tax havens.

The fictitious fabric of money has been spun to a scale shocking even to some of the financial technocracy. Bank of England chief economist Andy Haldane (2012, p 21) wrote: 'the increase has been particularly steep over the past thirty years, peaking at well over 500 per cent of GDP'. As governments are now the only stakeholders with sufficiently secure funds to insure banks against risk of failure, bank operations are now de facto creatures of the state. Yet they can act largely autonomously because of the political fiction that they are private businesses rather than the publicly supported and guaranteed institutions which they really are. The fiction is necessary because it justifies high earnings per share to shareholders, executives and, mainly foreign, investors, as well as, fortuitously, massive bonuses for bank executives.

The classic social democratic/socialist reaction to this scandal would be public – usually state – ownership and control. The political, ideological and ethical objections raised above caution against such a blanket strategy. An alternative would be a variation on the mutual and stakeholder enterprise governance suggested in the chapters by Cumbers and Jones. As outlined by Haldane, company constitutions which joined long-term financial investors and representatives of a more diverse range of interests – customers, small businesses, employees, community and environmental groups – could achieve more responsible and socially productive banking practice (Haldane, 2012).

The Bank of England's social goals need resetting; but so does its managerial structure. A new system would presuppose reform of the governance of the Bank of England; or at least of its powerful Monetary Policy Committee (MPC). As Thompson (Chapter Seven) described, the Bank now has a wider macroeconomic role than neoliberal monetary policy. Yet it is allegedly 'independent', at least from government diktat. In practice it is a technocracy suffused with views of appointed, usually 'market' – read neoliberal – economists. The composition of the MPC and the government-appointed Court of Governors could be widened to include (suitably qualified) experts from outside the financial and big business sectors. The Court has one token trade union leader, but elected nominees from local government, NGOs and consumer groups would add both democracy and wider socioeconomic perspectives. Financial institutions would still be organisationally remote from the values of lifeworld communities, but at least representatives from their culture could feed those values into policy deliberations.

Labour and employment

The supply of labour stems ultimately from the lifeworld of human relationships and families. Businesses cannot control directly the supply of individual units of labour. So to maximise its exploitation they must engineer longer or more intensive forms of working. Exploitation of what civil society regards as autonomous moral subjects leads to individual and social suffering amongst workers, through mental and physical fatigue, stress and disrupted personal relationships (see Introduction and Chapter Five). Inevitably, argued Polanyi, social protest eventually provokes counter-movements to challenge workers' treatment as mere commodities.

Neoliberal regimes have progressively removed many statutory and trade union forms of worker protection, intensifying labour's commodity status: through longer and antisocial working hours, lowered pay, casualisation and contractual arrangements such as 'zero-hours contracts'. A mildly social democratic regime could restore some trade union rights within firms, possibly extended to some representation in corporate decision making. As part of the democratic accountability paradigm, the 'social licensing' of foundational economy firms (Johal et al, Chapter Ten) could include contract conditions for a living wage and enhanced employment conditions – perhaps buttressed by the corporate codes of conduct for multinationals' suppliers in developing economies (Hoang and Jones, 2012), with joint policing by local authorities, trade unions and living wage campaigners such as Citizens UK to offset enforcement problems.

Unions and such civil society agencies would also need assistance to develop services to support the expanded army of genuine and bogus self-employed workers, through provision of legal, tax and commercial services. Some trade unions are already attempting such support for the self-employed. Another approach would be to promote representative organisations similar to the 'artisanal associations' which support microfirms in Italy (Jones, 1997, pp 217-243). The trend towards alliances between trade unions and social movement campaigns (Parker, nd), cited in Chapter Twelve, indicates the feasibility of such cooperation between new and old social movements.

Democratic principles can be successfully applied to make work itself a less demeaning, more varied and self-managed experience, as the much-praised example of the Suma worker cooperative shows (Walker,

2006). However, involvement of all members of an institution is of limited value if that organisation ignores obligations to, and impacts on, the wider society. Mutual organisations, such as the worker-managed cooperatives in the former Yugoslavia or the John Lewis Partnership in the UK, illustrate this defect (Jones, 2015). Participatory democracy therefore also needs to be accompanied by revitalised forms of external *accountability*, like those demanded for corporations by the Coalition for Corporate Responsibility (CORE) described in Chapter Nine by Johal, Moran and Williams in their proposals for the foundational economy.

Political and institutional challenges to alternatives

Three major impediments hinder the kind of societal rebalancing advocated here. Firstly, as has been argued throughout this book, a defective political democracy has been largely captured by interests with much to lose from any serious change. Secondly, potent and progressive alternative policy sets are either thematically fragmented or unpopular because neoliberalism has ideologically discredited or infiltrated and corrupted the paradigms – like 'socialism', with which they are associated. In this context, conventional social democratic paths to greater equality which rely on redistribution based on higher economic growth seem to be inherently problematic. Thirdly, neoliberal ideologies dominate national and international governance systems, including business regulation, and privilege financial and market forces, supported by mass media allies.

The bastions of neoliberal authority – larger corporations and state departments in the thrall of neoliberal hegemony – would strongly oppose even a mild reversal of public policy towards state fiscal activism,as implied by the different proposals of Crouch (see Chapter Ten), and Hain and Hutton discussed in the Introduction. There is also the endemic problem for left-radical politics of the national media, from which a majority still take their 'news'. It is systemically predisposed – even in public broadcasting – towards neoliberal assumptions (see Mills, 2015). Perhaps surprisingly, however, in view of its widely accepted 'non-death' (Crouch, 2011) neoliberalism's erstwhile adherents are less than united. As Farnsworth and Irving show (Chapter Five), the IMF was increasingly backing away from the proto-austerity policies it had promoted for much of the previous 30 years. In the case of Greece and other overindebted European economies, it was the new austerity hawks in the EU which had to stiffen the back of an ambivalent IMF against relaxations of public spending and welfare cuts. Our analysis of the EU crisis, in Chapter Six, dissects the extent and logic of its neoliberalisation. If the UK resigns full EU membership but remains within the latter's European Economic Area it will still be subject to the EU's neoliberal and ordoliberal authority. Complete withdrawal may be worse: isolated subjection to globalised trade pressures without any meaningful social safeguards.

We agree with other observers (Fotopoulos, 2015) that the network of trade and finance pacts in which the UK economy is now embedded, together with the international financial system, could continue severely to constrain social democratic macroeconomic policies. These alternatives could also be complicated by the proposed marketising of public services in the ongoing negotiations for a Transatlantic Trade and Investment Partnership (TTIP) (http://eu-secretdeals.info/ttip/; EurActiv.com, nd). However, such constraints would not preclude adoption of several ideas in this book, such as Cumbers' local mutuals, Jones' corporate governance reforms and the foundational economy focus of Johal, Moran and Williams. The latter make the crucial point that some critical reforms away from neoliberalism can succeed precisely because they work with the household-serving and informal economy, which functions largely separately from the mythic monolith of the national and international 'macroeconomy'.

At a national level the UK central bank has, as Thompson shows in Chapter Seven, effectively abandoned the stringent monetarist policies on which neoliberalism rode toward hegemony in the 1980s. A commitment to economic growth and consumer recovery from the post-2008 recession has meant flooding money towards rather unresponsive investment institutions. The case for diverting this 'quantitative easing' away from the banks' own control has been made by a wide range of economic and political figures, from the Corbyn camp in the Labour Party (see Chapter Ten), as far as members of the financial establishment (Haldane, 2015; Turner, 2015).

Indeed, there are signs that circumstances are pushing governments and policy makers to relax some of these neoliberal prejudices. Considerable state funding is being committed to capital projects, though of debatable public value in the case of nuclear power stations or the High Speed 2 rail line scheme (HS2). More interestingly, the then UK Chancellor George Osborne turned community groups' campaign for a 'living wage' into government policy in the 2015 Budget. In 2016, many employers had yet to adopt this measure. It is also partly a political cover for government cuts to tax credits for the low-paid. However, those that base alternatives on a more economically interventionist state should beware that such interventionism can be co-opted and subordinated into a broader neoliberal 'pro-market' policy set. (The same government has continued to privatise and to curb trade union rights.)

By contrast we argue that progressive change on a modest or large scale depends, ultimately, on winning political support for greater accountability, more meaningful, participatory, equality and corresponding wellbeing. Democratisation of economic power is a crucial element of accountability. As institutional or 'common' democracy, this would involve equality of participation in multiple decision-making spheres. It would be aimed at both 'vertical' dimensions of inequality – between income and wealth groups – and horizontal ones – between genders and ethnicities. A more embedded social democratic regime to govern a much moderated capitalist system would mean reducing, checking and circumscribing the powers of capital and the elites by strengthening rival economic institutions, such as mutuals, and democratising capitalist ones.

Realisation of these elements of a 'vision' depends on perception, dissemination and political traction and, ultimately, on the 'balance of forces'. At the moment the governing institutions, national and international, predominantly staffed by the generals of neoliberalism cannot, or will not, even think outside the neoliberal paradigm. Mainstream political parties have corrupting links to the business elites which limit their appetite for defying neoliberal conventions and altering the trilateral relationship. The dysfunctional election system maintains the security of elite positions, and could thwart a government pursuing a pro-lifeworld agenda – as could the ideological dominance of pro-neoliberal media in electoral debates.

Yet there are reasons for optimism. Despite setbacks such as Syriza's failure to reverse Euro-austerity, socialistic and anti-neoliberal political forces have (re)established themselves in Iceland and city governments in Spain, and even erupted into the UK's previously, staunchly neoliberal Labour Party. These last two cases are especially significant as they seem to represent, as did the early phases of Syriza, the translation of a social movement ethos of equality and environmental and social justice into the mainstream political arena.

To tackle neoliberalism at EU levels there is also the recently formed DiEM25 (Democracy in Europe Movement 2025) which seeks a more democratic and transparent EU in the medium term. Social movements, international trade union movement, and political parties of the left are also campaigning to democratise the International Monetary Fund, the World Bank and the World Trade Organization. Such checks on the power of the interlocking global elites may someday be achieved through democratically constituted global governance.

More immediately feasible is extension of democratic participation and the redistribution of economic power at the national level. If 'another world is possible' so is a Britain in which society's needs replace the imagined imperatives of neoliberal markets.

A lot may depend on whether such 'upward' links can flourish and social movements can deepen their own roots in the non-political spheres of civil society: in charities, community activities and the caring roles of the lifeworld. Appropriate political vehicles might be a more expansive Green Party – whose 2015 manifesto was, essentially, mainstream social democracy – or a radicalised Labour Party. A less probable, but concrete manifestation of ideas expressed here is a new community-based party, such as the increasingly successful People Before Profits Alliance in the north and south of Ireland (see www. peoplebeforeprofit.ie/). Alternatively, a more effective vehicle for political expression might be a rainbow coalition of new and old social movements which agrees a charter to press upon traditional parties.

In sum ...

Translated into more vernacular and media-friendly terms, the values in this alternative discourse should appeal already to a civil society vanguard: to many of the thousands active in trade unions, campaigning NGOs, community and voluntary organisations, amongst the 15 million people who regularly undertake voluntary work in the UK (NCVO, 2013). These could be the equivalent of the intellectuals whom Hayek advised his shock troops to convert before working on politicians. Or they could act as an analogue of the Labour movement which propelled and sustained the social democracy of the mid-20th century. Such a 'bottom-up' approach is essential to break with the elitist thrust of neoliberalism's top-down advance. Electoral reforms or realignments, or Jeremy Corbyn's Momentum activists, or similar networks, could deepen such links with the wider civil society. The kinds of equalising policies to restore measures of popular control sketched out above – for housing, employment and finance – assume civil society involvement to define and oversee them. Adaptation and elaboration of the various ideas and perspectives in this book can be schematically summarised in the following medium to long term aims.

1. Follow the advice of Johal, Moran and Williams and Coote: cease reliance on macro-management for growth of that unmanageable entity, the national economy; instead promote wellbeing and equality through the foundational or core economy.

2. Begin to equalise power through wider and deeper democratic participation in all spheres and at all levels, in economic, social and political institutions – with appropriate material incentives, such as a citizens' income, to displace overextended market relationships in the key nodes of social and economic life: in schools, in public bodies and popular finance, with smallscale but critical changes to decision making in corporate governance (see Jones, Chapter Eight) and collective resource enterprises, such as the municipal and mutual energy enterprises described by Cumbers.

3. Within the 'core economy' identify the key needs of family, relationships and community 'lifeworlds'. Campaign for these objectives – caring tasks, environmental health, personal security – in the language of the lifeworld, instead of the abstract jargon of market economics.

4. Focus specifically on rebalancing gender roles to achieve some of these objectives by engaging with and mobilising the many women who now work in these sectors, or who represent those women in unions or charities, or the public sector.

5. Champion these groups, alongside the wider green, feminist and social justice movement campaigners, as the new social force for a revised social democracy to augment or replace the diminished role once played by the labour movement.

In late 2016 such aspirations may seem fanciful. However, at some point solutions will be needed to respond to a crisis which neoliberalism cannot resolve. The crisis might be economic, from the dysfunctional, international economy, or from the politico-economic disarray following the EU referendum result. This 'democratic' decision means 16 million people, out of an electorate of 46.5 million, voted 'Leave': 26% of the *total* population decided the political and economic future of the other 44 million. Instead of the promised return of some power to Britons, complete 'Brexit' would actually increase native elites' power, while diminishing the already minimal popular influence over international market forces; influence which the EU institutions, described in Chapter Six, currently provides. We believe this whole process and the outcome only emphasises the case for the broader and deeper democratic decision making advocated above. A coherent and perceptibly relevant progressive paradigm is needed against the Brexit-induced and more ominous alternative of xenophobic right-wing populism. In the coming years, and unlike the missed opportunity of the 2008 crash, civil society campaigners and, hopefully, more open-minded social democrat politicians, must not 'let a good crisis go to waste'. They need to be ready with ideas and projects similar to those detailed in this book – not, however, as a precise blueprint, because the democratic alternatives proposed are both means and ends. Or, in the words of the social movements which inspired some of them: we must build the road we travel.

References

AMA Research (2015) *Housing associations market report – UK 2016–2020 Analysis*, www.amaresearch.co.uk/Housing_Assoc_14s.html

Brindle, D., Kelly, L. and O'Neil, S. (2014) 'The *Beveridge Report* revisited: Where now for the welfare state?', *Guardian*, 7 July, https://www.theguardian.com/society-professionals/2014/jul/07/-sp-beveridge-report-revisited-where-now-for-the-welfare-state

Coote, A. (2015) 'People, planet, power: Towards a new social settlement', New Economics Foundation, www.neweconomics.org/publications/entry/people-planet-power-towards-a-new-social-settlement

Crouch, C. (2011) *The strange non-death of neo-liberalism*, London: Polity.

EurActiv.com (n.d.) 'TTIP puts the EU's environmental and social policies on the line', www.euractiv.com/section/trade-society/opinion/ttip-puts-the-eu-s-environmental-and-social-policies-on-the-line/

Fitzpatrick, S., Pawson, H., Bramley, G., Wilcox, S. and Watts, B. (2013) *The homelessness monitor: England*, www.crisis.org.uk/data/files/admin_uploads/research/HomelessnessMonitorEngland2013_ExecSummary.pdf

Fotopoulos, T. (2015) 'Are austerity policies the problem or is it neoliberal globalization?', *International Journal of Inclusive Democracy*, 11 (1/2): 75–81.

Garland, C. (2016) 'London's housing crisis: 4 problems and 6 solutions', Novara Wire, http://wire.novaramedia.com/2015/04/londons-housing-crisis-4-problems-and-6-solutions/

GMB (2014) '1.9 million families on the housing waiting list', www.gmb.org.uk/newsroom/housing-waiting-list

Hacker, J., Jackson, B. and O'Neill, M. (2013) 'Interview: the politics of predistribution,' *Renewal*, 21 (2/3): 54–64.

Haldane, A.G. (2012) 'The doom loop', *London Review of Books*, 34 (4), 23 February.

Haldane, A.G. (2015) 'How low can you go?', Bank of England, www.bankofengland.co.uk/publications/Documents/speeches/2015/speech840.pdf

Hoang, D. and Jones, B. (2012) 'Why do corporate codes of conduct fail? Women workers and clothing supply chains in Vietnam', *Global Social Policy*, 12 (1): 67–85.

IPPR (2014) *The condition of Britain: Strategies for social renewal*, London: IPPR.

Jones, B. (1997) *Forcing the factory of the future: Cybernation and societal institutions*, Cambridge: Cambridge University Press.

Jones, B. (2015) *Corporate power and responsible capitalism: Towards social accountability*, Cheltenham: Edward Elgar.

Krugman, P. (2013) *End this depression now*, London: W.W. Norton and Company.

Mills, T. (2015) *Taking power back: Putting people in charge of politics*, Bristol: Policy Press.

Monbiot, G. (2016) 'Neoliberalism – the ideology at the root of all our problems', *Guardian Review*, 16 April.

Murphy, R. (2015) *The corporate tax gap. Tax evasion in 2014 and what can be done about it*, PCS, www.taxresearch.org.uk/Documents/PCSTaxGap2014Full.pdf

NCVO (2013) 'How many people regularly volunteer in the UK?', *UK Civil Society Almanac*, http://data.ncvo.org.uk/a/almanac13/how-many-people-regularly-volunteer-in-the-uk-2

OECD (2016) *Economic outlook*, 2016 (1), www.oecd.org/eco/outlook/OECD-Economic-Outlook-June-2016-general-assessment-of-the-macroeconomic-situation.pdf

Ostry, J.D., Loungani, P. and Furceri, D. (2016) 'Neoliberalism: Oversold?', *Finance & Development*, 53 (2): 38–41.

Parker, J. (n.d.) 'The trend towards alliances between trade unions and social movement campaigns', www2.warwick.ac.uk/fac/soc/wbs/research/irru/publications/recentconf/jp__airaanz_paper.doc.pdf

Piketty, T. (2014) *Capital in the twenty-first century*, Cambridge, MA: Harvard University Press.

Pleyers G. (2010) *Alter-globalization: Becoming actors in the global age*, Cambridge: Polity Press.

Polanyi, K. ([1944] 2001) *The great transformation*, Boston: Beacon Press.

Pollock, I. (2008) 'Not such a good idea after all?', *BBC News*, http://news.bbc.co.uk/1/hi/business/7641925.stm

Stiglitz, J. (2015) *The great divide: Unequal societies and what we can do about them*, New York: W.W. Norton and Company.

Tayler, G. (2003) 'UK building society demutualisation motives', *Business Ethics: A European Review*, 12 (4): 394–402.

TUC (2010) *The corporate tax gap*, www.tuc.org.uk/sites/default/files/extras/corporatetaxgap.pdf

Turner, A. (2015) *Between debt and the devil. Money, credit, and fixing global finance*, Princeton, NJ: Princeton University Press.

Walby, S. (2015) *Crisis*, London: Polity.

Walker, J. (2006) 'The VSM guide. An introduction to the Viable System Model as a diagnostic and design tool for co-operatives and federations', www.esrad.org.uk/resources/vsmg_3/screen.php?page=homean

Zigmond, D. (2015) *If you want good personal healthcare – see a vet*, Whitstable: New Gnosis Publications.

Index